THE NATURE OF HOME

The Nature of Home

TAKING ROOT IN A PLACE

Greta Gaard

The University of Arizona Press / Tucson

The University of Arizona Press
© 2007 Greta Gaard

LIBRARY OF CONGRESS CATALOGING-IN-PUBLICATION DATA

Gaard, Greta Claire.
The nature of home : taking root in a place / Greta Gaard.
   p.   cm.
Includes bibliographical references.
ISBN 978-0-8165-2576-8 (pbk. : alk. paper)
1. Home—Psychological aspects.   2. Ecofeminism.
3. Social justice.   4. Gaard, Greta Claire.
5. West (U.S.)   I. Title.
HQ503.G22   2007
305.420978—dc22   2007025508

Manufactured in the United States of America on acid-free,
archival-quality paper containing a minimum of 50% post-
consumer waste and processed chlorine free.

12   11   10   09   08   07   6   5   4   3   2   1

CONTENTS

Preface

Written and revised over a ten-year period from 1997 through 2007, these essays explore the intersections of feminism, ecology, and social justice through the lens of personal experience. At the time that I began this volume, there was no queer feminist environmental writing. I wrote these essays, in part, to fill that literary gap.

Larger than essay, memoir, journalism, or poetry, creative nonfiction includes these genres and goes one step further: it allows writers to address topics of importance through the lens of their own life experiences. Creative nonfiction utilizes research and reflection, dialogue and narrative and anecdote, the techniques of fiction and the tangible details of contemporary life. Neither this nor that, creative nonfiction is a hybrid genre well suited to writers with hybrid identities, and writers who see culture and nature, social justice and environmental health, as inseparably intertwined.

Writing about places that have been or could be home to me, I wanted to explore the ways that humans, like other life on Earth, both shape and are shaped by our environments. But there are no wholly adequate frameworks for this exploration. Traditional Western psychologies describe identity development as a process of separation and individuation, equating maturity with autonomy. To me, these psychologies seem antiecological, implying that a separation of self from environment is not only possible but desirable. Feminist psychologies in this same tradition provide an alternative view, describing women's identity development as taking place primarily through relationships, and women's mature self-identity as a self-in-relationship, interdependent but not subsumed by relationship. For the most part, feminists have not explored the power of nonhuman relationships in shaping self-identity. For that perspective, we can turn to ecopsychology. Initially an outgrowth of deep ecology, ecopsychology shares that philosophy's emphasis on wilderness, and focuses on the shaping power of wild places in forming human self-identity. But environments are both wild and cultured, both ecological and economic. Bringing the environmental justice movement's definition of environment as the place where we "live, work, and play" to a feminist ecopsychology of human development, we can begin to ask questions about the shaping power of place in all its dimensions—social, ecological, economic.

These essays approach the relationship to place as a primary relationship, seldom acknowledged and yet potentially equal in force to any marriage, partnership, or family relationship. As a relationship with a mate defines a marriage, a relationship with place provides the foundation for our sense of home. And what if place changes, as it does for so many of us in an era of increasing mobility? How do these fluctuating relationships to place affect our human relationships and our self-identity? And how do we reestablish relationships with place so that we can be at home wherever we live?

Bioregionalists suggest several strategies that in my mind parallel a process of courtship and commitment to place, and the essays in this volume attempt each of these strategies separately or in combination. To nourish the process of "inhabiting" the places I have called home, I sought to learn the land (in "Wilderness," "Climbing," "Whatcom Creek," and "Silver Lake"). I paid attention to the cultural and ecological histories of place (in "Family of Land," "Whatcom Creek," and "Explosion"). I invested time in getting to know the inhabitants ("Body, Midlife," and "Silver Lake"), exploring local economics ("Silver Lake" and "Food and Shelter"), and practicing engaged citizenship ("Looking for Home," "Women/Water," and "Food and Shelter").

At the same time that I was exploring my relationship to place, employing the strategies I thought would make me feel at home, I overlooked the reciprocity of the process: I too was changing. The spaces of wilderness I found most welcoming at 27 were not the same places of wild earth I sought out at age 37. The place I had considered to be home as a youth was less satisfying at midlife. And the places where I had built only temporary relationships had influenced me nonetheless, affecting what I wanted from my home place, and what I wanted to give in return.

To convey these shifts with any accuracy, I chose for this volume a spiraling narrative that brings together place and perspective in a loose chronology. Life develops this way, too, not in a linear progression but as a spiral: questions return again and again, each time finding different answers. Accordingly, in each essay, place shifts; the essays explore one or more specific environments, both social and natural. Time shifts; explorations from the past are mapped onto the present. Identity shifts. Our "authentic self" is no more static than our experience of home.

Ultimately, I found a sustainable relationship with place that balanced work, community, and ecological environments. My hope is that these essays may serve as a map for others seeking to do the same.

Looking for Home

As long as humans have been around, we've had to move in order to survive. Early hunter-gatherer cultures had to follow the food source, leaving an area when it had become overpicked or overhunted, allowing the plants and animals to regenerate. In more recent times, whole groups of people have been forced to leave home to survive. Irish immigrants left home during the 1845 potato famine; Oklahoma farmers left home for California in the 1930s; and throughout the twentieth century alone, Mexican farmworkers have had to follow the harvest across California, Oregon, Washington, Texas, even into Minnesota, searching for work. When the economies of a region—the water, the crops, or the industries—no longer support a people's existence, inhabitants are faced with a very simple choice: leave home or die. Under the looming threat of globalization, some communities are creating a third choice by developing locally owned, sustainable economies. These structures give people more control over their lives, more control over the social and environmental practices of businesses. They allow people to "stay put."

A migrant of a different sort, I moved to Bellingham, Washington, for work, hoping to find home. After five years of a weekly commute through farmlands, forests, and lakes stretching 150 miles between my partner's house in Minneapolis and my job in Duluth, both Shawn and I wanted a home together. We imagined somewhere with mountains and pine trees, progressive culture and activism, work and career opportunities, friends and family. We knew we'd have to sacrifice something. And we decided to move west.

In my lifetime, I have lived in three distinct areas: Southern California, small-town and metro Minnesota, and now the Pacific Northwest. Each of these places has both shaped and raised questions about my understanding of home.

In that part of the San Fernando Valley where I grew up, the single most distinguishing feature of the landscape was the mountain range that ringed the valley. From my earliest sense of myself and my place in the world, I am a person who feels at home in the embrace of mountains.

During the seventeen years that I lived in Minnesota, I felt strangely disoriented. Whenever I saw dust on the prairie horizon, I interpreted it as fog or smog hiding the mountains. My eyes continually sought for and projected the sight of mountains that weren't there. The mountains were inside me, a part of my identity, and without them around me I was not my true, original self. I was not home.

For many years my family spent summers and holidays in Palm Springs, in the days when the desert sands were still covered with sagebrush and cactus, and the freeway ended in Palm Canyon Drive. Sometimes we took the tram to the top of the San Jacinto Mountains and entered a world of fir and pine, with snow-covered needles and gray chipmunks above instead of sand and lizards below.

After twenty years of life in Southern California, I chose to go to graduate school in Minnesota to learn more about my father, who had grown up in Minneapolis and had passed away in my youth. I went, simply, in search of my roots—and found them. In Minnesota, unlike California, people seemed to know how to spell my last name, and there were lots of us (instead of only one) in the phone book. In Minnesota I uncovered my Scandinavian heritage, learned to appreciate *kumla* and *lefse* (but never lutefisk). Learned to "talk Minnesotan" by spending hours discussing the weather with people who spoke in monosyllables, my voice acquiring the Minnesota accent (distinct from a Midwestern accent generally by its unique rerouting of vowels *a* and *o* to a cranial exit entirely separate from the mouth). I learned more details of my father's life and family—stood in front of the very houses where he had lived, visited the schools he had attended, contacted his old chums. I learned to love winter—real winter, with minus-40 wind-chill factors—and I learned to play in it, to cross-country ski and to skate. In the culture of Minnesota, I found a society that shared the values I had been raised with: hard work, community responsibility, citizenship, neighborliness. I learned how to be an activist, and formulated my own feminism in the context of a rich populist heritage of labor organizing, farmer and worker solidarity, feminist and queer communities.

I learned to expect to see lakes and clear streams. I learned the cycle of the seasons: hot, humid summers marked by thunderstorms and tornadoes; excruciatingly beautiful autumns, lasting up to two months; then six months of snow, punctuated by severe wind chills and the January thaw; and finally spring, beginning with mud season, rain, and lilacs. Minnesota—the culture and the land—shaped me. It shaped me simply because I loved it, and I allowed it to hold me.

Part of going home means finding your own people—not just your blood relatives, but your whole family. When I left Los Angeles for Minneapolis, I thought I would find my people through researching my heritage. And that search was important. What took me longer to realize was that my people, my own family, extended both vertically through the blood lines and horizontally to include other residents of the land, both past and present. In 1980s Minnesota, there was no visible Latino community like the one I had grown up with in Los Angeles. I missed hearing the rapid cadences of Spanish, reading the bilingual street signs, listening to the salsa music on the radio, seeing the colorful clothing, and hearing the stories of my Chicano neighbors. Without a community conversation, I lost my never-too-fluent Spanish, and along with it the insights and perspectives of a culture with whom I shared my first home. When I moved to Minnesota to follow the blood, I lost these homegrown relations.

What I did find was family of a different kind. In Vipassana meditation *sanghas,* in WomanChurch gatherings, and in the Greens, I found communities of conscience and spirit. At Poetry Harbor in Duluth I found wild grassroots poets overgrowing the confines of the university. And on Lake Superior's red rock cliffs at Shovel Point and Palisade Head, I found a community of climbers who cared about the rock, left the chalk at home, and dropped their ropes far from peregrine falcon nests. This web of human relations encircled me like a mountain range, and yet I yearned for the landscape of my childhood home.

In search of mountain valleys and sustainable townships, I began visiting different places in the West to explore their possibilities. My criteria were many. The place I could call home would have its own renewable water source, and not be a blight on the environment; cities like Phoenix, Palm Springs, and Los Angeles were immediately ruled out. Both Shawn and I would have to be able to find fulfilling work. The social community would have to be politically progressive and culturally diverse, with an arts and spiritual community as well. And there would have to be mountains.

Our explorations circled through northern California—Humboldt County, the coastal redwoods, Mount Shasta, Arcata, Chico, Sonoma. In Weaverville, I was astonished to find a Chinese temple, built over a hundred years ago, and from this temple I began a discovery of the Chinese and Japanese presence in shaping California. None of my grade-school history had prepared me for this. In the elementary schools of the 1960s, we learned about the Spanish missions, El Camino Réal, and the Jesuits like Father Junipero Serra, who brought "salvation" to the Indians. What I uncovered through these later-life visits was a history of Native American enslavement, Chinese labor, Japanese internment, Chicano organizing and repression. I described the experience to a friend: it was like discovering that for generations the patriarchs of my family had been keeping other wives or mistresses, fathering other children, and yet acting as if *we* were the only ones. A whole other side to the family had been kept hidden.

Years ago, freshly sprung from high school, my partner Shawn had moved from Minneapolis to the Rockies and spent two years living in a tent and later a cabin, high in the mountains above Denver. When we visited Bellingham together, she saw the snowy peaks of Mount Shuksan, magnified by their watery reflection in Picture Lake, and recognized the image that had companioned her childhood, wallpapered on her family's basement wall. The lure of living with mountains beckoned us both.

Now standing amid ferns and moss-covered Douglas fir in our new back yard, Shawn and I worry: will we be able to make a home in the coastal rainforests of western Washington? Or with our family scattered between Southern California and Minnesota, will our histories and human relations become a stronger force than our ecological desires? How will our new relationship to place change our relationship with each other? And we make a pact: we'll give ourselves five years to build the relations of home. In five years, we'll choose again, Midwest or Pacific Northwest.

For me, returning west was like completing an unfinished love story. Too many questions remained: Where was the land I had dreamed of in childhood, the land with bare granite rocks and tall pine trees? Would I ever feel like my authentic self without mountains and ocean surrounding me? And why was this relationship to place the most compelling force in my life? This image of craggy granite mountains and soaring pines had interrupted all my relationships in Minnesota, whispering that the Midwest was only temporary, that no lasting relations could be formed because one day, I would be called west again, called back in search of home.

The questions wouldn't wait any longer.

A single thundering crash resounds across the valley, startling the animals and shaking the lamps and dishes in the house. Was it a gunshot? A sonic boom? Logging? The last great trees in this region fell years ago. It must be the work crews, blasting the mountainside to build a new logging road.

Living inside a logging culture is new to me. I don't know the sequence of events, what to expect, or how to intervene—but I am learning fast. At a public information meeting one wet, dark night in January, spokesmen from the state's Department of Natural Resources (DNR) announced their plans to clear-cut 212 acres on the mountains above Lake Whatcom, Bellingham's only drinking-water source. If approved, the DNR plan would include building 65 acres of new logging roads to clear-cut stands of old-growth fir in large areas around Austin Creek. On the DNR maps, I recognized the area of their proposed clear-cut: it extended upward from the old logging road where Shawn and I often walked our dog, Sequoia. I pictured the steep slopes lining the road, the enormous sawed-off stumps that appeared at irregular intervals, the tall snags and stands of alder that marked this area as cut-over second growth. If I wanted to protect the forest from further logging, I would have to learn the history and the economics of logging in the Lake Whatcom watershed.

Austin Creek, the main natural tributary into Lake Whatcom, was once a major spawning bed for cutthroat trout and kokanee salmon, but recent logging had added so much silt to the stream that the kokanee were gone, and the cutthroat severely reduced. If logging were to continue, there would be questions about the presence and safety of long-eared bats, pileated woodpeckers, marbled murrelet, osprey, bald eagle, beaver, and mink. Ten years ago, after a summer of heavy logging destroyed habitat for fish and wildlife in this same area, Austin Creek had flooded, sending eight billion gallons of water rushing down eroded slopes, taking loose soil and slash from the cuts along with it, in a process called mass wasting. What we do to the animals and the earth, we do to ourselves: The flooding destroyed roads, bridges, and lakeside homes, a disaster that cost the county $8 million. But the DNR paid no fines. This forest above Lake Whatcom was "school trust" land: instead of having state income taxes, Washington funded public schools by clear-cutting public lands. Education and deforestation for educating future generations—these seemed a paradoxical bequest.

One cloudy but dry afternoon, I hiked the logging road beside Austin Creek, hoping to get a better view of the proposed clear-cut. Not far up Lookout Mountain, a dense forest canopy shaded the creek's cascading water and cooled the air. Around a hairpin turn, the logging road crossed the stream and began its steep switchbacking climb uphill. Then there it was, affixed to a thick tree trunk by inch-wide pink ribbon and staples: the sign that read TIMBER SALE BOUNDARY. Beyond, the thick forest of conifers and understory of ferns was slated for clear-cutting. Through deeply shadowed recesses of hushed forest, the neon-pink ribbons usually associated with breast cancer survivors were now tied to trees just beyond the logging road, proclaiming the news of their imminent devastation. On one downed log, someone had spray-painted a neon-orange happy face.

This defense of water and forest, this test of local democracy, would be my first experience with engaged citizenship in Washington State. Through this struggle, I hoped to make myself at home.

What do we mean by *home?* A place of rest. Of food, warmth, safety, and belonging. A place to be our "real" selves. Or so the story goes. For women of many cultures, home has had a different meaning.

A place for work. For caregiving, in our roles as wives and mothers. And for a third of all women, a place of early or repeated sexual violation. For women in one out of six marriages, home is a place of physical abuse. Haven; prison.

All these meanings are carried into our understanding of Earth as home.

Just as Western culture has expected women as wives and mothers to be self-sacrificing caregivers, the makers of home, men and women have carelessly demanded more and more of Mother Nature. Today, there are indications that women and nature are exhausted, that there may be consequences from this relentless conquest. Worldwide, the temperatures are beginning to rise. The water levels, the pollution levels, the extinction levels are beginning to rise. The women, too, are beginning to rise.

After only eight months of living in Bellingham, it seems presumptuous for me to call this my *home*—the word implies an intimacy, a kind of knowledge of place, a set of relationships and commitments I haven't yet earned, though I am wholeheartedly engaged in the process. My partner and I have hiked many of the local trails, explored the region's cities and towns, joined in local activism, studied the watershed management plans, and listened to the birds. Here, I recognize some familiar feathers from Minnesota: the great blue heron, the snowy owl, the redwing blackbird, and the mallard duck. Other birds are new to me: the varied thrush, the American coot, and Steller's jay. The trees, too, are both familiar and strange: western red cedar and Douglas fir, blue spruce and madrone, white birch and alder. Unique to the area is the astounding variety of rhododendrons, the wild blackberries and raspberries that grow abundantly in summer and fall, the colorful array of flowering fruit trees.

I imagine I will not be a true resident until the cycle of seasons evokes a corresponding cycle in me. But the mountains already hold me. Slowly, with patience, I am learning to speak a new language of home.

YEAR ONE *History and Identity*

If the desert were a woman, I know well what like she would be:
deep-breasted, broad in the hips, tawny, with tawny hair, great masses
of it lying smooth along her perfect curves, full lipped like a sphinx,
but not heavy-lidded like one, eyes sane and steady as the polished
jewel of her skies, such a countenance as should make men serve
without desiring her, such a largeness to her mind as should make
their sins of no account, passionate, but not necessitous, patient—
and you could not move her, no, not if you had all the earth to give,
so much as one tawny hair's-breadth beyond her own desires. If you
cut very deeply into any soul that has the mark of the land upon it,
you find such qualities as these—as I shall presently prove to you.
                                        —Mary Austin, "The Land"

If I had influence with the good fairy who is supposed to preside over
the christening of all children I should ask that her gift to each child in
the world would be a sense of wonder so indestructible that it would
last throughout life, as an unfailing antidote against the boredom and
disenchantments of later years, the sterile preoccupation with things
that are artificial, the alienation from the sources of our strength.
                                        —Rachel Carson, *The Sense of Wonder*

Women/Water

During the campus interview that eventually brought me to the Pacific Northwest, a retiring faculty member from the search committee took me on a tour of Bellingham, ending at Lake Padden. That January afternoon was darkly overcast but dry, and when Michael pulled his Jeep onto the narrow two-lane drive to Lake Padden's shore, the darkness poured through the car windows, and we were drenched in a thick green tunnel of fir and cedar branches. Lake Padden was encircled by a walking path of about two-and-a-half miles, Michael informed me, grassy and open to the sky on the north and east sides, but densely forested on the south and west shores. I imagined jogging here with my dog, or taking cool green after-dinner walks in summer, but the thickness of the south shore's forest worried me. Were the lake's trails a safe shelter for women? My host hesitated before telling me that, in fact, there had been a couple instances of rape here.

Within a year of my move to Bellingham, in the fall of 1998, a twenty-year-old woman came to visit relatives in town, traveling here from Massachusetts in order to explore the area and the college. With her first visit, she knew this land, this region of forest and water, was where she wanted to live, and she made plans to attend the college the following year. Delighting in her newfound home, she was walking alone around Lake Padden one Friday afternoon when she met a gardener, a man in his late forties, who invited her to join him in errands to his employer, his friends, and then to go out for a beer. Two days later, her lifeless body was found alongside the Mount Baker highway near Glacier, her skull bludgeoned with a gardening tool, her body showing signs of sexual violation. The gardener had disappeared.

Keri Lynn Sherlock. Twenty years old. When I walk at Lake Padden, I imagine the joy she felt in finding this place. I want to remember her adventurous spirit, her trust in the kindness of strangers, her love of the earth. I don't want to think about men's violence against women. I want to think about water, Douglas fir and western red cedar trees, bracken and sword ferns, mosses and mud. I want to unfold my secret self in the arms of trees, be renewed by the deep kiss of rain on my lips, wind in my mouth and throat.

But in the forested slopes around Lake Padden, I see the jagged remains of once-great trees, sawed-off stumps with the springboard slots still visible. At one time, like Keri, this land could not protect itself. The interdependence of water and forest, the dreams and goals of a young woman: these became resources for meeting someone else's desires.

This history will shape my relationship with water and with place here. Other women's stories of water and place affect me, for water has always been a sign of home.

When I became aware of water in my first home, the San Fernando Valley, water wasn't called *water*. It was called *the wash*.

At the very bottom of a concrete-walled trough, another narrow trough traveled along the center, and in that cavity, a trickle. The Los Angeles River.

Growing up in an automobile culture, the only glimpses I got of the river were from the back seat of the Rambler as we drove down Coldwater Canyon, Laurel Canyon, Fulton, or Whitsett. Just before crossing Moorpark, we drove the bridge over the wash, and I peered out the window each time to see if the water was running. To see if it was even there. Later, as I was allowed to walk the two blocks to grade school, I discovered the wash ran just a half block beyond my school. Some days after school, if I had time, I would dash down to the bridge and peek over the steel railing to see the muddy trickle, the weeds growing through concrete at the bottom of the channel. By the time I was bicycling to summer school in junior high, I was stopping regularly at the wash.

The water lured me. I wanted to get acquainted with it, befriend it, provide a witness, listen to the trickle and somehow get down there and put my hands in it, participating in the flow. It wasn't like the real rivers I had read about, with fish and dragonflies, beaver and muskrat, rocks and soil instead of concrete. But it held the memory of being a river, and the promise too: outside and above the concrete walls and chain-link fence there were wide sandy spaces fringed with oleander bushes that bloomed pink and red. If you entered through the oleanders, you could walk the sand above the concrete trough with the little trickle and pretend that this was wilderness. Surely, it had been so, once before.

When she found out about my attraction to the river, Mother warned me not to go there. Strange men could hide there, and a small girl hidden by oleanders from the passing cars would be easy prey. After that, I only slowed my bike across the bridge over the wash, looking quickly at the little trickle below. What more could I do? We were both gasping and straitened by the concrete of Los Angeles—but I would get out. Already planning my escape, I felt guilty that I would be leaving this water behind. It was like betraying a friend.

One late August morning I woke at dawn, dressed, and climbed the 118-step staircase down the Encinitas sea cliffs to a place called Swami's Beach. Wading into the Pacific Ocean so that the waves hit my thighs, I pried open the cardboard box that held my father's ashes.

The ashes were black and gray and white. Some of the ashes were sand. The box was already light when completely filled, and when I pulled out the first handful of what used to be my father's body, the ashes sifted or were blown through my fingers and scattered on the frothy waves. Of course we were outlaws, my father and I: ocean burials were forbidden, at least this close to the shore. But I pulled handful after handful, now walking slowly in the waves along the beach, singing songs my father had sung to me for all my sixteen years. This is the burial he had wanted—no gravesite, no memorial stone, no storage vase or marble wall slot for his cremated self.

Don't visit me at a grave, he had told me. Let me go. Scatter me in the ocean at dawn, and whenever you want to talk with me, come to the water and walk along the beach.

And so I did.

Twice in my life, I've been unwillingly escorted away from water, annoyed by the thought that perhaps my father has served as chaperone. The first time, Rosemarie and I had taken blankets down to the beach in Santa Monica and lay down together in the sand. There were other lovers on the beach, other blankets scattered along the night sands, and we took some time to place our blanket in darkness, at a reasonable distance to preserve privacy. Some time later, the loud *whoosh* and *aaah* of ocean waves silenced the whisper of automobile tires on sand, until a glaring searchlight exploded our embrace. Fully clothed but fearing criminal punishment or worse, we grabbed our blankets and ran for the car.

Ten years later, wearing just swimsuits and shorts, Mary and I bicycled through the heavy velvet darkness of a humid Minnesota summer night. At Lake Josephine we dropped our bikes and our clothes beside an oak tree and raced each other into the lake. Swimming skin to skin with water under a starlit, moonless night, I felt a rightness with place and passion. This is how I was meant to live: naked, in water. And then the searchlight skimmed the lake until it found us.

When I moved to Minnesota to find my father, I found water instead.

The university that drew me to the Midwest had draped its campus across both shores of the Mississippi, and there were whispered stories about the English department's famous professor who had ended it all by jumping off that university bridge. Even in town, the Mississippi River created its own urban wilderness. On the west bank below the Franklin Street bridge, a homeless camp flourished, complete with a fire ring, scattered chairs, the occasional blankets left behind, and elaborate footpaths that persisted year after year. Across the water from the homeless, men walked singly, met, shared pleasure. Their stretch of the river resisted the efforts of city planners who paved the paths, set park benches and trash cans, cleared out the underbrush. The men still walked, though their pleasures took place farther south.

The first inhabitants here, the Ojibwe and the Dakota, had names for the water. *Minne sota,* for the milk-white color of the Great River (*Missi sippi*) at flood stage. *Kitchi gumi,* for the Great Water most European Americans know as Lake Superior. *Owah-Menah,* for the falling water later named St. Anthony's Falls by a Catholic priest and explorer, Father Hennepin. By 1852, the European explorers had settled. Combining their heritage with this new place, they used the Dakota *Minne* and the Greek *polis* to name this the City of Water. In 1884, with the publication of *Huckleberry Finn,* the Great River's attributes as wild nature and home to outlaws alike became the celebrated subject of Mark Twain. At the falls in Minneapolis, the Great River's tumultuous power put an end to the upstream journey of Twain's storied steamboats, leaving a wilder, less traveled river farther north. At the Great River's origins, the water began as a creek so small it was rumored you could walk across it on stones.

Some day, I vowed, I would visit the headwaters of this river that divided a continent. The source of its 2,552-mile journey from Lake Itasca to the Gulf of Mexico would have something to teach me.

Named for two legendary Dakota youth, the parallel streets "Hiawatha" and "Minnehaha" run from downtown Minneapolis to the waterfall where Minnehaha Creek crosses Hiawatha Avenue and pours into the Mississippi a half mile later. Development has extended Hiawatha a mile beyond the falls to the Crosstown Highway, but the two-becoming-one marriage myth wasn't lost on the original city planners or turn-of-the-century honeymooners, who kept the tiny hotels around the falls in business well up until the highway expansion. Today a metal sculpture of Hiawatha carrying Minnehaha stands just above the falls, and a rose garden in the park is decorated with lines from the poem by Longfellow, who reinvented Hiawatha as "skilled in all the crafts of hunters," and his mate, "Minnehaha, Laughing Water" as the "Handsomest of all the women."

This romanticized legend of water as a Dakota woman was on my mind one spring day when I canoed Minnehaha Creek. For the creek's 22-mile length from Lake Minnetonka in the west, through south Minneapolis, and into the Mississippi, I wanted to hear "her" perspective, see the city from the viewpoint of water. For if water speaks, this might be the story.

Where the creek begins in Minnetonka, the houses along the banks mimic royalty. Massive three- and four-storied homes perch above the creek, with groomed lawns, statuary, volleyball courts, elaborate wooden jungle gyms, gazebos. Private Property. Keep Out. But after the big estates disappear, the creek reclaims its own banks. There are fallen logs, willow and cottonwood trees, redwing blackbirds swaying on cattails in the open marshy elbows of water. Mallard ducks float or rest in bachelor groupings, their beaks beneath their wings, beady eyes open or closed in sleep. Canada geese urge on fluffy yellow goslings that look nothing like their black-and-white parents. And then the trails begin to appear, first dirt footpaths for a good distance, and much later, paved bike trails to reduce the impact of humans sharing the shaded banks. Beginning in aristocracy, Minnehaha Creek ends in democracy. The commons. The falls are part of a public park, and the last half mile of the creek is edged with recycled plastic boardwalks and foot-hardened dirt paths all the way to the Mississippi, where people gather to fish or watch the boats go by. That's the story.

For ten years I walked around the lakeshores in Minneapolis and St. Paul. In winter I skated their groomed surfaces, scoffed safely from shore as friends showed me how to walk on water, bike on water, even drive and build ice houses on water. In summer I swam and sunned, canoed and floated on inner tubes. Not once did I consider drinking that water. My relationship with water was pure aesthetics, pure recreation.

For my first job after university, I moved to a town on the shore of Lake Superior, about three hours north from the community of family and friends I had developed in Minneapolis. Here in Duluth, the winters were one month longer coming and going, with snowfall possible by late September, and the lilacs of springtime not blooming until June. For a Southern California native, Lake Superior's winter was too much of a good thing, and the town offered little diversion. Aside from the environmentalists, poets, and outdoor enthusiasts, the town itself was a cultural mismatch for me, and for eight years I poured myself into my work. But the several creeks that flowed through town from the hilltops to the great lake offered woods, hiking trails that doubled as ski trails in winter, and sweeping vistas of steel-gray water and even darker skies. On weekends when I wasn't commuting to Minneapolis, I skied, hiked, climbed, and made friends with the land.

Lake Superior was not like any water I had known before. A cross between an ocean and a polar bear, Lake Superior was like a great moody animal, her heavy breathing visible in summer waves, her winter's hibernation frozen and heaving at the shore. The Ojibwe considered Lake Superior a great spirit, a grandmother, and it was said she would give you what you needed, if you asked.

One New Year's Eve, disheartened by five years of dating and short-term relationships after my divorce, I resolved to be single and celibate (two different things, I made a point of confiding to friends) until I met someone truly significant. And for five months I skied, hiked, climbed, wrote poetry, taught, organized, and socialized, often spending weekend nights alone with my own personal video showing. Without much of a cultural scene in Duluth, that was about all you could do.

By mid-June, I was running out of resolve. I couldn't see how I would find a future mate by following the course of action I had chosen. I would have to act more decisively.

On summer solstice, when the air was still cool off of Lake Superior and the light lasted long after sunset, I went down to the shores of the lake and stood on the smooth round stones of pink, blue, and cream-white, Superior's characteristic eggs. Behind me, the lakewalk curved inland from the three-mile sand spit called Park Point, where tiny summer cabins from the turn of the century had been reinforced for year-round residents. Connecting Park Point with the mainland, the aerial lift bridge allowed ocean-going ships to pass between Lake Superior and the bay. Next to the lift bridge was the Shipping Museum, and the lakewalk began just outside, where seagulls waited raucously for tourists to throw bread and popcorn on the grass. From the Shipping Museum, the lakewalk followed the shore inland past a half-sunken stone warehouse called Uncle Harvey's Cribs, and then turned north to the old Fitger's Brewery building, now converted into a hotel, restaurant, and shopping mall. Standing at any point on the lakewalk, you could see arms of land embracing the lake, Minnesota's north shore on one side, Wisconsin's rolling land mass on the other. But the arms never touched: to the north and northeast, steel gray water met inky blue horizon.

Summer was tourist season in Duluth, and on weekends the lakewalk was throttled with families walking its narrow path, riding in horse-drawn buggies, roller-blading, pushing baby strollers, and pulling dogs. Park Point and the aerial lift bridge were reportedly the most touristed spots in Minnesota. But on summer weeknights, the lakewalk belonged to the locals, and there weren't many of us out that night. You could still feel alone with the lake.

Kneeling by the water, on pink and blue and cream-white lake stones, I invoked the Ojibwe stories of the Lake as a great-grandmother, a powerful spirit who would give you what you asked if you asked from the heart. It was a moment I did not take lightly. First I thanked the lake for the gift of place, for the unembraceable enormity of silence and spaciousness. I promised to give back to water, to work as an ally and a granddaughter. And then I put both my hands in the lake, and asked.

I met Shawn the next day.

Up the scenic North Shore highway, past the Lester River, the Duluth water-treatment plant modestly hugs the shore. Looking something like a gymnasium, the red limestone building with its rounded arch windows and crenellated turret is now used as a pump house, bringing in water through the original steel pipe placed sixty-four feet deep and 1,560 feet out into the lake, and letting it settle. Transported to the newer red brick building across the street, the water then enters a process of flocculation, filtration, and chlorination. And then we drink it.

Originally, the process was much simpler, and the results were less favorable. From a bulletin published in July 1930, city engineers reported the annual death rates from typhoid fever among towns taking their water from Lake Superior. Tracing the typhoid to "coli," the engineers noted the "great number of sewer outlets along the north shore" and the direct line in water currents carrying the lake water to the pumping station. The seasonal distribution of typhoid fever could be linked to the prevailing winds that moved water close to or away from the intake pipe. Treating the water with chlorine was the engineers' only solution, though they warned that "notwithstanding its vastness and phenomenal purity, Lake Superior water cannot assimilate a large amount of pollution."

The next problem for water began in 1955 when Reserve Mining started dumping taconite tailings into Lake Superior. Located fifty miles northeast of Duluth, the mining company dumped approximately 67,000 tons of taconite waste per day until 1980. Why did they stop? In 1973, asbestos fibers were discovered in Duluth city water. As with the sewage, the prevailing winds and the counterclockwise circulation of water in Lake Superior carried the taconite tailings right down the shore to the drinking-water intake pipe.

As recently as 1999, researcher Julie Stauffer in *The Water Crisis* describes the problems facing the Great Lakes in terms of pollution. Persistent organic pollutants such as PCBs, mercury, dioxins, dieldrin, furans, benzopyrene, hexachlorobenzene, DDT, alkylated lead—the International Joint Commission (IJC) on Great Lakes Water Quality has expressed concern based on the persistence of these chemicals in the environment, their toxicity to wildlife, and their potential effects on human health. Starting with Lake Superior as a site for zero discharge, the IJC has recommended that industry phase out all toxic chemicals. Involving the public in demanding cleanup and prevention is crucial, since the IJC has no enforcement capacity.

Now the problems of pollution have been joined by a newer problem: what if the water *leaves* the Great Lakes?

In Stanwood, Michigan, Ice Mountain Spring Water bottling plant has been drawing as many as 400 gallons of water every minute—up to 575,000 gallons a day—from groundwater that accounts for 80 percent of the stream flow that feeds Lake Michigan. The little plastic bottles are taking Great Lakes water, water that has been part of the commons, and taking it backward, back to the big estates, and selling it for corporations like Nestlé.

Bottled water isn't safer than municipal water. It isn't healthier. Most of the plastic bottles aren't being recycled. And Michigan has no mountains like the one pictured on Ice Mountain's plastic water bottle. Perhaps bottled water would be less of a problem if its production and consumption were limited to the same ecoregion, ensuring the water would recirculate, and if the profits were used to maintain the public water works. But most of the water bottles leave Michigan, with Nestle making the profit and the ecosystem paying the cost. Water bottling raises questions about water ownership, water profit, and water's purpose.

When I left Lake Superior for the Pacific Northwest, I took a small vial of lake water as a reminder of the grandmother. And I started asking questions about other women's relationships with water.

Around the world, water that has been flowing freely in rivers, lakes, or underground streams is being captured, treated, and divided into small plastic bottles. At the same time that some women purchase the water in the plastic bottles, other women spend three to five hours each day hauling water to their families and their fields. The women who purchase the bottled water flush toilets that carry their waste water to sewage treatment plants; these women have no waterborne illness, and their children generally live past the age of five. The women who carry water use all day the same amount of water that the bottled-water women use in one toilet flush. But the comparison falls short, because the women who carry water have no sanitation. They fear for their children's health, for the risk of intestinal parasites, diarrhea, dehydration, and death. Many of their children do not live past the age of five.

Today, both groups of women are excluded from decision-making processes that affect their access to water. But the women who can buy the bottled water aren't feeling the effects of their exclusion. Yet.

In the map library at the university, Janet Collins shows me her earliest file photograph of Lake Padden, taken in 1941. The southern slopes are still densely forested, indicating that if the lake were indeed clear-cut, the logging would have taken place in the first fifty years of settlement. At the Whatcom County Museum of History and Art, Jeff Jewel shows me another photo from the turn of the last century. Again, the south shore is forested, and there are about six or eight homesteads visible on the north and eastern shores. There were no setbacks in those days, and the homesteads run right down to the water line. Jeff pulls out map after map of Lake Padden, and we see the lake has two inflows, one from an unnamed stream entering on the north side, another entering the lake's southeast corner at the present "dog exercise area," where the old Valley Shingle Company was to stand in 1914.

One map from 1922 shows six different areas around Lake Padden already platted for development: Highland Park, Sea View Lake Park, and Parker's Lake Padden on the north, a Lake Shore Addition running along the eastern shore, with Highland Glen and Walla Walla Additions platted on the steep forested slopes along the south shore. Amid all this planned development, the map also shows the Fairhaven Water Company's intake pipe, its long drinking straw entering the lake from the northwest corner. The people were going to build on, and drink from, the same lake.

Of the various sections proposed for development, Highland Glen was the most ambitious. Platted in 1889 for investor-owners Will and Elvira Jenkins, this imaginary community had zoning for hotels, churches, public school buildings, boat houses, and public parks. With a Grand Boulevard planned along the lake's southern shore where the packed-dirt walking trail now runs, the streets of this development sparkled with names like Diamond, Ruby, Garnet, Pearl, Emerald, and Crystal Avenues. Selective cutting of the biggest, sturdiest trees began the process of deforestation. Luckily for the lake, the Jenkins's glittering community never fully developed, and in 1903 an order vacating the Highland Glen plat was passed by the Fairhaven City Council. Today, Garnet Avenue is a fallen branch in the horse trail, knocked down in high winds during a rainstorm. Emerald is the mossy pond of standing water, Pearl is the mushrooms that grow beneath the ferns, Ruby and Diamond are the spotted deer who venture down to the lakeshore in late afternoons.

Bellingham drank Lake Padden until 1968, when the Whatcom Falls water-treatment plant made Lake Whatcom the town's primary drinking-water source. Preserved as a city park in 1972, Lake Padden's safety is temporarily ensured. The park's law protects all of nonhuman nature within its boundaries, but not the women who walk there.

Every four or five days at the food co-op, I fill a five-gallon jug of drinking water from the co-op's water filter. With all the pesticides, logging and mining residue, the storm-water runoff, and findings of mercury and crypto-sporidium in Lake Whatcom, I've decided to take the water-treatment plant's water through one more filter. At the co-op, the water filter uses activated carbon, reverse osmosis, and ultraviolet disinfection. It costs me an extra two dollars for every five gallons, and some effort in hauling water. My uneasiness around water quality is shared with others, and on weekends we stand three and four deep in line for water.

If our industrial and economic practices continue on their present course, this four-person line is only the beginning. New trade laws have declared water to be a commodity, making it possible to sell water across ecological and economic boundaries, profiting from those whose water sources have dried up or become too polluted to drink. Cities unable or unwilling to maintain their water and sewer infrastructures are quietly selling off public utilities to corporations who are operating them at a profit. Under private enterprises, water and sewer rates go up, water quality goes down, and the poorest customers may now be cut off from any water at all. I imagine huge ships hauling gigantic sacks of water across the oceans. I imagine thirsty people pouring into the streets in protest, demanding water. I worry about water, about the creatures who live in water, and all those whose lives depend on water. I worry about our culture's carelessness with this irreplaceable element of life.

When I heard the dynamite blasting Lookout Mountain, walked the logging roads and found the pink ribbons tied around tall stands of old cedar and Douglas fir, I became deeply involved in the fight to stop a planned clear-cut of 212 acres around Austin Creek, a prime tributary to Lake Whatcom. To challenge the proposed cut, we would have to gather research about water and soil and wild animals, speak the language of logging, show the numbers.

And we did. We found data about wildlife, about marbled murrelet and native cutthroat trout. We analyzed the route logging trucks would take to exit the cut, running directly past four elementary and middle schools, and we challenged the route's safety. We looked at slope stability, and found historical information about flooding and landslides from clear-cuts not fifteen years earlier. We looked at water-quality reports. We attended the Forestry Forum, the city and county council meetings. We wrote letters. We created petitions. And we kept at it.

Around the same time, questions arose from another front about the quality of drinking water from Lake Whatcom. The county health officer presented serious charges about cryptosporidium in the water, was ignored, and resigned. Studies were published on the deteriorating quality of Lake Whatcom's water by the local university's Institute for Watershed Studies. Two months later, other scientific studies were commissioned and published, assuring the public that the water was safe. Forums were held.

Committees formed. Scientists debated. For a while, it seemed like something might happen.

Amid all the arguments was a great silence. It was a silence about why we were fighting at all, why Linda Marrom was taking time away from work, away from single parenting, why Fairhaven students were going to county council meetings, why Sherilyn Wells was writing legal briefs to end development on Lake Whatcom, why Marian Beddill and Tim Paxton and Larry Williams formed the Initiative Group in the hope of raising enough funds to purchase the entire watershed. If we told the truth about why we fought the developers, the DNR-commissioned loggers, the investors who wanted more sewer lines extended around the lake—if we told the truth, we would lose. Our scientific credibility would be marred by emotion. Everyone knew it.

Here were the stakes. On one side, there was a desire for financial gain, coupled with a willingness to deny the consequences of that gain. Beneath that desire for finance was fear—fear of economic insecurity, fear of job loss, fear of losing status, of losing control, losing face. Economic profit, fear, denial. On the other side, those who defended the lake worked for free. They spent their own money copying petitions, doing research, calling representatives in Olympia. Some worked to create a name for themselves, but most worked without thought of fame. They saw the beauty of the lake, the vulnerability of the streams, the relationship between ecosystem health and animal lives, including their own. They thought about connections. They thought like water.

What we know is that all bodies of water in an ecosystem share the same flow. When you open a tap anywhere in Bellingham, the water that comes out of that tap comes from Lake Whatcom. The water I drink today was soup for settlers a century ago, rained down on blackberry fields outside of Lynden, washed over Lummi canoes and Nooksack woven baskets. This is the water that the Haida and Tsimshian warriors saw falling as rain when they came down from their northern islands and coastal villages to capture slaves from the Lummi, Sammish, and Nooksack. This is the water that Captain George Vancouver saw in 1792 when he first sailed into Bellingham Bay. This is the water that Henry Roeder used to power his sawmill in 1853, that John Whichtalum claimed with his tribal land under the Homestead Act of 1884, that Rabbi Joseph Polakoff drank at the new

Beth Israel Synagogue in 1908, that Emma Goldman walked through in puddles when she was jailed here that same year, water that Harry Okamoto used to run his laundry on State Street before Executive Order 9066 drove him away. The human body is 70 percent water, and our blood, 83 percent water. Living in place, we embody the water we drink. In Bellingham, we are the water of Austin Creek, Carpenter and Smith creeks, Olson and Beaver and Brannian. We are the water of Lake Whatcom. The Nooksack River flows through my blood. The Deming Glacier chills and melts in my body as it does on Mount Baker.

But water also flows through air, evaporating from the ocean and lakes, from creeks and streams, evaporating up into clouds that flow east and south, precipitating down in rain and snow from clouds that have flowed here from Alaska, from Asia and the Pacific. Who owns this water? Who owns that water? And where does the water own itself? If you listen, the water will tell you. In words of raindrops and splashes, bubbles and ripples, water speaks a language that is the beginning of all life on Earth.

When early explorers saw the Nooksack River, they wrote that "the three forks beckoned like the crooked fingers of a witch, daring man to venture into the rugged, mountainous shield." Believing the water had magical powers over humans, they thought nothing of its vulnerability. Now, we know differently. The water witch beckons no one. She moves with her own purpose, and if we can learn to respect her flow, we too can flourish.

For Keri Sherlock

Family of Land

Soaring 30,000 feet above the lush Cascadia region of volcanic mountains, over the checkerboard of forest and clear-cuts, then the sprawling urban masses of Portland and San Francisco, I finally recognize California's central valley. Near Lompoc, I watch as the Los Angeles aqueduct pours through its channeled course across square and rectangular pieces of farmland, through Thousand Oaks and Valencia, making its way defeated and diminished into the concrete channels of the San Fernando Valley. I recognize these bare brown hills, crisscrossed with fire roads and flanked with new housing. I know the dry greens and browns that shelter rabbits and birds, lizards and snakes, red and brown ants, earthworms and sow bugs. I've never learned the names of these scrubby hillside plants, but I know their woody smell and sharp branches, their tough roots that reliably sustain the toehold of a child climbing vertically to the hilltop.

When we land, I feel the familiar mixture of comfort and captivity that accompanies every return to my birthplace. Escaping Los Angeles for graduate school at twenty years old, I had crammed my records and turntable, books and clothing into Grandma's four-door Plymouth Valiant and headed east for Minneapolis. But as the lights of Los Angeles receded in my rearview mirror, I realized that everyone and everything I cared about was still there. For many years after my departure, I believed that if "the big one" ever destroyed Southern California, I would have to drive west from wherever I was living, wade through the rubble to the very edge where California had finally fallen off into the ocean, and throw myself in. A seismologist of the heart, I felt that without those earliest loves, those people and places as reference points, my life would become unmapped territory. A blank.

Now inching closer to my origins with each move, I empathize with that emblem of the Pacific Northwest, the salmon, whose heroic quest of separation, initiation, and return finally explains my own movements, formerly incomprehensible even to me, but with each step clearer, responding to the inexorable call to return to the birth waters, lured on by smell, that oldest of memories, and by the life force of sexuality itself. After thousands of miles and adventures of years, place, season, and struggle—finally we return, the salmon and I, because we can't find what we are seeking anywhere else, because our lives and our futures (if there is one) require it, this coming to terms with the past.

When Mother turned off the air-conditioning in the Rambler and rolled down the windows, I would quickly thrust my hand outside to feel the desert's dry heat. Greeting the air ritually marked our arrival into Palm Springs.

On summer evenings, after the sun dropped behind the San Jacinto Mountains, and their shadows stretched out to cool the desert valley, the temperature dropped as well, falling from the day's high of 115 to a comfortable eighty-five or ninety degrees. At night, the palm trees along Palm Canyon Drive were illuminated from the base, their glowing fronds magically lighting the streets. My parents liked to join the promenade of people wearing sandals, sleeveless shirts, and shorts, walking and window-shopping along Palm Canyon Drive. Often my father would buy us ice-cream cones to savor as we walked: chocolate for Mother, strawberry for him, peppermint or chocolate chip for me. I reveled in the freedom of hot dry air against bare skin, cold ice cream melting on the tongue.

If I finished my cone by the time we reached the Welwood Murray Public Library, I was allowed to enter while my parents waited outside. I liked the library's Spanish-tiled roof, the white stucco exterior, its rounded doorways, the cool rough surface of interior stucco walls, the sight of rows and rows of books all lined up, ready to be taken home and read. Except for the senior citizens, the library was usually empty. The younger people and families were out on the street, shopping.

The library was located on the corner of Palm Canyon Drive and Tahquitz Canyon, the heart of downtown Palm Springs. Once, my father and I had driven up Tahquitz Canyon Road as far as it would go. At the base of the mountain, we parked the car and hiked into the canyon, following a tiny stream up to a large pool and waterfall hidden inside the mountain. In the waterfall pond, we found three hippies bathing naked. A large mound of beer cans squatted nearby. Earlier that week, we had seen hippies bathing in the fountains outside of the Bank of America building. My father took one look at the waterfall and hiked back down. When we were out of hearing range, he said some harsh words about the hippies, their beer cans, and their garbage, which had destroyed the beauty of this natural spot. Evidently he believed our cars and shops, hotels and restaurants had only enhanced the desert. We didn't keep our garbage by the pools.

If you followed Palm Canyon Drive south, instead of curving southeast with the traffic going to Cathedral City and Rancho Mirage, you would find the road's real namesake: Palm Canyon. Along this canyon's stream, palm trees grew densely and at random, unlike the ones we saw in town. Instead of spotlights, these trees had thick skirts of desiccated palm fronds at the base, and dead or dying fronds beneath their dusty green tops. Accustomed to the highly controlled appearance of the trees lining Palm Canyon Drive, I was slow to appreciate the look of wild palm trees in the real Palm Canyon. There, the empty, spacious feeling of the desert, the possibility of meeting snakes and lizards and coyotes, the canyon's streambed and wild palm trees offered an image of how the land must have looked years before.

Curving around the area that is now Palm Springs, these canyons of the San Jacintos—Palm, Tahquitz, Andreas, Murray, Chino—are home to the largest concentration of palm trees in the world. For centuries past, they were also home to the ancestors of the Agua Caliente band of Cahuilla. My father said the Cahuilla Indians had used the hot mineral springs downtown. It was hard for me to imagine a mud or adobe shelter thatched with palm fronds in a spot now occupied by the plush Desert Spa Hotel. The Cahuilla still owned the hot springs and surrounding land, as well as numerous squares of land set out in a checkerboard pattern throughout Palm Springs. But we never saw the Cahuilla unless we went to Palm Canyon to go hiking, or drove out to Indio for the Date Festival.

Years later, I would learn that the Agua Caliente Cahuilla had developed extensive communities in the desert, moving between sites near the hot springs in winter and the canyon's cooler air and abundant water in summer. They had grown melons, squash, beans, and corn. They had gathered plants and seeds for food, medicine, clothing, basket weaving. They had hunted rabbits and deer. They had painted and carved in the canyon's rock walls. And they told stories about an evil god, Tahquitz, who lived in one of the mountain peaks and made the mountains rumble. For many reasons, this history, this relationship between people and a place I loved was important to me. But my parents traced their Palm Springs history in a different way, looking not to the land but to the history of white vacationers, convalescents, and sun seekers on the land. Movie Stars.

Western settlers originally came to Palm Springs for health reasons, Mother told me. The hot springs and the desert air were thought to cure tuberculosis and other sicknesses. I believed her. Any time I had a cold, it cleared up after a day in the desert. The dry heat, clean air, and pure sunlight made a healthful elixir.

Looking at a geological map, I can trace the San Jacinto fault line running behind the San Jacinto Mountains. In the high valleys of Idyllwild, and in front of the mountains, where Palm Springs lies nestled at the base, runs the San Andreas fault. The hot springs come from a deep place of molten fire and transformation, of life and death and healing.

After health, there was recreation. In the thirties, movie stars like Al Jolson, Constance Bennett, Charlie Chaplin, Janet Gaynor, Ralph Bellamy, and Marlene Dietrich began coming to play tennis in the sun. Some stayed for the entire season, which ran only from November through April because there was no air-conditioning. In the 1950s, recreational interest shifted from tennis to golf as the movie stars aged, and golf course after golf course appeared. The names of these movie stars glitter like stars in the sidewalk: Liberace, Mae West, Nat King Cole, Jerry Lewis, Sammy Davis Jr., Alan Ladd, Hoagy Carmichael, Desi Arnaz. And my mother.

Born and raised in Omaha, my mother couldn't wait to leave Nebraska and become a Hollywood starlet. She made her first visit to Hollywood at the age of seventeen, and though forced to return for a year of college at Lincoln, Mother was persistent. During her twenties, she played bit parts in movies and in stage shows, even acting in one film with the Three Stooges. Her glamour photos portray a blond beauty with dimples, bright-blue eyes, sharp nose, full lips, and straight white teeth. If beauty were the sole criterion for actresses of her time, I never understood why Mother didn't become a star.

As a child, when I looked at my mother's acting photos I was struck breathless by her untouchable beauty, her flawless figure, the haughty tilt of her head. Elegant in 1940s suits or furs, hats, and gloves, Mother posed for photographers, her perfectly arched eyebrows and dark-red lipstick making her simultaneously desirable and unattainable. Long after she had given up acting, she still wore the same color of lipstick. I used to watch, mesmerized, when she used the lipstick brush to outline the contours of her full lips, painting in the swelling curves, and finally pressing her painted lips together against a tissue.

On December 7, 1941, the day the Japanese planes dropped their bombs on Pearl Harbor, my mother celebrated her eighteenth birthday.

Driving in the car, I can follow the history of Palm Springs through its place names. McCallum Drive bears the name of John Guthrie McCallum, who moved in 1884 from San Francisco to an adobe cabin near the mineral waters of the Agua Caliente tribe, hoping to cure his son's tuberculosis. As the first white settler, McCallum bought over 5,000 acres of land and named it Palm Valley Colony. Murray Canyon and the public library are named for Welwood Murray, who leased some land from McCallum and built the first hotel, a ranch-style adobe capable of sleeping twenty-six people. Street names like Arenas, Andreas, Belardo, and Morongo come from the Mexican and Agua Caliente residents. Chino Canyon was named for Pedro Chino, the Agua Caliente medicine man who lived to be 120 years old, though most people know the canyon simply as the route to the Palm Springs Aerial Tramway.

As the city expands farther southwest, the movie stars take over. First it's Gene Autry Trail, then Frank Sinatra Drive, Bob Hope Drive, and then their favorite recreation creeps in. Golf Club Drive, Country Club Drive, Dinah Shore Drive. At last count, there were more than eighty golf courses in the desert. Now the development has shifted farther southeast, skipping Cathedral City and Rancho Mirage, and centering on Palm Desert. There, people come to the desert for the flowers and bright-green golf courses, the dazzling display of fountains and pink flamingos at the big hotels.

Just beyond Windy Point, at the northwest entrance to Palm Springs, near where Highway 111 splits from Interstate 10, the mountains are growing wind turbines to convert the power of high desert winds into energy that can be used to cool hotel rooms, shopping malls, and restaurants. Although wind power is a means of energy generation more sustainable than nuclear, hydro, or coal, my throat constricts when I enter the chilling air-conditioned interiors of Palm Desert's opulent boutiques. I mourn the loss of the desert's own warm breath, its sunlight and silence, and the impact of this new population on the original inhabitants, the Agua Caliente Cahuilla, the coyote and rabbit, lizards and snakes, mice and red-tailed hawks and roadrunners. I remember the wild audacity of sandstorms transforming vast stretches of tranquil desert into swirling clouds of dirt and tumbleweeds. I remember summer's illusory mirage of shimmering water concealed in every dip of highway, in every basin of sand.

On our last night in the desert, Mother and I went to see the Palm Springs Follies, a stage show and musical revue performed in the original Plaza Theater on Palm Canyon Drive. Mother had heard that all the show's dancers and performers were in their fifties, sixties, seventies, and eighties. This excited her. She wanted everyone to know that aging didn't necessarily mean losing your spunk, style, or mobility. To me, this message seemed like just another repackaging of California's youth-obsessed, appearance-oriented culture, where everyone had facelifts and dyed their hair after age thirty-five. I agreed to see the show, and prepared myself for an evening with senior citizens trying to be young.

Instead, the show brought me face-to-face with European American youth of the 1930s and '40s. Featuring the songs of Irving Berlin, dancers in "There's No Business Like Show Business" and "Puttin' on the Ritz" showed us all the glamour of the lavish Hollywood musical era. Wearing headdresses as large as their own bodies, women appeared costumed as trees, as huge flowers, as animals, sphinxes, and queens. The poverty of the Depression was recalled in songs like "Remember My Forgotten Man" and "Brother, Can You Spare a Dime?" But the show's real energy picked up in the songs of the 1940s, as the youth came of age dancing to "Jukebox Saturday Night" and "Two O'Clock Jump." Their innocent exuberance ended abruptly with the experiences of war.

The prejudices and pitfalls of their time were performed as proudly as they had been sixty years before. "Sayonara" was performed by a white woman in exaggerated Japanese drag, while other white women dressed as "Orientals" and pretended to be Salome to the music of "Caravan." During one intermission, the emcee told drunken Irish Catholic jokes, fat jokes, sexist jokes, Native American jokes. My mother sneaked a sideways look at me, probably hoping we wouldn't have to discuss these jokes after the show. Then the emcee asked the oldest and the youngest persons in the audience to identify themselves—ages eighty-seven and fifteen, respectively. To the fifteen-year-old he said, "I'll bet you don't approve of these jokes. Your generation doesn't tell such jokes. They're politically incorrect. Well, our generation doesn't have those four- and five-lettered words you have. We can't even *do* them."

What their generation did do was fight a world war. In songs like "Oh, How I Hate to Get Up in the Morning" and "This Is the Army, Mr. Jones" we watched young men adjusting to military life. Musical numbers like "You'll Never Walk Alone" and "Don't Sit under the Apple Tree" showed us the experience of young sweethearts, wives, and mothers as they waited and worried about their soldiers. The show culminated in a fervor of stars and stripes, a musical medley blending the "Battle Hymn of the Republic," "God Bless America," and "America the Beautiful" with the full cast of performers dressed in red, white, and blue. A cannon dropped its phallic barrel and ejaculated red, white, and blue confetti. Tissue-paper stars and streamers rained over the audience when "The Star-Spangled Banner" began to play, and everyone in the 350-seat theater sprang to their feet to sing with all the patriotic passion of their lives. When dancers uniformed as the Marines, the Navy, the Army, and the Air Force marched into the finale, the audience yelled and applauded wildly.

I stood silent, realizing where I was, and who I was with.

These people are the embodiment of the twentieth century's first fifty years.

They are a generation who believes in the myth of America.

They created segregated drinking fountains, the atomic bomb, the Japanese internment camps, DDT, and the family of Father-Knows-Best.

They grew up in the Roaring Twenties, survived the Great Depression, came of age for World War II.

They gave their lives for duty, for honor, for love of family and nation.

They still cover their hearts when reciting the pledge of allegiance.

When they die, these first-hand experiences will die with them.

These are my parents.

Mountainsides made of granite, the boulders and dry dusty earth home to pine trees of soaring heights: my earliest memories are of this place. Here,

I can see my father climbing a steep dirt trail, beckoning to mother and me. He moves nimbly over the boulders, taking pleasure in the freedom of each step. In these memories, my father is the one with the headful of thick, dark-brown curls, while I am the one with thin, lighter-colored hair. Fifteen years later, these roles would be reversed, and I would ease him through the final stages of cancer. In the time intervening, he would work too hard, putting in seven-day workweeks, coming home to tense family meals and a walk with the dog, falling asleep in the recliner after a few hours of television. I worshipped him. I yearned for him. I never got enough time with him. He was always working.

But in the High Sierras, he is laughing joyously. When he picks me up and sets me on his shoulders, I am on top of the world.

For a long time I thought the images of boulders, mountains, and gigantic pines were a secret fantasy life of mine, something I had dreamed up. I told no one. Then I found some scallop-edged black-and-white photographs taken in June the year that I was two. No one has photographs of their dreams. These photos were marked "the High Sierras" in Mother's careful handwriting. Years later, I borrowed an old sixteen-millimeter movie projector, and Mother sent me reels and reels of home movies. There, in one of those movies, was the landscape of my dreams: a clear mountain lake set against granite mountains fringed with tall pines, yarrow, and sage. I viewed the movie again and again as my father quickly panned the town, trying to catch a glimpse of a sign, anything that would tell me where this was. Then I saw it, a sign atop the hotel. June Lake.

I am returning to June Lake the way adopted children seek out their birth parents. I return to find a part of myself that was born here.

Sketching the western slopes in 1772, the missionary Pedro Font named the mountains *una gran sierra nevada,* a great snowy range. When my parents used the phrase "High Sierras," it had an air of mystery and reverence. I thought it was our secret name for an otherwise unknown location. But *High Sierra* is actually a specific term for the alpine region of the Sierras, an area above the main forest and generally above 8,000 feet, where the peaks, lakes, basins, and other rock formations carved by the glaciers can easily be seen. *High Sierras* means rock.

Driving from Seattle to June Lake, I followed the eastern flanks of the

Sierras on U.S. 395. The landscape around Mono Lake, with its arid salt flats and weird tufa formations, looked more lunar than my much-dreamed-of memories. Too late to turn back, I realized that I was expecting June Lake to have remained frozen in time, like a snow globe that I could just shake and make come to life. The real June Lake could destroy my dreams.

At the town of Lee Vining, past the turnoff to Tioga Pass and Tuolomne Meadows, the road began to climb. The land was still, arid, desiccated, clearly the stuff of the high desert. Amid the granite boulders, only a few tall pine trees dotted the mountainside. Warily, I turned west at the June Lake Junction and held my breath. The road dipped and began a long, gradual ascent. Tall pine trees like none I had seen in recent years stood spaced apart, then clustered together. My throat tightened, then closed. In my mind, images started falling into place. Past a sign for "Oh!" Ridge, at the crest of the hill, the lake sprang into view.

From "Oh!" Ridge, you can look directly across the basin of June Lake to the sheltering smooth granite shoulders of Carson Peak, elevation 10,909. The mountains to the lake's south and west reach to forested heights, but on the north side of the lake, the land is lower, the boulders and yarrow more prominent than pine. On that day in late August, all the colors of June Lake came into sharp relief beneath the clear blue sunlight of mountain skies: rich greens and golds of pine needles, the gray-blue of sage, white granite boulders, burnt orange and brown underbrush, the yellow flowers of yarrow and broom.

The road into town followed the lake's south side, cresting another small hill. Behind a sign that announced "June Lake—population 614—elevation 7,650" stood two huge boulders, one balanced atop the other like an old-fashioned double-scoop of ice cream. The town of June Lake was about three blocks long, with two short streets leading down to other cabins and motels built on the small patch of land connecting June and Gull lakes. Along with several lodges and motels, the town sported a General Store, the Sierra Inn Coffee Shop, the Tiger Coffee Shop and Cocktail Bar, June Lake Automotive, Ernie's Tackle and Ski, a video rental/ice-cream store, a real estate office, fire station, a public library and community center. Two campgrounds dipped just below Main Street.

Walking the town of June Lake, I was filled with an urgency to find the exact places I had seen in the home movies. Where had my family stayed?

Where was the trail my father had first taken me hiking? I looked at every building through half-closed eyes, squinting as if I could superimpose the town of forty years ago onto the town of today.

In the General Store, I found a small paperback titled *Horseshoe Canyon: A Brief History of the June Lake Loop,* edited and illustrated by Betty Bean and sponsored by the June Lake Loop Women's Club under the advisement of Mrs. Maria Combes, historian. The back of the book was completely blank. No famous writers praised its elegant phrasing, its meticulous documentation, its significance to historians. Nor was the editor's biography of sufficient importance to merit a few lines. But on the book's front cover was a wintertime photo of Balanced Rock, the trees and boulders snow covered, a dogsled team and driver in the foreground. Inside, the book's pages were illustrated with sketches of mountainsides and clouds, skiers and fishermen, foxes in snow, tracks of various kinds. It was the kind of book you would laugh for the sheer joy of finding.

That night, in a log cabin just beyond Balanced Rock, I curled up with Betty Bean and read the history of June Lake.

Using *Horseshoe Canyon* and a topo map, I learned that June Lake was the highest of four lakes in the Loop. The entire curve of Horseshoe Canyon had been shaped by Rush Creek Glacier, a mass of ice that must have sat where June Lake is today. In its heyday (the Pleistocene), Rush Creek Glacier extended twenty-four square miles and supplied all of the ice reaching Mono Valley. Following the path of the glacier, from June to Gull to Silver lakes, water flowed toward the Sierras, not away from it, a phenomenon so unusual the flow was called Reversed Creek.

After the glaciers, humans began shaping the land. First, the Paiute lived on the eastern Sierras, collecting tubers and pine nuts, caterpillar larvae from the Jeffrey pine forest, fly larvae from Mono Lake. Known by the foods they ate, the Paiute were called Menache, or "fly people," by tribes to the north. They made arrowheads from the glossy black obsidian found in the Mono Craters and Glass Mountain area, and gathered willows to make baskets.

Betty Bean didn't explain why the Paiute way of life ended.

The first known white men in the area were surveyors from the U.S. Geological Survey in the 1870s. After June Lake had been surveyed and mapped, word of its beauty spread. Anglers made the three-day drive north from Pasadena to June Lake Junction, traveling the rest of the way into the valley on foot. In 1915, construction began for a power house on Rush Creek. In 1917, a power-house employee, Roy Carson, started the first private resort. And in 1921, his friend Frank Lewis rode a horse to the area's highest peak, planted a U.S. flag at the top, and named it after Roy. After the U.S. Forest Service built a dirt road from the highway to June Lake in 1924, power-house employees pushed the road through to Silver Lake, and summer cabins began springing up along the lakes. The Department of Fish and Game built a fish hatchery on Fern Creek, producing a million fingerling trout a year. With more fishing, the town grew.

Reading Betty's history, I tried to find the moment where it had all gone wrong, where the new residents of June Lake began to take too much from the land. Was it 1924, when the oil magnate, Mr. MacMillan, built his retreat on Lakeview Drive and hired a Japanese houseboy to care for it so that Mrs. MacMillan could entertain guests? Was it 1928, when workers on the Owens Valley Project began living in the June Lake Loop, later patronizing Mr. Dumbrowski's Hog Ranch, the area's red-light district? Or was it 1935, when the Los Angeles Water and Power Company built the fourth of the lakes in the Loop, Grant Lake, using it for storage of more water to feed the Los Angeles aqueduct? What about the first building, the Rush Creek Power House, now owned and operated by Southern California Edison to generate power for Southern California and parts of Nevada? Maybe it all came back to the anglers, as Betty Bean kept insisting—"it was the avid fishermen who really led to the development of the Loop." Maybe it went even further back, to the first white surveyor, or to Pedro Font himself.

The same people who took too much from June Lake also loved it, in their way. In the 1940s, the Loop community cherished its own local poet, Bear-Bait Hartley, known for singing his poems around an old wood stove, prompted by a cup of coffee and a slice of homemade pie. His 49-stanza poem, "The June Lake Loop," was reprinted in full in Betty's book as one of the few chronicles of local history. In the 1950s, the area's local character Stew-Pot Slim became known as the best handyman in town, a "one-man cement-mixer, brick-layer, and general construction company," wrote Betty Bean. And in 1963 the June Lake Loop Women's Club formed, committed to a ten-year project of raising money for a community center, and appointing Mrs. Maria Combes to gather materials for a book of local history.

Betty Bean made no mention of my parents. I would have to find that history for myself.

Jeffrey pines are unique to the eastern slopes of California's Sierra Nevada, at elevations ranging from 5,000 to 9,000 feet. Mature Jeffreys can grow to soaring heights of sixty to 170 feet, with branches beginning at twenty feet above ground. When the Jeffreys grow in pure stands, as they often do around June Lake, they form an open forest with very conspicuous trunks. Jeffrey pine bark smells like vanilla—warm, burnt vanilla—or like amaretto. Whenever I got the chance, I pressed my nose between the wedges of bark to breathe in this tree's warm scent.

Everything about these trees amazed me. Looking up to their high branches I saw silky needles clustered in pom-pom fistfuls around double pinecones the size of cantaloupes. Jeffrey pinecones looked like perfect little Christmas trees, thick and full, each scale ornamented with an in-turned prickle.

In these vanilla-scented pines, I recognized the trees of my childhood.

With only four days to explore the June Lake Loop, I wanted to visit every place that might unlock a memory for me. It was like receiving one of those Advent cards with all the little doors for each day leading up to Christmas. Each day I hoped that this day would be the one, that I would open the little door and find my father standing behind it, alive and laughing.

If my parents came for a long weekend at June Lake, surely they would have taken day-trips to explore the surrounding areas. Searching road maps and topo maps, I settled on Mammoth Lakes. Its combination of shops and hiking seemed about right for my parents.

In Mammoth Lakes, memories opened at every turn. There, kneeling by the sign "earthquake fault" are my mother and me. She is wearing a white silk scarf over her hair and has me wearing a pink one just like it. We are smiling and waving. When I cross the log bridge over the ravine, I see us again. Here, I am grinning in bright sunlight, the scarf is gone, and my doll is waving too.

Walking this landscape of memory, I find that though all photographic attention seems to be focused on the two-year-old, I am trying to catch my mother's eye. I am now older than my mother was on this trip, and I can speak to her freely. Take off your scarf, I want to say to her. Your hair is the color of sunlight. The wind wants to touch you. The dirt and the rocks, they know your body. Nothing will hurt you here.

I take the shuttle down to the valley formed by the San Joaquin River, and another little door opens. I see my father standing at the base of Devil's Postpile, a gigantic rock formation about 300 feet long and 200 feet high. He is explaining to my two-year-old self how basalt formed from a volcanic eruption that had flowed molten lava and cooled into rock many, many years ago. Then a glacier, a moving mass of ice, had sheared off one side of this cooled lava, so that we could see the tall, six-sided columns standing here today.

He kneels down and puts one arm around the child, pointing her attention to the Postpile and the fallen columns that lie in pieces at its base. "Columnar basalt," he says carefully, picking up a rock so that she can feel it. Small fingers touch the rock, then touch the father's cheek. When he stands up, she sees that his head is level with the top of the Postpile. No wonder that she reaches for him with both arms, demanding "Up!"

And suddenly I am looking at another volcanic formation, the columns and crevices of Devil's Tower in Wyoming. With the fingers of memory, again I feel the coarse surface of rock. I sense its radiant energy. Then I am moving, climbing beyond thought, acting within the sensation of that first step up onto the rock, hands and arms reaching up, fingertips searching for holds on crevices, gripping onto ledges, jamming my toes sideways into cracks and then twisting my feet upright so that I can stand, pushing my hands into crevices and clenching them into fists, twisting them into place, and then leaning back into air, into movement, trusting the full weight of my body to this tightly wedged relationship with rock.

Finally, I am sitting on top of my father's shoulders.

Standing at the base of Devil's Postpile, I wonder if my vertical desires took root here, in cooled lava, in the connection of touch between coarse rock and whiskered cheek.

My father never talked about the war. After his death, I found that for the last thirty years, he had carried in his wallet a laminated photo-reduction of his honorable discharge. From 1942 to 1946, he had served in the southern Philippines as a technician fifth grade. Under "other military occupations," the certificate also listed "Entertainment Specialist." In addition to a medal for good conduct, and a bronze service arrowhead, my father had been awarded two theater service ribbons.

The second of three children, my father grew up during the Depression. Soon after his birth, my paternal grandmother divorced and remarried, bearing another daughter with her new husband. Unable to keep all three children, the new family sent the first daughter to the grandparents, and my father grew up in foster homes. His elementary-school grades were erratic, rising and falling with each new address. But during high school, my father showed an interest in writing poetry, and began acting in school performances. After graduation, he wrote several plays, and performed in the downtown Minneapolis theater district. Then he enlisted for service in World War II. At twenty years old, he was already married to his first love, Iris. His service photo shows him as a young man with full-lidded brown eyes and dark, curling hair.

When he met my mother in 1952, they were both entertaining the troops headed to or from the Korean War. After their marriage, they slowly put aside the dreams of their youth and took on the duties of adulthood. They went to church. They had a child. My father began selling real estate.

The Heidelberg Inn sits on the south slopes above June Lake, between Main Street and Lakeview Avenue. Originally opened in May 1928 as the June Lake Rod and Gun Club, it became known simply as the June Lake Lodge. Its raw-log lobby boasts the largest four-sided fireplace in the world, a stone construction reaching up the full two stories, adorned with the heads of deer, elk, and moose around its upper level. The lodge offered fifty guest rooms, building cabins nearby to house the housekeeping staff. Decorating the walls of the lobby, numerous photos attested to the lodge's elegant past. In the 1940s, it had been a magnet for movie stars such as Betty Grable, Buster Keaton, Sam Goldwin, Jimmy Durante, Ingrid Bergman, and Charlie Chaplin. Frank Capra liked June Lake so much he bought a cabin there. The lodge housed Bob Hope, Bing Crosby, and Dorothy Lamour while they filmed *Road to Utopia;* the land around June Lake was cast as Alaska. June Lake was also chosen as the setting for *The Call of the Wild,* starring Clark Gable, Loretta Young, and Dorothy Lamour.

I imagined the wide split-log stairway and plush lobby along with the lodge's movie-star past would have been very appealing to my mother. I imagined my father would have paid anything just to get Mother out into the mountains. If she could be comfortable, she would be happy, and he could go hiking and fishing without guilt. As I got older, those camping trips—to Death Valley, Lake Cachuma, Big Bear—happened less and less often. Mother didn't enjoy roughing it, and my father worked seven days a week. Sometimes my father and I would go camping alone, trips I cherished not only for our hikes in the mountains, but for the boxes of Cracker Jack and cans of cream soda my father always hid under his sleeping bag as our special treat each night.

In the lobby of the June Lake Lodge, wild with yearning for my father, for the love of earth and pine that acted like a belay rope between us, I rang the bell to summon the desk clerk. Perhaps the lodge had kept its guest registries from over the years. I wanted to see my father's flamboyant handwriting, touching through his signature a place where his hand had once rested.

A pretty woman in her mid-fifties, the clerk was in a conversational mood. Yes, the lodge had been converted in the 1970s and now it was a timeshare. Many people came back to the lodge, she said, and the management had made every effort to preserve its history. She nodded to the sheets of real estate listings I held, saying that many people who had come here as children now owned vacation properties. I felt exposed—certainly, that had been my first thought when I picked up the information sheets outside the real estate office, but the prices made that idea impossible. She wasn't surprised. Developers who had turned Mammoth Lakes into a beehive of condominiums and shops were running out of room, the clerk told me, and the demand for vacation resorts in this area was still soaring. Lots around the June Lake Loop were being snapped up by developers to build more high-end condos. Already several new, half-million dollar "luxury rustic" homes were being completed along the main road overlooking the lake. In the next five years all the land around June Lake would be sold. The desk clerk only worked half time at the inn; the other half-time job she held was at the realty office. She felt lucky to be getting in on the ground floor of such hot property.

Sickened, I thanked her and walked outside. The granite boulders, the yellow blooms of yarrow and broom, the silver-blue sage, the embracing Jeffrey pines greeted me silently. The Paiute had been driven from these mountains just a century ago. Now, June Lake's history as a place for big fish, a three-days' drive north from Los Angeles, was being erased by developers. I had come back in time to witness the end of another era. It was a change I could do nothing to prevent.

That afternoon, I hiked up the Fern Creek trail to Fern Lake from behind the old fish hatchery. All along the ascent, I was rewarded with clear views of Silver Lake, Gull Lake, June Lake, and even Mono Lake. On the sandy beach of Fern Lake, I sat and sketched the mountains. In the shallow water by the shore I saw small rainbow trout. Behind me, a chipmunk skittered past, while in the trees the squirrels chattered and threw pinecones. I listened to the voices of aspen leaves, to the dance of Fern Creek making its irregular descent down to the valley. Scarlet penstemon trumpeted their colorful message. Beside the log I used as a backrest, vivid blooms of lupine complemented my cast-off purple wool socks. And everywhere I could smell the heated scents of pine trees, water, and sun-warmed dirt.

I didn't find my father on the hike that day. Instead, I found the silent beauty of the High Sierras in the configuration of stark blue skies, craggy granite peaks, an alpine lake ringed with sierra juniper, red fir, aspen, and Jeffrey pine. This image was the one waiting behind the last door on the card. And when I opened the door and looked inside, I saw my reflection in its tiny mirror.

In time, my parents found their dreams transformed into places where they could be the people they wanted to become. In Palm Springs, my mother lived like a movie star. In the High Sierras, my father found a stillness more profound than the silence of exploding bomb shells, ringing telephones, the hoots and laughter of an expectant audience. And through these places, my parents each shared a part of themselves with me.

As much as my father's brown eyes and curly hair, or my mother's full lips, this land is ancestor to my flesh and bone, blood, breath, and hair. When I look at the photos of my mother, posed as a starlet reclining on her chaise lounge, I see the brown mountains of the desert draped in the folds of her long velvet gown. And in the Jeffrey pine, in the mountains of granite and basalt, I reach up to the tall arms of my father.

Because of this land, these parents, I am.

YEAR TWO *Place and Workplace*

We travel light into a new starvation.
From the dark land   the luminous bodies
From damaged water   earth and flesh
There is a damage
A slow scream issuing from the body and the earth.
Something heavy moving through the shadows
Something half invisible seems to be appearing
        In a long journey   a long night
Under the nuclear rain
The old misused and corned-out cottoned-out soil
Seems to rise in us like an organ tone.
There is no life apart from our common destiny.
        —Meridel Le Sueur, "Asking for the Stories
                of Our Mother's Rebirth"

Whatcom Creek

The little city of Bellingham was conceived at the joining place of waters, on the shore where the freshwater of Whatcom Creek splashes down its sixth and final fall, entering the saltwater of Bellingham Bay. When the European Americans Henry Roeder and J. E. Peabody decided to build their lumber mill here in 1853, they learned the name "Whatcom" or "noisy water" from the Lummi chief Chowitzit and accepted the falls and the surrounding land from him even though the land may not have been his to give. But that's all water under the Holly Street bridge, water sinking into mercury-laden silt, sands sinking with dioxins.

Like freshwater joining saltwater, the cultural and urban histories of Bellingham converge here as well: Native American with European American, Asian American, African American, Mexican American. After the Roeder-Peabody mill began operations, European American entrepreneurs hired laborers to mine coal from the mountains and quarry stone from the foothills. Fisheries and canneries were constructed around the bay, employing a thousand Chinese workers from 1901 until 1905, when Edmund Smith of Seattle invented a machine to replace them, naming it the Iron Chink. In December 1906, a colony of 100 black laborers settled in boxcars on the south side of town, brought here from the South to work on extending the railroad between Bellingham and Vancouver. White workers weren't happy with the influx of cheap labor. By January 1907, the colony of railroad workers had been moved to the outskirts of Ferndale, an area well north of Bellingham. Six months later, a mob of between 400 and 500 white men drove hundreds of Sikh mill workers out of their boarding houses in the middle of the night, out in their night-shirts to hide in the tidal flats beneath C and Holly streets, waiting until the morning trains for Oakland, Seattle, Vancouver could take them away. By 1910, only fifty-six African Americans made Bellingham their home, living and working in the blocks nearest Whatcom Creek's estuary, a section called Old Town.

Like other ethnic groups that settled around Whatcom Creek, the European Americans battled among themselves about race, religion, economics. When European American organizers of the Tulip Festival narrowly succeeded in barring the Ku Klux Klan from marching in the 1926 festival parade, more than 780 Klan members formed their own mile-long procession down Cornwall Avenue past Assumption Church, a statement of open defiance against Catholicism and African Americans alike. Three years later, in 1929, Bellingham mayor John Kellogg addressed a Klan convention at the Eagle's Hall, where he presented the Klan's grand dragon with the key to the city. Water under the bridge? Hardly. In a migrant farmworker camp in Whatcom County, a wooden cross was set ablaze in 1994. This time, a multiracial coalition formed, defending human rights across differences of race and class, gender and sexuality. Coming together hasn't come easily, but we are learning.

Urban history records a similar uneasiness of union. Contemporary Bellingham was once four cities: Whatcom and Fairhaven at the north and south ends of the bay, Sehome and Bellingham in the middle. As the towns grew, the trails and roads that were once knee-deep with mud became planked with logs or made passable by rails; the convergences began. In 1889, the year Washington Territory became a state, the towns of Fairhaven and Bellingham became Fairhaven. Sehome and Whatcom became New Whatcom, but new became old, became simply Whatcom. In 1903, Whatcom and Fairhaven became Bellingham. Today, Whatcom refers simultaneously to a 2,180-square-mile area of land surrounding the bay, the Lummi language, the noisy waters of the creek, and the lake above it. Bellingham references a British naval officer, a body of water, a historic town that no longer exists, a modern city of 66,000. Say what you mean. Here in Bellingham you can't say water without meaning land, mountains without meaning trees, salmon without hawks, humans without nature, without meaning. Like water, meaning meanders. E pluribus unum? When you say American, when you say Bellingham, the words are in motion.

After the Roeder-Peabody mill on Whatcom Creek burned down in 1873, Henry Roeder sold the mill site to a group from Kansas who wanted to build a utopian colony on the same economic base that financed the culture they sought to transform. The group succeeded in building a mill and a mile-long wharf out into Bellingham Bay, but they ran into difficulties: Roeder's own claim to the mill site was tied up in litigation, the local economy was in a slump, and Kansas families weren't moving to the Washington Colony in great numbers as planned. In 1883, Roeder tried again, discharging his responsibility for the 4.5 acres around the falls by giving the land to the city as a potential park. But the water and the land quickly became a garbage dump for European Americans. Sewers were channeled into and across Whatcom Creek, blocking salmon from returning to their spawning grounds; refuse was left on the stream banks. And though many lamented the despoliation of the water and renewed calls for planting trees, shrubbery, and grass, the lower mouth of Whatcom Creek still tumbled through garbage. In 1947, the city built a sewage-treatment plant on the filled land and operated it with only one expansion until 1974. Then a new fish hatchery was built, the stream was cleaned up, and a fish ladder was constructed so that salmon could pass over the sewer line, and the few survivors, wild and hatchery salmon alike, began returning to the birth waters of Whatcom Creek.

Creekside restoration for the park began in 1990, when the Nooksack Salmon Enhancement Association cleared the stream banks of refuse, garbage, and blackberry brambles, and planted a variety of native species: red osier dogwood, black hawthorn, nootka rose, sitka mountain ash, trillium and twinberry, pacific willow and large-leaf lupine. Now, schoolteachers and parents bring children here to learn the plants. There are benches here like life-sized Lincoln logs, one end-notched log laid atop two middle-notched logs, perfect places to sit, learn, gaze.

On this day in early September, I am standing on the bridge that used to connect Whatcom's Thirteenth Street and Sehome's Holly Street, standing above wood pulp and sewage and garbage that was dumped here for nearly a century, filled and topped over for another fifty-some years. Behind me to the south is Georgia Pacific, another timber-dependent corporation gone silent except for its tissue-producing plant. On the flats below the creek bluff, rolls of grass have been laid out to cover the land, green lawn carpeting over once-sandy delta. By the Holly Street entrance to the park stands Gerard Tsutakawa's fountain sculpture, *Confluence*. From the narrow apex atop this silver sculpture widening down to its base, where river rock and pebbles lie scattered, water tumbles continuously down between outspread silver legs, a pulsing tribute to the fertility goddess of Whatcom Creek.

Farther upstream, closer to the falls below the post office and the county art museum, is a twenty-foot-tall cedar totem pole carved by Lummi woodworkers Jewell James and Cha-da-ska-dum Which-ta-lum. The totem of Raven, Salmon Woman, Bear, and Steelhead was placed beside Whatcom Creek in 1997 to honor those who work to protect salmon. The totem also contains a warning in the story of Salmon Woman. According to legend, Salmon Woman and Raven saved each other from death, married, and returned to Raven's people, who were starving at the mouth of the river. Salmon Woman gave her children to feed Raven and Raven's people, but warned them not to take her children from their spawning beds. For many years the salmon came to the village, and the people caught all they needed, obeying Salmon Woman's request. But when Bear violated the promise to Salmon Woman and fished in the spawning beds, the salmon died: as Bear touched each species of salmon, all of its kind died and drifted downstream. Raven rushed upstream to stop Bear, throwing black powder on him just as he was about to take the last salmon, Steelhead. From that time forward, Salmon Woman allowed only one species of salmon in the river at a time, and Steelhead is the only salmon that returns to the ocean after spawning. On the totem pole, Salmon Woman clasps two steelhead salmon to her breasts, tears streaming down her cheeks.

From culture to culture, legends tell of a god who gives his son, a goddess who gives her children that humans might be spared. And from culture to culture, the humans abuse the sacrifice, taking more than they need, disregarding the covenants they have made. In Shel Silverstein's *The Giving Tree,* a tree that is Mother gives and gives to a boy child—shelter and branches for climbing, fruit for eating, timber for homebuilding, and finally a stump for rest. How long will the humans take and take from this giving creek, and still be forgiven? Lummi carvers placed the pole here to honor the creek, honor the salmon, to signify the ancient way their stories prove their relationship to the land, their culture's longstanding presence, and to teach nonnative residents of the land: this is how the salmon must be treated. This is how the land, the water, the animals must be treated. If we hope to continue, if the salmon are to return, they must not be taken from their spawning beds.

Seen at a certain angle, the totem pole behind the silver steel sculpture, Salmon Woman and *Confluence* seem to merge, interpenetrate, offering a reconfiguration of images from ancient fertility cults, evoking comparisons with the artifacts from legendary goddess cultures of Malta and Crete. Both sculptures honor the fertility of the water. Both sculptures beckon a return for the salmon, for the increase of the land.

On the banks of Whatcom Creek today, people are fishing, striving to take the returning salmon regardless of the sculptures. In Whatcom Creek, chinook and coho return September through October, and chum salmon return October through December. Chinook are the largest of the returning salmon, living nearly six years and weighing up to forty-five pounds when they return. Coho salmon are smaller, weighing anywhere from six to sixteen pounds and living only three years. When coho return to spawn, the males are noticeable for their hooked snouts, red bodies, and slightly humped backs. Chum salmon become tiger striped, with olive green and purple markings. I know this only because each September I find their broken bodies in the stream's muddy margins.

Below the nicely repaired riparian zone are orange mesh fences, trampled and torn by fishermen in muddy knee-high plastic boots and hip waders who stand on the banks and out in the stream, hoping to catch salmon. My golden retriever, Sequoia, darts into the bushes, sniffing and licking a foot-long salmon lying dead and discarded in the mud. Its belly has been split, pink salmon eggs spilling out wasted on the ground. The Maritime Heritage Center fish hatchery has tried to control the rapacious practices of local fishermen by placing limits on salmon, by requiring catch-and-release above these limits, by offering to take the eggs and milt out of the salmon for life to continue at the hatchery before the fishermen take the carcasses home to fry. On weekends I have seen the banks as thick with fishermen as the creeks once were thick with salmon. It was said, You could have walked on their backs.

Instead, I want to follow the creek, from Bellingham Bay back to its outflow from Lake Whatcom, four and a half miles. I can see the creek's path on every city map, but the blue line that wavers and thins doesn't tell me what it means to be a creek in this city. I want to companion the water back to its origins.

Looking up across the creek's estuary to the north bank, I see the ReStore and Northwest Recycling standing just east of Holly Street, with the Maritime Heritage Center fish hatchery beyond them. The banks where the fishermen are standing, leaning, or casting are animated by the tinkling sounds of broken glass, the metallic crunch of aluminum cans. It's a soundtrack of waste and reuse providing odd commentary on the visual of fishermen casting for diminishing returns. There are a few salmon visible in the creek, a few ripples made by tails and fins, but only a few.

Above the falls by the post office, Whatcom Creek passes under the first of many roadways, this one leading to the city's center: city hall, the police station, the firehouse, the public library. By this section of the creek, Wayside Park, another sculpture of an eagle, *The Watcher,* bears silent witness to Liam Wood, the eighteen-year-old who went fishing on June 10, 1999, after picking up his high-school diploma. When the Olympic pipeline exploded, Liam was overwhelmed by gas fumes and drowned in the water before the flames of the explosion could engulf him.

The Watcher's presence here is a signal of things to come farther upstream, a sign that all is not well, and was not well for a time. The cedar of this sculpture recalls the old-growth forests that once lined the stream. The eagle represents the drowned teenager, the frog at his breast represents Whatcom Creek, and the salmon in the eagle's claws represents the interdependence of survival. Butterfly wings carved on the totem's back represent a mother's love for her child, and the burned area on the side of the totem recalls the explosion.

Behind city hall on Lottie Street, there is a steep embankment down to the creek. The parklike appearances continue only for the seat of city government. In 1907, residents praised the area for "its rugged wilderness," praised "the clear water" that "runs so rapidly and murmurs so merrily." Once I leave this privileged city center, stream access becomes more difficult. As the city developed, Sylvan and Canoe streets were renamed Commercial, Elk Street became State Street, old-growth trees became buildings and benches. Past the public library, the creekside trail vanishes, reappearing in a different form behind the Bellingham Athletic Club at Halleck and Ohio streets. Here a gravel path runs high above the creek, without cozy log benches for contemplation. The stream is too far down, the banks too high and bramble covered; no one wants to sit here, only to pass through. The air smells of chlorine, and behind the gym's parking lot is the first trash I've seen—plastic sacks, a potato-chip bag, a pop bottle. This stretch of the creek is the last restored riparian zone for homecoming salmon. For the next two miles, Whatcom Creek looks more like the Los Angeles River, a wide gutter channeled between straitened concrete banks.

Nearer to York Street, Whatcom Creek is surrounded by bank build-ings, loading docks, construction-supply buildings. Behind a bank's drive-up teller machines is another bridge over the creek, its drains stamped with the motto "Dump No Waste—drains to stream." It's hard to imagine people dumping out coffee cups, soda cans, ashtrays, oil pans, being so culture-focused that their eyes wouldn't see through the drain grating to the creek running silently below. But the warnings must be needed. Over the bridge I see a bike path leading north on Ellis, another industrial street, while Whatcom Creek winds south and away. To find it again I must cross the tangled intersection of North State, Ellis, and York streets, which meet in a kind of triangle rotary. At the center, on the former site of the York-Ellis mill, squats the Puget Power substation, its Frankenstein cylinders and metal spirals, buzzing electrical lines and barbed wire signaling a more powerful but unseen danger, the electromagnetic fields pulsing down to homeward-bound salmon. The business of an industrial culture puts water and its creatures in the background, behind parking lots and garbage cans and fences. From downtown to the I-5 overpass, Whatcom Creek flows through the industrial heart of Bellingham, past car dealerships and ath-letic clubs and office complexes. Its stream banks are shaved and exposed, immobilized and confined by concrete, without protection from industri-ally transmitted diseases, fuel spills and car exhausts, pesticides and pet feces and unfiltered runoff from pavements.

I walk past Village Lighting, through its parking lot by the labor hall, and find a slightly trammeled path through the last patch of blackberry brambles, pulling Sequoia now by the leash. The blackberries by this part of Whatcom Creek have not even been picked, and although it is late in the season there are dozens of plump, ripe berries hanging at every turn.

I stop to pick some for Sequoia, who has acquired a taste for blackberries and will sometimes eat them off the branches if invited. We are feeding each other and smiling, intent on our harvest, when I hear a splash from the creek below. It is a summons, and yet I have to see to believe. Beneath the tangle of blackberry branches there is riprap, huge bales of rocks held together with wire mesh. At eight feet away from the water I can see there is a little rill, a stair step in the creek, though from this height I cannot tell whether it is one or two feet high. Four salmon are attempting to jump this step, leaping, splashing and falling back, circling, returning, trying again. Their tenacity, their persistence, the scent of home powering them past any other hunger—they humble me. They know that any obstacle in their way must be challenged, surmounted, overcome. They have traveled the world, breathed in water as far north as Alaska, swum with the big ones, eluded the hooks and the nets. After all they have seen, done, journeyed, the scent and aqueous memory of home, of birth waters, is what they will live for, will die for.

Here, behind Village Lighting, behind World Gym and Michelin Tire, here is the basic epic of life, the journey. Sex, death, rebirth. The covenant, in water. These are the children of the goddess. And who are we?

Just above the intersection of Woburn, Yew, and Iowa streets, where Cemetery and Whatcom creeks converge, Whatcom Creek returns to the sheltering green arms of Whatcom Falls Park. Here, the force of Whatcom Creek has carved fingers of water through the Chuckanut sandstone that runs everywhere beneath Bellingham. The loose rocks have swirled into sandstone kettles, and the damp earth is covered with ferns and firs and dappled light. Here, sunlight filters through dense cedar and Douglas fir, bounces off moving water, reflecting diamonds on the undersides of trees. Here the landmark stone arch bridge was rebuilt in 1939, using labor from the New Deal's Works Progress Administration to move sandstone arches from the burned-out Pike Building downtown. Now, through these arches pours the pounding heart of Whatcom Falls.

Sequoia and I walk beside this creek almost daily, in rain and wind, sunlight and shadow. We know the large grassy field where the trail first begins, where Lake Whatcom becomes Whatcom Creek, near the swimming beach at Bloedel-Donovan Park. We know the blackberry bushes that grow thickly along the path near Scudder's Pond, a wildlife refuge donated to the city, a daughter's living memorial to her father. Here, great blue herons and Canada geese find food and shelter among sedges and willows. Red-winged blackbirds sway on cattails, and above them bald eagles, downy woodpeckers, and belted kingfishers fly among black cottonwood and bigleaf maple trees. We know the winding wooded paths that pass the creek's first waterfall over the old hydropower dam, the new concrete footbridge and crumbling railroad trestle. We know the pond where children first learn to fish, the open-grated footbridge over the pond's waterfall outflow, the salmon hatchery and the swings and picnic tables farther beyond. We have followed the creek from the stone arch bridge to the lower creek gorge, where the falls have created a whirlpool and swimming hole. Each summer when the water is high, boys swing out from ropes on trees high above the whirlpool, to let go over deep, cold, rushing water.

Across from the swimming hole is the city's water-treatment plant, and just below this, the oil pipeline crosses the creek.

The water level in the creek varies unnaturally. Sometimes it recedes below the banks, and Sequoia has to wade far out into the stream just to cover her paws. Other times, the water nearly reaches up to the dirt paths, flooding over picnic-table benches and stream banks. This variance in water levels has little to do with the season, the amount of rainfall, the runoff from glaciers high in the North Cascades. The stream's volume is controlled by engineers who regulate the water entering Lake Whatcom through a diversion dam built off the Middle Fork of the Nooksack River. It's an unnatural regulation, a disorientation that makes me recognize my urge to read the seasonal health of the stream through its speed and volume. It's like trying to gauge the happiness or emotional health of a friend on amphetamines.

Despite its natural beauty, Whatcom Falls is an intensely managed park, with leaf blowers clearing its paths, a water-treatment plant filtering and chlorinating twenty million gallons a day, and a pipeline, set to blow.

Wilderness

The Buddhist practice of insight meditation, or Vipassana, is a deceptively simple process of paying attention to the breath, and noticing what comes up in the mind. Through the process of increasing mindfulness, the practitioner becomes more skillful at recognizing those thought patterns that cause suffering, and consequently, more willing to let go of such habits of mind.

After two decades of teaching in the university, I was suffering. Trapped in an endless cycle of researching, publishing, and activism that became more voracious the more I fed it, I began to recognize that I would never be able to do enough to secure my own worth in that system. Indeed, the entire structure was intended to encourage relentless, ever-increasing feats of publication, whose merits lasted less than a semester before the expectations for more production began again. Like rBGH for cows or genetically engineered seeds for crops, this demand for ceaseless production was both antiecological and unsustainable. If my body-mind was truly a part of nature, it would not be able to keep pace with these limitless demands. Breaking my dependency on production, on doing, meant reconceiving my self-identity.

For this, I turned to Vipassana. Simply by skillful observation of the mind, the Buddha had realized the emptiness of self and the interconnectedness or dependent co-arising of all things; he had become enlightened.

I was less ambitious.

In sporadic weekly sittings and an occasional weekend retreat, my meditation practice had shown me that when the mind quiets down, the real apparatus of self becomes more visible. The longer I sat, the more I saw. On a ten-day retreat, I imagined I would gain greater self-knowledge, discover an identity that lay at the root of all my actions, beneath my writing, my beliefs, my personal history. I could travel through an inner wilderness simply by watching the mind.

Twelve years after my first wilderness expedition with the National Outdoor Leadership School (NOLS), I packed my Synchilla camp jacket from that long-ago journey and drove four hours south of Bellingham, to sit a week in silence at the Cloud Mountain retreat center in southwestern Washington. Just shy of Oregon, the retreat center was secluded by county roads, rolling hills, and a dirt-and-gravel driveway through a thickly forested tunnel of shade. Half a mile later, a small parking area divided the gardens below from the dining hall and kitchen above. The cars in the parking lot here reminded me of another parking lot in Lander, Wyoming, where we left our cars to become hot and dusty for ten days in the sun.

From the Minnesota prairies to Wyoming's Wind River Mountains, it was a twenty-hour drive. Dan-the-wolf-man had agreed to accompany me, partly because he wanted another solo backpacking experience in the Winds and I was his ticket to ride, and partly because he didn't think I'd make the trip alone. "After a ten-day wilderness expedition with NOLS," Dan assured me, "you'll be able to walk back from Wyoming. My job is to get you there."

Dan's faith in the transformative powers of wilderness told the story of his life. At the time we became friends, he had already soloed for months in Minnesota's Boundary Waters, hiked and canoed every inlet on Isle Royale, and worked in Ely on the wolf project, tagging and tracking endangered animals. Dan never held a job longer than the next backpacking, canoeing, or camping trip, and kept his living expenses to a minimum by choice and by necessity. His four-room apartment above a garage on St. Paul's Summit Hill—"it's a 'carriage house'," Dan always corrected me—was stuffed with camping gear of every kind, with topo maps, photos, leaves and rocks lining his bookshelves, supported by books on environmental philosophy and wilderness travel. My friendship with Dan kept reminding me of the person I had intended to become, but had somehow lost track of in the pursuit of an academic career. The "me" that I had lost was crafted in relationship to a specific topography: mountains. When Dan urged me to sign up for the NOLS course, and described the Wind River Mountains of Wyoming, his words evoked the landscape of my earliest love: the craggy peaks of the High Sierras, the smell of sunbaked dirt and pine needles, the sight of smooth gray boulders, fir trees, and wild mustard bushes. In a ten-day wilderness-skills course, the National Outdoor Leadership School could teach me how to be at home in the mountains. If Dan wanted me to go to NOLS, he obviously knew his business.

Just outside of Lander, Wyoming, I drove Dan up the mountain to the Popo Agie Wilderness boundary, and we said our good-byes at Stough Creek Lakes trailhead. Watching Dan's backpack disappear up the trail, I felt the weight of my aloneness thrown across my shoulders like an old army blanket, stiff and warm and ill fitting.

The NOLS pretrip meeting that evening confirmed my isolation: every one of the eleven campers seemed devoutly heterosexual, white, and middle class. The men outnumbered the women six to one, if you included the leaders, Clark and Jack. And I began to wonder why I was paying good money to spend ten days in the wilderness with a group of guys. The NOLS leaders, introducing themselves through their stories of unlimited hiking, mountain climbing, and wilderness travel, actually seemed like deadbeats to me, drifters in life—sort of like Dan, whose lifestyle I envied and yet would never be able to emulate. Like me, of course, the other paying campers had full-time jobs, yet we were here to learn from these aimless teachers.

After breakfast the next morning, we were issued equipment at the "barn," where NOLS kept all its gear: backpacks, lash straps, tents, sleeping bags, tarps, cookstoves, boots, clothing. Once we'd all gone through the barn and accumulated our group gear, Clark and Jack helped the new hikers by sorting through our personal gear, removing items that we only thought we needed (like toilet paper), showing us how to load a backpack, and weighing our packs on a meat hook suspended from the porch of the staging barn. My pack weighed sixty pounds, slightly less than half my body weight. This ratio was desirable, since we were using external frame packs and thus could carry more weight, particularly in food, allowing us to stay longer in the wilderness. I slipped on two pairs of wool socks, heavy leather hiking boots (weighing at least five pounds per foot), and hauled on my pack. The journey, in short, seemed impossible. There was simply too much weight.

An old converted school bus dropped us off at the same trailhead where Dan had vanished into the wilderness, and our group hiked in through a darkening tangle of trees and boulders for at least an hour before setting up camp. It was still light out as we ate our brown-bag dinners and made small talk. Nearby, we could hear the sounds of a small stream. After dinner, the leaders gave each camper a tiny bottle of "potable aqua" tablets and explained their uses—one per water bottle—in preventing the dangers of *Giardia*. Without safe water, our sojourn in wilderness would be next to impossible. I had never considered the safety of my drinking water before; I just turned on the tap. The idea that something as basic as water was now an immediate concern shifted my attention from fears about personal appearance or comfort to more fundamental concerns, like survival. My very life depended on what I took from the land, and how skillful I was in traveling through the wilderness. The tiny bottle of potable aqua seemed like a veritable amulet. The journey had begun.

On the first evening of the retreat, our teachers Kamala and Steve explained the daily retreat schedule—a cycle of sitting meditation, walking meditation, meals, teacher interviews and dharma talks from 5:30 a.m. until 10:00 p.m. For ten whole days, I would join fifty other yogis in silently doing nothing, just sitting and walking, eating and sleeping—"accomplishing" nothing. The very idea of it seemed to strike at my sense of self as one who accomplishes many things in a short period of time. If I could not be someone who does things, but who simply exists, I did not know who I would be, or how I would be any different from anyone else. The so-called individuality on which I prided myself as an American, and which I had spent half a lifetime in developing, would erode and disappear. I would be no one. It was for this experience that I had come.

Steve explained the ground rules that would provide the foundation for our practice. Throughout the retreat, we would keep "noble silence," refraining not only from conversations with other retreatants, but from all forms of external communication that could disturb our practice of concentration and mindfulness: writing, reading, and all but emergency phone calls. We were to enter fully into experiencing the wilderness of our own minds, hearts, bodies. In the silence created when we let go of all distractions, we would be able to watch our minds' incessant busyness, and find out what lies underneath. Clearly, I found this idea frightening: to a retreat where we were not supposed to read, write, or speak, I had brought a journal and five books—spiritual books, of course—hoping I wouldn't have to use them. To give up reading and writing—this was unthinkable, even for ten days. Like NOLS instructors, Kamala and Steve were going through our packs, pulling out the things we didn't need for this expedition, helping us to lighten the load. As usual, I was not happy about letting go of the things that gave me comfort.

For this retreat, Steve told us, we would become *renunciants,* meaning those who accept what comes into our lives, and let go of what leaves our lives. Every day, we seek refuge from suffering in the diversions around us: food, shopping, work, sex, alcohol or drugs, socializing, and activities of all kinds (reading, I added, and writing). Renunciants are those who give up or renounce these ways as unsatisfactory, as temporary and ineffective means of ending suffering, and instead take refuge in the "three jewels": the Buddha, not localized in one person but also representing our own potential for enlightenment; the Dharma, or the truth of all life's dependent origination; and the Sangha, the spiritual community of yogis. Our lasting refuge from suffering will be found only through these.

To make the retreat a safe place for all participants, and to live a moral life that supports our meditation practice, we would also take the five precepts. With these vows, repeated and recommitted each day, we would express our intention and commitment to refrain from killing, from stealing, from sexual misconduct, from wrongful speech, and from any form of intoxicant. Taking the five precepts gave us a foundation of respect. Together, we would form a moral and spiritual community, a sangha. And each day, we would meditate, watching the mind in accordance with the simple philosophy of Vipassana: look. Look to your own experience. There was no dogma, no credo, no deity to worship. Our meditation practice itself would show us the way.

Along with its insistent emphasis on paying attention to the body and to the present moment, these features of the Vipassana practice spoke to me in a language both foreign and familiar, like a voice from long ago, calling me home.

After breakfast on our first morning, all eleven hikers gathered atop a rocky outcropping in a sunny meadow to hear Jack's class on map reading. Jack stood at the center of a boulder, near a smooth level part of the rock on which I expected him to unfold and flatten the map he held in his hand. Jack stuffed the map in his pocket, and gestured with his arms.

"Look around you," Jack commanded us. "The first rule of map reading is to look closely at the land." Jack gave us a few minutes to look in every direction. "What do you see?"

"Mountains. Trees. The stream," volunteered one novice.

"I know the trail is back there," another gestured, "though I can't see it."

"That's okay," Jack replied patiently, "that's a good start. But what features of the land will you use to orient yourself when we hike off trail?" Jack paused to let us consider that dreadful possibility. The trail was our last link to civilization, and some of us were not ready to let go of that security just yet.

"Always start with the mountains," Jack resumed, "start with the shape of the land itself. Streams, lakes, and wetlands can dry up from one year to the next, but the land changes more slowly, and the way that water has shaped the land changes slowly too. Where is the highest peak? Where do the mountains curve or recede? What do you really see here?"

From Jack, we learned to see the land as it really was, learned to estimate the different heights of peaks and to look for drainages and glaciers, tree line, meadows. When he was fairly convinced that the landscape had emerged into focus for us, Jack asked, "How would you draw all of this if you were looking down at it from a plane? How would you make a two-dimensional drawing of a three-dimensional wilderness?"

As we puzzled over this question, Jack took out a pen and began drawing all over his hand. Thinking this maneuver was yet another minimum-impact technique, perhaps for saving paper, a few campers exchanged smirks. But Jack surprised us again.

"This is what you might draw," said Jack, crouching down and showing us the flat back of his hand. "And here's what it looks like from where we are," Jack continued, closing his fingers into a fist so that the circles and lines on his hand rose upward into three-dimensional form. "These are the mountain peaks," Jack explained, using the pen to point to the circles around each of his raised knuckles. "These are the drainages, where the snowmelt from alpine lakes and glaciers comes down in streams that cut into the mountains," said Jack, showing us the lines coming down in V shapes between his fingers. "The lines follow the elevation contours of the land, and each part of the country measures the distances or intervals between the contours differently." Now, Jack spread out the map on the rock, and we all gathered around it with new interest. "What is the distance between contour lines—the contour interval—on this map?"

"Forty feet," someone answered confidently, reading the map.

"Can you find our trail?" Jack persisted, gently bringing along the camper who had thought to navigate by road signs alone. "Can you look around you now and imagine a drawing of those peaks, this valley, that stream, and the trail?"

Only when a few people had nodded did Jack allow us to find our location on the map and show us how to orient the map so that it corresponded to the land around us. In the process, two different groups emerged, each convinced they had found our location on the map. The topo moved from side to side on the rock. Jack refused to settle the argument but instead asked us more questions. "Why do you think that's the spot? What are the features of the land that lead you to believe that? If we really are there," said Jack, pointing to the map, "then where do you find that little peak over here?"

"But over here there's no green meadow," the soon-to-be-disoriented group's leader protested. "This whole valley should be green. The map shows it."

Jack smiled. "Remember: the map is not the territory. Look at the land first, and see what's really there."

The next afternoon we climbed a mountain of granite, up to an elevation of 11,546 feet. Ascending over boulders larger than my arms could hold, finally scrambling up the ridge line to the summit, I wrestled with the fear that I would jump, that I would be seduced into the void, just to experience the thrill of weightlessness, the rush of gravity calling my body back home. Each time it seemed we were reaching the summit, a new peak appeared behind the one we had just climbed. Ilyse finally asked Jack,

"When will we get there?" and Jack replied, "Right now, we're here. Be there, then."

The idea struck me as delightful. For ten days, we would have arrived at our destination, in every moment. It seemed too good to be true.

At the summit, the air smelled like mint, and the view opened endlessly in every direction. Each hiker fell silent, stunned by the enormity of snow-capped, jagged mountain peaks and sky all around us. The distance offered a kind of communion, allowing us to see vast expanses of mountainsides and valleys that dwarfed our small bodies. There are tangible places in this world where one's entire past falls into perspective, illuminating the inevitable logic of the paths we have taken to where we are standing. "The Big Picture," Jack called it. The granite boulders and rocks around us reminded me of bones, as though we were sitting on the earth's own skeleton. How very alike all the elements of the earth are, and how clear it seemed there, on that summit, that we are made of the same stuff: bone, wind, sky.

In the first three days of the expedition, I became uncomfortably aware of how unlike myself I felt. I envisioned our crude bunk rooms in the NOLS hotel the night before we left, with my toiletries and cosmetics neatly stacked across the shelf below the mirror, my wrinkle-free outfits hanging modestly on a hook behind the door. Now, for an entire ten-day course, we were allowed only four pairs of socks, two pairs of underwear, two T-shirts, one pair of shorts. I had to buy or borrow the rest of my drab wardrobe: a wind shirt, wind pants, rain poncho, two polypropylene long-sleeved shirts and one pair of leggings, a synchilla jacket, wool gloves and mittens, and a wool cap that I would never use, as such things flattened my hair. It was like one of those nightmares when you find yourself at work in your pajamas, hair tousled, face unwashed, teeth unbrushed.

After three days without toilet paper, everyone noticed how hard we were working to secure the necessities that we used to take for granted: safe drinking water, shelter, dinner, cleanliness, a flat space to lay one's bed. Each day we did strenuous hikes with full backpacks, sweating in shirts that had already been sweated in, urinating and defecating without toilet paper. Once every few days we arrived at a campsite in midafternoon and with a couple hours before dinner, we were allowed to rinse (without soap) our dirty socks or shirts in a stream and hang them on a tree to dry.

If there was time to use soap to wash hair or critical body parts, we had to haul water 200 feet away from the water source, soap up, and rinse. Some of the guys found soap to be too much trouble, and simply went swimming in the icy-cold lakes with all their clothes on. For the most part, our clothes retained the pungent smells of our bodies, reheated the next day as we warmed up on the hike. Jack said that the person who bathes too often is punished by more readily noticing the smells of other people. Our best strategy, Jack advised, is to accept that bodies smell. For the guys, this acceptance seemed to come more readily than for the women.

Being on a wilderness expedition was like being stripped of all external gender. My face became oily, my hair dirty, my movements heavy with the weight of camping gear and hiking boots. The expedition had made me leave behind things that I had thought were essential aspects of who I was, things that I relied on and took for granted—not just clothing, makeup, and hair styling, but also sleep, privacy, reading, autonomy, bowel regularity, and even silverware (each camper was allowed only one Permaware tablespoon and a Swiss Army knife). How irritable I would be at home to be deprived of these things. Here, it was part of the journey.

After awhile, I had to let go of appearances and fasten my aspirations on something I actually had a chance of getting: occasional and partial cleanliness and a good night's sleep. When I lowered my expectations to this level, the trip got a lot easier. But I still didn't feel like a woman in the wilderness. And I found myself dreaming of soap and mascara.

On the fourth evening after dinner, Clark told me that he'd been watching me hike, and that I needed to take more chances. He said I seemed to need secure footholds, that I wouldn't take a step until I was sure of my footing, and that I could move faster if I would accept transitional footholds, ones that weren't 100 percent sure but would support me temporarily. The advice seemed familiar: what else was like that in my life?

The next day I watched some of the guys hiking across high alpine meadows, through dazzling blooms of scarlet, lavender, yellow, and white flowers, and noticed the difference: many of the guys moved more quickly than I did. Not only did they have longer legs, but they took more risks with footing and balance. They stepped without hesitation. And I realized that something long ago had told me not to trust the power of my own body.

The same messages that told me when I could feel attractive and womanly were the ones now telling me I wasn't at home in the wilderness.

I began taking more risks. I stopped dreaming of mascara.

The resonating sounds of a bell bowl, rung three times, ended our morning's meditation. Retreatants shifted in place, stretching cramped limbs, releasing long-held coughs or sneezes, rearranging pillows. Steve spoke first.

"Now it is time for walking meditation, a practice of mindfulness equal in importance with sitting. I know," Steve began to smile, "that some people may think of walking meditation as 'recess time,' a break from the real work of mindfulness." A few guilty chuckles rippled through the dharma hall.

Walking meditation was a way of bringing the mindfulness of sitting into one of our most common daily movements. The purpose of walking meditation was to cultivate an awareness and immersion in the many aspects of our immediate experience—in this case, walking. We were not here to become better walkers, Steve joked, but simply more mindful of the fullness of our experience. Paying careful attention to the minute details of lifting the foot, moving it forward, placing the foot, and shifting the weight would require us to live fully in the present moment.

"Don't walk to 'get' anywhere," Steve advised. "Find a space about ten paces long, and walk back and forth. We spend all our lives walking to get somewhere, so we pay no attention to the walking itself. But here on retreat, there is nowhere to go!" Steve observed, with a twinkle in his eyes. "So, be mindful of your walking in this next session." And he bowed to us all.

Outside the dharma hall, I chose one of the paths that sloped steeply up the hill, well sheltered from the soft patter of rain, and began walking. Going uphill, I noticed the tension of muscle at the backs of calves and thighs. Going downhill, I felt the upper thighs tense to brace me with each step. And before long, I noticed the difficulty I had at the end of each stretch. Turning around to repeat my path seemed to cause a certain discomfort. As long as I was moving in one direction, I could pay attention, but I seemed to take the ends of the walk in one swift motion. I discovered I was uncomfortable with change, unwilling to stay with the uncertainty that came when I had completed one course of action and had not moved on to another. Of course, I was very comfortable with walking—it involved doing something, even if I wasn't getting anywhere. What I needed to learn was how to find comfort in the spaces between doing, when time stood still. I made a practice of stopping at the end of each direction, noticing the discomfort, and just being with it.

During walking, there were other things I noticed. Moss, for one; it was drier than it looked, almost brittle. And snails. There were two types at Cloud Mountain, the snail with its conchlike spiral shell midship, and the banana slug, four to five inches long, varying in colors from tawny to striped to leopard. I hadn't noticed this much about my immediate environment since childhood. Paying attention to bamboo, I saw it had a spine on each segmented piece, first one side, then the other, with different segments alternating the two patterns. And on the undersides of fern leaves there were rows and rows of tiny black velvet buttons. There was so much to notice in the world, so many details of beauty. For too long, I had been too busy to pay attention.

After only two days in meditation, I found I was not able to observe things without judging them, and then liking or disliking them. Not only did I have to have an opinion about everything, but my opinions were accompanied by an entire narrative. Sitting at the back of the dharma hall for the first two days, I was already irritated by several other yogis whose inability to sit motionless for the full forty-five-minute sitting was disturbing my concentration. Putting my training in eighteenth-century literature to good use, I invented names for them all. There were Mr. and Mrs. Noisemaker, who always fidgeted, exchanged blankets, or came in late. There was Mr. Manypillows, who was using not only a camping chair but an assortment of pillows inside it. And there was Mistress Movesalot, who had the annoying habit of arriving after we had begun the sitting and then ripping the Velcro bindings off her sandals just outside the open windows of the dharma hall.

When a space opened up at the front of the hall, I moved my *zafu* forward, hoping to put as much distance as possible between me and these irritating yogis.

On the third afternoon, Kamala instructed us in the practice of loving-kindness, or *metta,* starting with ourselves, a benefactor, and a dear friend. The practice of loving-kindness was intended to open our hearts to experiencing the good will we have for others, an experience that often was separate from our abilities to safeguard their well-being. Practicing metta didn't relieve us of the desire or responsibility for seeing those good wishes brought into being; it simply allowed us to love, to work, and yet to let go of our attachment to outcome, or of evaluating the quality of our metta based on our power to control the circumstances of others' lives.

After dinner, I took a walk up the country road from the meditation center, noticed the familiar metal gate used in Washington to close off a logging road, and jumped it. Hiking in across the bridge over a wide stream, I came up to a slope that had been entirely clear-cut. With its stumps of trees and dead branches, the hillside looked as though a box of giant matches had been tossed over it, smashing down the ferns and salal bushes beneath sticks of dead trees. The area had been ravaged.

Powerless to change the past, I knelt down to put my hands on the ground and said the metta phrases for the forest, for the earth:

May you be safe and protected.
May your body be healthy and strong.
May you be at ease in your life.
May you be happy.

The poignancy of the words unlocked my deepest grief. It seemed like a bitter mockery that my species had done this damage, and yet here I was, "wishing" the earth well. Angry and tearful, I didn't want to wish; I wanted to do something. It wasn't enough to be in touch with my feelings of good will. And I thought again about how many years I had used rage as the force for my activism—how powerful it had been for me, and how much it had cost me emotionally. I wondered if loving-kindness could ever be a force more effective than rage.

Although all fifty yogis had taken the vow of noble silence, a feeling of community began to develop by the fourth day. Silently, we understood how difficult the mindfulness practice could be. Each day we heard someone sniffle or sob in the dharma hall as they faced their own inner struggles. Just as if we were talking, there were some yogis I disliked, and some I wanted to get to know better: Barbara, an older woman who walked with a cane; Lucy, a woman in her fifties, who gave up her seat in the dharma hall to a yogi who complained about a draft where she was sitting; Evan, one of the retreatants working here, who took as many walks as I did; the guy with the EarthSave vegetarian T-shirt; a couple of women in their forties who also liked to walk after meals. I found the loneliness, the yearning to have a conversation with someone, seemed to come up primarily after dinner. The daytime had an intentionality all its own, but in the evening, I felt more exhausted, more in need of solace and conversation.

Because I could not communicate with any of the other retreatants, nor was I supposed to write, I contented myself with sending imaginary postcards to Shawn and all of my friends. Instead of the usual vacation message, "having a wonderful time, wish you were here," the retreat message would read "being in the present moment with the way things are, and just noticing that."

One evening after the dharma talk, Steve surprised us. Usually we sang the metta chant, sat for another five minutes, and left for bed. That night, with no warning, Steve kept us there for a full forty-five-minute sitting. Every moment of Steve's surprise was rich with the experience of noticing aversion. After what was surely ten, then twenty minutes, I wanted to check my watch to see what time it was, but I already knew the answer. It was the present moment. Our entire purpose was to pay attention, no matter how long the sitting. After Steve finally rang the bell signaling the end of meditation, he spoke to us kindly, encouraging us to stay for yet another hour. Evidently the practice of mindfulness was so restful, it reduces the amount of sleep we actually need. On longer retreats, yogis could sit far into the night. Steve spoke passionately: every one of us could achieve enlightenment in our lifetimes if we chose to—there was nothing stopping us.

That night, as the possibilities for our practice increased and the limits seemed to fall away, the mood in the dharma hall intensified. I could feel the power of our collective intentions, the power of the sangha. This was what I had come for.

Each day opened up more spectacular vistas: pristine alpine meadows snuggled between steeply rising mountains, their contours shaped by the stream that still flowed through the valley. With full packs we ascended above timberline, crossed mountain peaks, and came to rest for lunch at the summit of Thorofare Peak, elevation 12,058.

Playtime. Jack pointed to the glacier below us, removed his sleeping pad from its lash straps on his backpack, and pushed off. Anxiously, I watched him disappear beneath the slopes and bulges of the glacier's snowpack, exhaling only when the speck of him reappeared on the flat field far below. The other hikers whooped and waved to Jack, then quickly stowed their lunch bags and pulled out their sleeping pads. I froze: if someone were injured while glissading, it would be several days before they received medical help. Rescue would depend on the chance of flagging down a low-flying plane by waving our jackets in circles around the wounded hiker, or on the ability of the fastest hikers to make it back to trailhead, ride with strangers into town, and return with help.

I pulled out my Ensolite sleeping pad, sat down on the snow ridge, and pushed off. The pad quickly gained speed. Faster than thought, my body leaned into the curves of the glacier's surface, did a double rollover to shoot between two suddenly visible rocks, and came to rest, laughing, on the flat snowfield at the base. I had to do this again.

Glissading down glaciers taught me to let go and trust my own power, the responsiveness and agility of my own body. Later that afternoon, I remembered Clark's advice about taking risks in my footing, and allowed myself to boot surf across shifting slopes of shale and boulders with that sixty-pound pack, positive and certain of myself. I felt free and alive.

Moving through the mountains with my pack, I thought about what it would be like to live this way: nomadic, with all one's possessions limited to whatever could be carried in a pack. Mentally, I walked through my apartment and looked at all the things I wouldn't be able to carry: the blue couch, the wing-backed chairs, books and bookcases, pots and pans and dishes, closets full of clothing. I tried to imagine how life might have been for the Western Shoshone, moving through these mountains before the days of conquest and colonization. In this vision of fewer possessions and a life based in relation to the land, a simplicity of living, and a different kind of social community emerged. I needed and used all the objects in my apartment because of where I worked, and where I lived—my culture emphasized separation and independence. But here in the mountains, in community, I could do without most of those possessions. The possibility of merging the two places, the two ways of relating to place and to people—of bringing a wilderness sensibility back to my city apartment—enlivened me. I was imagining the freedom of nomads.

Through the teachings of the Buddha (the dharma), I had struggled for many years to understand right relationship to place. On retreat with my teachers in Minnesota, Washington, and California, I had asked the same question: when was it right to change the circumstances of one's life, and when was this dissatisfaction with place just a mask over the basic unsatisfactoriness of life, or *dukkha?* And at each retreat, I didn't get answers I could understand. All life was suffering (dukkha), and our attempts to avoid suffering were like moving furniture inside of a jail cell, when the more skillful act would be to let go of our attachment to "having everything right" before we were willing to be happy. As long as our happiness depended on conditions, we would always suffer.

I understood this much. What I didn't understand was how some teachers who were unhappy with where they lived eventually moved to tropical destinations, like Hawaii. How did the dharma illuminate their decision? Quite earnestly, I asked. But their answers were not applicable to my own dilemma: I couldn't seem to bring together the places where I worked and the places where I felt most connected to the earth. And until I could find this balance, this right relationship, I was suffering.

On the sixth day, it seemed our hiking group had finally begun to cohere as a community. At noon, Larry, Ilyse, Eric, Chris, Jerry, and I all gathered around, looking at the map. After a few moments of silent study, Chris said, "Wow, look at that. We've come a long way."

Larry, munching, asked, "Really? Where are we?"

"I don't know," Chris replied, "but we've sure come a long way."

But later that afternoon, our group splintered when we came upon a herd of elk grazing on the mountain across the valley. Their wild beauty seemed almost unreal, like a nineteenth-century painting of the Old West before the white people arrived. I could see several young calves grazing or nursing from their mothers, and just beyond the herd, a lone elk with great antlers stood still, watching them.

Meanwhile, on our side of the valley, the guys were talking about the "dominant" bulls. I didn't see any domination taking place, but the guys assumed if there was a bull, there was bound to be domination. This belief did not bode well for our own community of hikers. I stepped closer to listen.

Explaining to the others that "if you blow on a blade of grass, it sounds like a calf in distress, and the cows will come to you," Jerry began searching for a wide blade of grass. A few of the guys thought this was a good idea. Ilyse and I exchanged dismayed glances. Jerry found his blade of grass and began blowing.

"Jerry!" I spoke sharply, but he ignored me, though I was ten feet away. "Jerry!"

He paused from blowing. "What?"

"I don't want you to blow on that blade of grass," I explained. "If it really does attract the cows, you could be endangering all of us. And you are deliberately tricking the elk. How is that 'minimum impact'?"

"Oh," Eric snorted, "get real."

"I don't think that will be a problem," Jerry replied coolly, and he resumed blowing even more loudly than before.

Ilyse murmured, "Isn't the purpose of observing wildlife to leave them undisturbed in their natural habitat?" But she did not confront the guys.

Completely irritated, Ilyse and I resumed hiking, leaving the guys to blow grass, or whatever else they wanted. I was disgusted. Why was Jerry blowing the grass? If he really believed it would work, why couldn't he visualize the confrontation between a herd of elk, one if not two bulls, and six hikers? If, on the other hand, he thought the grass-blowing was ineffective, was he doing it just to impress the guys? Was he trying to commune with nature? Did Jerry secretly feel like a calf, and wish that a cow would come over? Try as I might, I could not think of any good reason for Jerry's behavior.

At a rest break, the guys caught up to us, still discussing the elk—this time in terms of food. They debated how they would eat the elk, how big an elk was, or how much "meat" the bull would provide, and how once the elk had been killed, its body would have to be immediately dismembered because a horse (of which we had not a single one) could not carry all that weight alone. The fact that we had all the food we needed for the trip did not seem to stop them from wanting more.

These were the people who supposedly loved wilderness. No wonder our world was in such a state. And I felt suddenly alone, hiking with people who look upon wild nature and think about killing it, people who look at life and think of death. How could I ever speak to such people? We had nothing in common.

Some of the oldest rocks on earth—three to four billion years old—have been found in the Wind River Mountains. On the backs of these ancient ones, we were given a lesson on "bouldering." Walking over and around what appeared to be largely horizontal boulders, feeling their surfaces through our thick leather hiking boots, we noticed the rocks were anything but flat: slopes and bulges, cracks and ridges, tiny shelves and wedges broke the surface of most rocks, making it that much easier for a hiker to find a foothold. When the instructors were satisfied with our attentiveness to the rock, they led us over to a low-lying rock wall, and we exchanged our heavy boots for tennis shoes. Working with a partner, one person was to traverse the entire length of the rock wall without stepping on the ground. The partner was to spot the climber, holding his or her hands up in readiness to catch the climber if she slipped. This challenge seemed simple until the leaders had us go back along the wall in the opposite direction, letting us see if we could climb with equal strength on both sides. The trick was to use our hands and arms for balance, letting our feet and legs do the work.

Eric and I teamed up as climber and spotter, taking turns in traversing the wall. Yesterday Eric had been one of the grass blowers; today I held my arms up behind him to catch him if he should fall. Then he did the same for me.

Traversing the cracks and contours of this granite wall, I discovered that I liked the rock. I liked touching rock, feeling the nuances of nubs and surfaces. The rock was rough and solid, cool and sharp to the touch. Tomorrow, the leaders said, we would be ready to climb.

One morning, after a teacher interview with Steve, I got a cup of tea and sat mindfully by one of the ponds. Under ferns and beside the paths, moss-covered stone shrines reminded retreatants of our purpose here. Nestled into the bamboo by the goldfish pond, one shrine even held little wrapped Hershey's Kisses, offerings to the Buddha. The calico cat came over to see me, jumped on my lap, sniffed my tea. Mindfully, I noticed all of this, but my heart leaped when I saw behind the shrine just the sandaled feet and shawl of another yogi. It must be my teacher Kamala, I thought. She too must be sitting outdoors. Overwhelmed by gratitude and loving-kindness for her, I sat for a time with my eyes closed, sending metta to the figure behind the shrine. When the bells rang signaling the end of the meditation period, I heard her footsteps as she got up to leave and opened my eyes to catch sight of her before she left. Instead, I saw Mistress Movesalot.

What would it mean to send metta toward my harshest enemy? How would I feel? Perhaps, even—how might she feel?

During the first three days of the retreat, all my meditations were littered with plans for what I would do when I got home, work I would accomplish that summer, courses I would teach in the fall. Simultaneously, I spent many sittings lamenting the things I had not brought to the retreat (candy, mints, different clothes), things I had or had not done before I came. I called these thought patterns "planning" and "reviewing," noticed how these patterns kept me focused on the future or the past, and tried to return to the present moment when I was walking. Lifting, moving, placing the foot, shifting the weight. How uninteresting. And I was off again into a fantasy future.

"There's a cartoon of two monks sitting in meditation," Steve told us, "and the elder monk says to the other, 'Nothing happens next. This is it.'" Steve chuckled along with us, then paused. "The present moment is the only moment we have," he continued, emphasizing each word. "What prevents us from experiencing this moment in our lives is called in Buddhism 'the Five Hindrances.'"

Far from being another exercise in mathematics, I found, the Five Hindrances were some of my most intimate and faithful companions. Attraction, Aversion, Sloth and Torpor, Restlessness, and Doubt—they sounded like the Seven Dwarfs. In fact, the Hindrances helpfully categorized every problem I was experiencing in keeping my attention focused.

Perhaps my biggest struggles were with Attraction, otherwise known as desire, wanting, or grasping. We think we will be happy if only we can have this or that thing, this or that person, house, car, or job, Steve explained. But after we get this thing, we still aren't happy. We still want something more, something else, and this wanting has nothing to do with the quality of our experience in the present moment. Why does wanting continue? Because after our basic needs have been satisfied, wanting only produces more wanting. Wanting and contentment are antithetical. They cannot coexist. It is the wanting mind that tells us there is something more than this present moment. And if we believe it, and follow it, we will never be fully present.

After the talk on the Five Hindrances, I had an opportunity to work with Restlessness the very next day. I felt I couldn't sit or walk mindfully for another moment. Having run out of topics from the past or the future, I was finally stuck with the present moment, where there was absolutely no stimulus. I began thinking about what I was going to wear—as if there were a choice. After dinner (my most vulnerable time of day), I started making up stories to provide the retreat with some sensationalism. Mr. Manypillows would leave the retreat in the middle of a sitting, throwing his pillows and disrupting everyone's concentration. Mr. and Mrs. Noisemaker would sneak off together and be discovered in amorous embrace. The chocolate Hershey's Kisses would disappear from the Buddha's statue, and accusations would be made. And the next time Missy Movesalot came late to the dharma hall and ripped off her Velcro straps, every yogi would turn around to look at her and name their experience, whispering, "hearing, hearing, hearing."

That day was "dukkha" day for me, a day of suffering.

Five more days. We were right in the middle of the retreat.

Renewing my intentions to practice mindfulness, I got out of bed when I awoke at 4:00 a.m. and went to sit in the dharma hall. Many yogis were already up and about. The young hiker was out doing stretches; people were walking mindfully on the paths, or sitting in the dining hall. Yogis supported each other through furtive smiles, kind gestures, someone putting my bath towel on a hook nearer my shower stall. One yogi stepped onto the gravel in stockinged feet so that Barbara could have the path with her cane. I smiled at James (as I've named the yogi who sits so quietly beside me) when I came upon him plucking fresh red thimbleberries and stuffing them in his mouth.

Sitting silently with whatever came up in the mind, we were each climbing our own mountains, burdened with the weight of our own packs. The heroism and the camaraderie went unspoken, but the strength of the sangha was undeniable.

During one afternoon's sitting, I practiced with Aversion, staying with it long enough to notice how aversion has two different feelings in the body—a pulling-back motion, a recoiling, and a going-toward motion, a more active form of aversion. Then I noticed how Attraction has only a forward-going motion.

And then I noticed there is a pleasurable quality to forward-going aversion.

The insight took me by surprise. My dislike for Mrs. Noisemaker had actually given me pleasure, because I could say "I'm not like her." But, I *was* like her; I just didn't want to acknowledge those parts of myself. Through mindfulness, I discovered that when I was actively aversive to someone or something else, I reenacted cutting off and pushing away the parts of myself that I don't like. And this caused suffering.

The political implications were enormous. Racism, sexism, classism, homophobia—each involved a separation of oneself from another, a projection onto others of the qualities we devalue and would prefer to disown in ourselves. Hating those qualities in others elevated us above them; we were not like them. And it allowed us to deny the presence of the same qualities in ourselves.

The solution, clearly, was to develop loving-kindness for those parts of myself I had disowned or disliked, and thus for all others as well. This loving-kindness would allow me to recognize myself, whole, and to realize a richer sense of interconnection with others. For there was nothing I hadn't done or wasn't capable of doing. It was fear of those unwanted, ugly parts that caused me to close down, disconnect, disassociate.

Going out to that evening's walk, I passed Mr. Manypillows standing on the lawn, looking through a pair of binoculars. I paused, shocked: he too was a birdwatcher. Manypillows lowered his glasses and looked at me, then grinned. He held up two fingers and pointed to the trees. I didn't see what he was looking at, but I returned the grin.

The next morning I awoke to find my clothes blood soaked: underwear, polypropylene, wool pants. My period had arrived two weeks early. Before climbing that day, I would have to haul water 200 feet away from the stream, soak and rinse my clothes, and hang them out in the trees. The extra chores depressed me. If this was nature, I wanted no part of it. After all the others had left camp, I did my chores, and then hiked over to the climbing area where the lessons had just begun.

The leaders were showing us how to make climbing harnesses out of tubular webbing, how to tie in to the climbing rope with a figure eight, and how to belay another climber. This was enough information for one day; we weren't ready to learn how to set up top rope anchors yet. Clark climbed to the top of the rock face by going around the back of the mountain, where there was a dirt gully to scramble up. Jack stayed at the base of the climb, supervising the climbers. There were three ropes hanging down a forty-foot rock cliff and three teams of climbers. Jack handed me the running end of the rope and watched me tie in. To belay me on the first climb, I chose Don, one of my favorite hiking companions. I knew he wouldn't let me fall.

"Ready to climb," I said politely to Don.

"No," said Jack. "You've got to shout it. Imagine that the wind and the rock can absorb your voice. Shout like your life depends on being heard. Because it does."

"*Ready to climb!*" I barked.

"*Thank you!*" Don responded, still fussing with the belay device. I waited. "*Belay on!*" Don finally announced.

"*Climbing!*"

"*Climb on!*"

With two steps, I was on the rock. Don took up the slack so that the rope held me firmly. There would be no backing down until I touched the anchors at the top.

On that afternoon, time stood still. There was only the rock. Its rough surface, the occasional lichens. It had been there, silently, thousands of years before today. It would be there when we were long gone. I felt tremendous gratitude toward this rock for supporting my footholds, my fingerholds, my weight balanced with one foot smeared atop a rocky bulge. As far as I knew, the rock felt nothing for me in return. No sentiment, no hope for my ascent, no compassion were I to fall. I did not believe the rock was indifferent; I believed the rock was simply itself: timeless, content.

"*Up rope!*" I demanded, my moves outpacing Don's ability to take up the slack in the belay rope.

"Slow down," a voice above me advised. And there was Clark, peering at me over the lip of the climb. "This is it. There's nowhere else to go."

Rappelling down the route, I thought, This is what a woman in wilderness does on the first day of her period.

For the trek out of the mountains, all the hikers decided to stay together, covering a distance of ten miles and a 2,000-foot elevation gain, a prospect that would have been unthinkable just ten days before.

Breaking camp by 8:00 a.m., we covered the six miles to Cub Creek in a little under two hours. With no more than 500 feet in elevation gain, a steady drizzle to start us off, and two stream crossings, our obstacles were few. At the first stream crossing, we simply removed our wool socks, loosely relaced our boots, and unfastened the waistband of our backpacks. This stream was only about ten feet wide, shady, and knee-deep. We crossed individually, doffed our packs on the other side of the stream, and sat down to empty the water from our boots and put our socks back on. After the early-morning drizzle, midmorning had become gloriously sunny. The clouds had scattered, revealing shocking blue skies and glittering peaks high above our path, winding at the edge of green meadows and wildflowers just below our trail.

The second stream crossing was a bit trickier: it was both wide and deep, unshaded and yet cold. In addition to the precautions with foot gear and waistband, we assessed the group's strengths and weaknesses, and decided to send Jerry across first with one of the walking sticks lying discarded on the stream bank. One of the group's strongest hikers, Jerry often volunteered to haul water for two food groups at the end of our longest days of hiking, nimbly bringing the four gallons of water straight up from the stream to our mountain campsites. Now, in the middle of this stream crossing, Jerry waded methodically over slippery-smooth stones at the stream's bottom, testing each step with the walking stick and allowing the current to flow across rather than against his body. At its deepest, the water reached Jerry's hips. This stream crossing had to be taken more seriously than a creek. We decided to cross in teams, hands on each other's shoulders for stability. The group emerged refreshed from the cold water. It was time for lunch.

I have only one photo from that day, taken during our lunch break. It's a head-and-shoulders shot of Ilyse, Larry, and me looking very self-assured. Ilyse has decorated her hair with a brown-and-white striped feather and a spray of tiny white flower buds. Larry stands in the middle with his arms around both women, his blue bandanna tied around his head so that the point stands straight up, as if he has been crowned King for a Day. His hands are open beyond our shoulders, and his face wears a half smile. I am beside him, wearing a Batman T-shirt with the sleeves cut off, my hair scooped up in a high ponytail atop my head. One hand rests on my hip. All three of us wear a rather defiant expression. We know the day's journey is only half over, and we are in it together.

After lunch, our triumph quickly faded into determination, as our chosen route took us off trail, bushwhacking up to a scree-sloped base of the mountain behind us, then straight up the mountain to a campsite and lake presumably just beyond the mountaintop. Last night, the route had seemed feasible. But as we progressed uphill, all reason vanished. Why had the leaders allowed us to choose this route? As if to mock our loss of faith, we heard thin calls far above us and looked up to see tiny specks of heads we recognized as Clark and Jack high above us, laughing and waving. Then they disappeared. It was the confirmation we dreaded: this, indeed, was the route.

Hiking up that mountain was timeless. Off trail, it was slow going. Low bushes pricked our legs, slopes slid, footing was unsure. For safety, we alternated leaders every hour or so, allowing each hiker a chance to select what appeared to be the easiest contours to traverse as we slowly ascended, creating our own single trail of switchbacks to minimize our impact on the land. Often, the route was at such a steep angle that I could extend one hand while traversing the slope and touch the mountainside beside me for support. I had never thought such steep hillsides were hikeable. Certainly not with full packs.

To make matters worse, it seemed we were making little progress. Every time we thought we were nearing the summit, a later glance would dash our hopes, revealing the false summit and the higher peak beyond. At one of these points, near two trees behind which a fallen log had come to rest in its flight downhill, I stopped, gasping. Along with the steep angle of the mountain, the log was at a perfect height for resting the base of my pack, easing the weight off my shoulders and allowing my back to breathe. We had learned the times and places for removing or resting one's pack. Here, given the slope and my fatigue, if I took the pack off now, I would never get it back on again.

Rest. Looking out to the valley below, with the stream winding through it, I could see we had made progress. Rest. Except for my feet, snugged into the hillside at an angle to keep me still, my knees locked back so the weight of my body rested on bones, every muscle in my body rested. Breathe.

Larry trudged up and sat down beside me, resting his pack and panting, taking in the view.

"Honey," I said after Larry's breathing had slowed, "I don't much feel like cooking tonight. Can we go out?"

"I know you've had a hard day," Larry replied sympathetically. "The office, the phone calls, the clients—and then the traffic on the way home. You deserve a break."

Larry paused as a bald eagle glided noiselessly above us, its head tilting as it watched tiny rodents far below.

"Why don't we order out?" Larry suggested. "We can call that organic pizza place you always like, I'll pick up a video, and we can just stay home."

"You're so good to me," I replied, meaning every word. Then we pulled on our packs and faced the mountain once again.

On the last night of the retreat, the ashes of Bill Hamilton, founder of the Dharma Seed Tape Library, were brought to Cloud Mountain. Bill had lived on Whidbey Island and had many friends in the Seattle sangha. In March of that year, Bill was told he had pancreatic cancer. A woman on the retreat outlined the story of his hospitalization and surgery, amazed at how affable and pleasant he had been through his suffering. Bill had wanted to be buried whole underneath an apple tree, but since such burials weren't allowed in Washington, a small apple tree was brought, a hole dug by the pond here, and his ashes were sent.

Bill's friend invited each of us to take a handful of his ashes and scatter them in the hole where the tree would be planted. Whether or not we knew him personally, we were part of the same spiritual community. As Bill's friend struggled to open the plastic cremation box, I stepped forward to help. My father's ashes had come in such a box twenty-three years before, and knowing how to open the box is not something you forget.

I wondered if I would be able to take a handful of this man's body and scatter it at the base of the tree. One by one, other yogis did so. Watching them, I recognized my reluctance to scatter the ashes was covering my resistance to death, particularly my father's death, and my unwillingness to accept that life is, after all, impermanent. I had been grasping onto my father's life for the past twenty years, unwilling to let go, unwilling to accept his death. No wonder I still felt such incredible suffering.

Only then was I able to step forward, take a handful of ashes, and scatter them into the ground. I focused on the present, on this man, Bill, and all his goodness.

It seemed a fitting way to end the retreat.

On our last night in wilderness, Clark took a climbing rope and asked us to sit in a circle. We were to hand a byte of rope to one person and thank them for something they had done during the trip. In this way, the rope gradually wove together all thirteen backpackers, and many of us got to thank more than one person. When all 150 feet of the rope had been paid out, Clark had us stand up, still holding onto our bytes of rope, and lean back. As we all leaned out into space on that cliff, the force of our gratitude for one another pulled us back from the abyss, keeping us safe.

Riding back to Lander on the NOLS bus, I looked out the window and wept. In ten days, total strangers had come together and found a way to survive, in a place that brought forth some of our deepest strengths and weaknesses. It demanded that we carry only the essentials, and showed us that these were more than enough. In ten days, I discovered a place and way of being that seemed so authentic, everything else seemed trivial by comparison. How could this wild self, this relationship to the land, the clear fact and necessity of human interdependence and the interrelatedness of our survival, be brought back to life in the city?

Driving the thousand miles home, I read the roads as contour maps, avoided public rest areas and instead chose places off the roadside to pee. I felt homeless, torn between wilderness and city, remembering the feeling of my boots on boulders, my fingers on rocky crevices. The sensual memory was indelible. Now, because I had allowed myself to open to the mountains, I felt I could not go on without them.

But as I entered the city, I realized my vision had shifted. Instead of seeing only highway and street signs, buildings and billboards, I focused on elm and maple trees, the thick swaths of wild grass between the highways, the wetlands with red-winged blackbirds swaying on cattails. The wild earth was right here, pushing up through the city. We hadn't killed it yet. I could bring back everything I had learned. Minimum impact ethics. Simplicity in personal belongings. Route finding. Concern for water. An awareness of arriving fully in every moment. The interdependence of all our lives.

On the final morning of the retreat, I arose as usual at 4:00 a.m. and walked the rain-wet gravel paths to the dining hall. The dark fern-filled forest no longer frightened me; I had seen more terrifying shadows in my own mind. Inside the dimly lit dining hall, I found Mrs. Noisemaker and Mr. Manypillows. I sat down and looked out the windows at the gray dawn. Mr. Manypillows, I reflected, just wants to be free from pain, as do I. But Manypillows hasn't realized it's not possible. He thinks more pillows hold that freedom. Often, I, too, adjust my posture in a sitting, looking for the same freedom. What we both haven't accepted is that freedom from pain can only be temporary.

Looking around the dining hall, I saw other yogis having coffee or tea, collecting their belongings for the shower. These were people who simply wanted the same things I want, who were here to make the effort to know themselves more fully.

Cloud Mountain was truly a recovery center, a detox unit where doers could sober up to their own being. Here, we had journeyed into the wilderness of our own minds and bodies, practicing how to live fully in the present moment, just as it was. In her book on *Lovingkindness,* Sharon Salzberg writes, "It is a state of peace to be able to accept things as they are. This is to be at home in our own lives."

YEAR THREE *Home/Economics*

The key elements in this vision are that people must first understand and internalize the linkage between environmental degradation and unsustainable livelihoods so as to make conscious efforts—driven by strong felt needs and convictions—to improve their livelihoods through environmental conservation.
                    —Wangari Maathai, *The Green Belt Movement*

In the face of globalization, we have moved toward recovery of local self-reliance.
                    —Winona LaDuke, White Earth Land Recovery Project

A feminist economics approach is particularly important in proposals for green economies that stress the local and the communal. Without gender awareness, local and communal could continue to be parochial and patriarchal, with women doing the most menial and lowest-status work.
                    —Mary Mellor, "Ecofeminist Political Economy:
            Integrating Feminist Economics and Ecological Economics"

Climbing

On the winding road up to Mount Baker, Roger shows eight would-be snow climbers how to make knots in the climbing rope while Bud drives the van. Girth hitches, butterfly knots and prusiks, figure eights—we learn or review them all. This snow-climbing class, and another weekend course on glacier travel and crevasse rescue, are mandatory for those of us hoping to be accepted for the Mount Baker summit climb in July. Between knots, we catch glimpses of the Nooksack River flowing wide and rapid, bulging with spring snowmelt off hillsides and the Deming Glacier. Rising steeply beside us, jagged outcroppings of andesite and basalt poke through snowbanks piled thirty feet or higher, reminders that snowplows have worked hard all winter to clear the roads. Stark blue skies bring the snow and rock of these volcanic peaks into clear relief on this bright Sunday in early May.

Bud says the North Cascades Range contains the most diverse collection of materials of anywhere he knows. The mountains were formed when an island the size of a small continent, complete with its own volcanoes, floated from the South Pacific and slammed into this part of the North American plate, pushing up mountains from the ocean floors, joining rocks of the north with volcanoes of the south. "See Table Mountain?" Bud points to a mountainous wall of rock and snow whose summit runs level like a platform rather than a peak. "The rocks up there are from the bottom of the ocean."

Because these diverse materials are already cohabitating, no one asks if they should be together or not. No one suggests that the rocks from the sea floor won't be able to make it at 9,000 feet in snow and sky, and they had better get back to the murky saltwater depths where they belong. No one questions whether the pressure of the subduction zone might not be too much for these metamorphic rocks. The mountains are here already, and they seem to have worked it out.

Unlike the mountains, our group of snow climbers is predictably homogenous. Six of the eight students are women in their late thirties to forties; of these, Beth and I are the only dykes, a difference that may be invisible to the others. As one might expect, the two leaders are heterosexual men. The leisure, the interest, the strength, the gear, the history—these are available to them. Another characteristic of our group is that, like the snow, everyone here is white. And everyone has paid money and time to be here.

For our first class on snow climbing, we stand knee-deep in sticky clumps of heavy snow, bright sunshine reflecting glare, squinting at the instructors as they explain the mechanics of ropes, anchors, and belay devices. Roger shows us how to set a dead-man anchor. Bud sets out stakes in the snow, ties on some webbing and a carabiner, then clips his rope to the anchor. On his belt are two belay devices, variously shaped metal or steel alloy that allow climbers to protect each other from falling as they advance their party across rock and ice. One piece is called a Sticht plate, a circle of steel with two elliptical holes inside it and a metal spiral below. The other is called a tuber, offering the same principle of elliptical holes in a circular metal shape, only this one is elongated, tubular. It's called an air traffic controller, or ATC, a title that conveys all the bragging that guys do about their feats on rock and ice, their sense of power, control, and authority. "This device is state-of-the-art," Bud tells us confidently.

I can't help but smile. I remember learning how to use two simple carabiners as a belay device (gates reversed and opposed) before locking carabiners were something everyone was expected to have. Locking carabiners cost two to three times what a regular carabiner cost, even then. For belays and rappelling, I used a blue or purple figure eight. It made sense to carry one double-duty piece of gear rather than several.

"Figure eights are obsolete," Bud informs us. "Climbers used them to rappel and they'd get the rope so twisted up the next person would have to untie completely in order to untangle the rope before it could be used again."

This problem never happened to me, to any of my group, or to anyone I climbed with. Everyone knew that tubers were just a cooler belay device than a figure eight. They were new. They cost more. Few people had them yet. Everyone wanted one.

My favorite climbing partner, Tom, had all the latest gear even though he was still finishing his undergraduate engineering degree and his work was sporadic. When most of our climbing community was still using hexes and stoppers for protection, Tom had a collection of camming devices. When he got his own #4 cam, the biggest one available at the time, he carried it around with him, demonstrating all the places one could use it to set an anchor: between tables in a restaurant or between cushions on a chair, underneath the stone steps leading up to his house, or even in Tom's mouth, if opened very widely.

When we met, Tom was a student in my technical writing class. One day Tom brought in photos from his most recent climbing trip, and we discovered our shared love of climbing and the outdoors. After that, we talked about climbing whenever there was a lull in the computer lab. On the last day of class, as I always did at the time, I came out to my technical writing students. First, I asked how many of them knew someone who was gay, lesbian, or bisexual, and after only three out of twenty-four students had raised their hands, I told them they could all raise their hands the next time. I told them this was a gift I was giving them. This information about difference hadn't really mattered during the class, but now that they had gotten to know me, they could add this information to what they already knew, rather than seeing everything about me through the lens of my sexuality.

Many of these students were from small towns in northern Minnesota, third-generation Scandinavians coming to the "big city" of Duluth for the first time. My announcement did not register on their faces. Some looked away. But Tom never took his eyes off me during the whole scene. After class, he asked me to go climbing with him. Later I learned from friends how impressed Tom had been with my courage that day in class. He said he wanted to climb with someone who could move through fear.

Class privilege and class differences are things our society thinks about even less than differences of race, gender, or sexuality. Because of the myth that we live in a classless society, these differences are harder to recognize. Almost everyone but the very rich and the very poor will say they are middle class, if asked. But class is not the same thing as money. As Joanna Kadi explains in *Thinking Class,* class identity comes from many places: education, values, culture, income, dwelling, lifestyle, manners, friends, ancestry, language, expectations, desires, sense of entitlement, religion, neighborhood, amount of privacy. Writing about class in *Sinister Wisdom,* Caryatis Cardea says that your sense of yourself in the world comes only partly from money. The rest comes from saying, My mother is a teacher, as opposed to, My mother cleans the toilets after school closes.

These differences in class, learned before the age of twelve, affect us all our lives. They affect how we think about the world, about our opportunities in the world, and they persist independently of the changes we may make in our later lives—regardless of how much money we make, how much education we get, where we live or work.

They affect how we climb, or if we climb at all.

Tom was working class and he wanted to climb—loved to climb, in fact, loved to be outdoors. He used to invite me to evenings at the climbing wall, where we could spend three hours working together to perfect our moves. Actually, perfection was his goal, and he was fanatic about it—but then, he was fanatic about anything he took an interest in, a quality that could work for or against him. He climbed routes again and again, making up games to challenge himself, informing his belayer, "Okay, now I'll climb it without using my left hand," or, "Now I'll climb it blindfolded," or, "Now I'll climb it without using those four holds" (the key holds on the route). He always wanted others to play along with him and sometimes I did, but Tom's standards weren't fun for me. They were painfully high. Now I wonder if they were even really fun for him, or just a form of self-punishment, a way of withholding self-acceptance until he reached some unattainable standard and was perfect enough to warrant being loved. It never occurred to me that Tom was able to attempt the wild stunts he did on the rock, on the bike, or even with his heart because he felt he had nothing to lose.

That first day on the snow, we learned the basics of snow travel: how to kick step, duck step, and French step our way up and down the mountains of snow and ice; how to use an ice axe to stop ourselves from sliding down the mountain, a process called "self arrest"; how to move across the snow when roped together in a climbing team, placing and cleaning anchors, and going into self-arrest when other climbers fell. We practiced sliding down slopes of snow and ice in every imaginable position—seated, head first, upside down and backward—to be sure we could use the ice axe quickly and safely to break a fall.

Some people were more comfortable than others in taking the risk of losing control, then trusting their own bodies and their newly acquired skills to save themselves. One woman had great difficulty even trying to slide. When Bud noticed this, he brought our group down to a slide about ten feet from the flat-packed snow base and had us practice there. Given a shorter distance to fall, the woman felt safe enough to let herself slide, lose control, then self-arrest. Bud's democratic approach to snow was working for all of us.

Finally, on a simple upright glissade from the hilltop, Bud and Roger showed us how to use the point of the ice axe as a brake, keeping the pick and adze out and to the side, well away from our bodies. When it was my turn, I chose to slide the chutes and bumps upside down and backward, feeling the rush of snow below me while staring up into clear blue skies above snow-covered peaks, allowing myself to gain more and more speed before pulling the ice axe up to my shoulder and flipping over, digging the pick and my shoulder into the snow. When I got to the base, laughing from the thrill of it all, Roger quietly told me I needed to be more careful with the axe point. Evidently I could have pierced my thigh, possibly even my femoral artery, from one wrong bump in the position I'd been holding the axe. Falling to death, or bleeding to death—I needed to learn how to avoid them both.

To me, this was adventure. To someone else, it might be unnecessary risk. Perhaps it all comes down to how we define adventure and risk.

In his book *Flow,* Mihaly Csikszentmihalyi explains *flow* as that balance between risk and skill, when the adventurer is pushing all available skills to their previous limits and moving just beyond them with an acceptable level of risk. Flow is the sense of working at the edges of one's ability and tolerance—but it is not doing the impossible, because by definition that cannot be done, and it's no fun to try and fail. Flow is about success.

Middle-class and working-class people, women and men, queers and straights, whites and nonwhites all have different senses of risk and adventure, and these are not inherent differences, but real assessments of safety and support, based on the social and material conditions of our lives.

A lot of mountaineers go into the wilderness with a knapsack of privilege that consists of tangible and intangible goods. Tangibles include the money to buy the knapsack itself, the Gore-tex clothing, climbing and camping gear, boots and helmets that make it all possible. Recent tangible accessories also include cell phones and the global positioning unit (GPU) that can spot one's location exactly and transmit signals to others if one is buried beneath an avalanche or caught in a whiteout. Intangibles include time: time to acquire the mountaineering skills, time off work and away from household duties, time to take the trip itself. The crucial intangible is the sense of risk and safety. Part of privilege is the confidence that you will be rescued somehow if anything "bad" happens. Few people go mountaineering believing this trip will be their last. This confidence in being rescued by unseen helpers is reinforced particularly in the lives of white, middle- and upper-class people: through employer-provided health insurance and long-term disability insurance, through car insurance and dental insurance, through inheritance and credit, people with privilege are constantly receiving signals that someone will rescue them. Mountaineers get search-and-rescued all the time. Their loss and recovery becomes a public, newsworthy event. But when a waitress loses her child support and day care, the rescue teams and TV cameras are nowhere to be found.

What do we see as heroic? What counts as meaningful risk?

Maybe it's human to want to take risks, to want to push the limits of what we can do, to challenge ourselves. Even the woman who was afraid of sliding and self-arrest wanted to be on the mountain. She just wanted a risk of a different size, one that would push her limits and yet allow her to reach her goals. When someone is already taking plenty of risks in her daily life, the idea of going up to a mountain to risk her life seems at best unnecessary, and at worst, redundant.

Poor and working-class people take risks with their lives every day. They take jobs without health care because these may be the only jobs available to them. They work without hope of getting ahead. Women take risks each time they walk alone at night. People of color know the risk of driving, let alone walking, in rural America.

No wonder that when someone working and living within these conditions of danger and risk sees photos of people rock climbing, he may rightly ask, "Why would anyone want to do *that?*"

For the glacier travel and crevasse rescue course, our leaders chose the Heliotrope Ridge trail, a four-and-a-half-mile hike up to an ice flow off Mount Baker's Coleman Glacier. When we parked the van and pulled on our backpacks at trailhead that morning it was already raining, but after two miles of hiking up trail, the rain changed to snow. Sweating inside raingear, panting up switchbacks, slipping on mud and slush as we stepped awkwardly over fallen trees while balancing our fifty-pound packs, the group sorted itself out. In the front were the hardcore hikers: Dave, a tall, balding mountaineer who kept a steady, quick pace; Laura, a small Italian woman in her midfifties, still strong from her years as an Outward Bound instructor; and me, a middle-aged college professor and aerobics junkie. We kept up good conversation and a good pace until we reached the snow field where we'd been told to wait for the others. There, we shifted gear, pulled out our ice axes and crampons, put on climbing harnesses, and roped together, four people on a 160-foot rope.

As before, Dave was in the lead, followed by me and then Laura, but now Beth tied in between Laura and me. Beth's knees weren't the strongest, she told us, so she carried ski poles for help in climbing and balancing. Crossing the first snow field, it wasn't long before I was pulling and being pulled between Beth and Dave, yanking on the rope behind me to urge Beth along, while looping up the slack ahead between me and Dave. Several times when Beth stalled unexpectedly, I lost my footing and slipped off trail. Then the sliding snow and bulky pack made it even harder for me to regain my balance.

I would have struggled on this way for the last mile and a half if Laura hadn't called out to me. To my surprise, she told me that the slowest climber was not the problem. Coiling the excess slack in the rope between Dave and me was making me the unsafe climber; if one of us fell into a crevasse and the others went into self-arrest, we would have to fall that much farther to take up the slack. To correct the problem, Laura suggested, I needed to start behaving in accordance with the way things were on the glacier: we were roped together for our own safety. I couldn't keep walking at my own pace without putting my whole rope team at risk.

Now I remembered: in the mountains, the values were reversed. Interdependence, not independence, was the key to survival here.

When Laura took over the lead from Dave, she set a slower pace, one we could all keep step together. And the rope stayed taut as we crossed the glacier.

Among the climbers on Lake Superior's North Shore, Tom was known for his full wardrobe of spandex shorts and tights, and his delight in the array of colors and styles he was able to mix and match. The years we climbed together, I remember him wearing red spandex shorts and a blue wind jacket, with a small fanny pack snapped around his waist. Tom and I belayed each other on the Needles of South Dakota, on Arizona's Mount Lemmon, and on Minnesota climbs at Shovel Point, Palisade Head, and Blue Mounds. In photos of those years, I can see Tom playing Hacky Sack at the top of a three-pitch climb in South Dakota; Tom leaning back off the second of seven rappels down a 900-foot climb, his tongue defiantly touching his nose; and one image of me belaying Tom on Palisade Head above Lake Superior, my attention casually focused on examining my fingernails. "This is my belayer," Tom loved to say, snorting, when he showed this picture, proof that he rarely needed the belay.

In my favorite photo, the faces aren't visible—only the silhouette of a rocky pinnacle, our two bodies against the sky, and the belay ropes dangling from our hands and harnesses. Tom and I wanted to do a "simulrap" down Tricuni Nail, a three-headed spire in the Needles. To do this, Tom had to lead the climb, belay me up the route, and wait for me to tie in to the summit anchors. Then Tom and I laid the two 9-mill ropes between the humps of the spires, coiled and tossed the running ends down opposite sides of the spire, put each other on belay, and undid the anchors. There was this awful moment at the top, when we were each leaning back on opposite sides of the spire, five feet away from each other but face to face, and we realized the only thing holding us there was the weight of each other's bodies. If one of us screwed up, we'd both fall the distance. Eye to eye, we paused.

"I've got you," Tom assured me.

"Liar," I taunted, "I've got you."

At Xuehua's Chinese New Year's party, I listened to two young white men from Environmental Studies exchange stories of their climbing trips. One man had gone climbing in China, another had gone trekking in Nepal, and both had gone snowboarding throughout the mountains of southeast Asia. One of the climbers, John, told our small cluster of aspiring mountaineers that of the five best ice climbers in North America, four of them were dead. We caught our breaths and exchanged glances of horror mixed with rapt wonder.

What does it mean when first-world climbers travel to distant countries where the majority of people live in poverty as a result of global trade agreements that benefit the climbers' own country? What does it mean to hire those people to guide you through their country's wilderness? Or to visit that wilderness without the benefit of native guides, and then leave the country, having accomplished the climbing that you came for?

Where does colonialism stop?

Is it reasonable to talk about class privilege only within the context of a specific society, or, in a global economy, can we talk about class privilege on a global scale?

Sky diving. Bungee jumping. Glacier travel. Living without health insurance. Which of these are acceptable risks? Which are meaningful risks? Which ones will inspire college students to gasp and say your name with reverence after you die?

Is it a more meaningful risk to climb a glacier and summit a volcano, or to change the structure of your economic life?

One night I dreamed I was in a three-story-high gymnasium that had a running track around the third level. In the center and from the sides from the ceiling hung suspended all sorts of gymnastic equipment: swinging bars, loops, and ladders. Extending lengthwise along one half of the gym, suspended just above the first floor, was a wide springy webbed net, rigged so the gymnasts on the third level could practice and push their limits, take risks, fall, and bounce in the net. The other half of the gym was free for basketball. I was running on the track across from the gymnasts, and when a swinging bar came my way, other joggers helped me up on the bar to swing out over the gym. I don't recall having any feelings about going out on the bar. It was as though I had done this before, and was confident about my abilities. But once I was in the air, hanging from the bar with my hands, I realized I didn't have chalk or wristbands. My hands began sweating and I began to slip. I called out for help, and people below me began trying to move the webbed net from one half of the gym to the other, below where I was swinging. But the net was big and heavy, and they weren't moving it quickly enough. I was slipping.

I woke up then, realizing the depth of the feeling that there is no net.

After crossing a few snow fields, our rope team arrived at the rocky brink of a lateral moraine. Below us, Coleman Glacier stretched out its frozen white-blue length, riddled with deep crevasses. This would be our training ground for learning crevasse rescue techniques. Now, it was time to set up camp.

Beth and I had decided to share a tent, but could find no level spot for setting it up. Everywhere the snow sloped gently or dangerously downhill. Dubiously, we watched the leaders set out snow shovels and explain the art of crafting a tent pad. Any site out of the obvious path of an avalanche would do. We would simply have to shovel out a level area large enough to accommodate our tent. Somewhat dismayed, Beth and I took turns shoveling until we had created a bumpy but reasonable tent platform. Then Beth pitched her tent and set up our sleeping pads and bags inside it, while I began cooking dinner. When she was done, she called me over.

That's when I discovered Beth's tent was made largely of screen.

At the pretrip meeting, Beth and I had agreed to be tent mates and divided up responsibilities for bringing our shared gear: tent, ground cloth, stove, fuel, food. Beth didn't inspect my stove; I didn't see her tent. We made some assumptions about each other's mountaineering skills and resources. Neither one of us owned winter-weight sleeping bags, but the leaders had assured us that inside a tent, our three-season bags would be warm enough for one night on the mountain. Of course, that assurance depended on the tent being fully enclosed.

Beth didn't seem worried about freezing to death in the night, and I tried to put such thoughts aside. We ate an early dinner and went on to the first crevasse rescue class, hiking a half mile away from our tents and onto the glacier.

As the leaders reviewed techniques for setting up ropes and anchors for the z-pulley rescue system, it began snowing. The wind picked up, blowing stiff and crisp over the glacier. The sun disappeared behind clouds, and the temperature plummeted. Climbing students stamped their feet, listened to the leaders, and pulled on caps and snow jackets. After the instruction, we were to practice climbing out of the crevasses using prusiks.

But I couldn't stop thinking about the tent, and how it was already being ventilated with wind and snow. When Roger was alone at the rope, I told him our situation. Unless the problem could be resolved within the resources of the group, I reasoned, Beth and I should be allowed to hike out now while it was still light, sleep in the van, and return in the morning.

Roger called to Bud, and the leaders stepped away from us to confer. Then Roger returned with their decision. Both of the leaders had brought winter-weight sleeping bags and a winter-quality insulated tent. They would exchange tents with Beth and me.

Telling the news to Beth, I practically wept with the generosity of the leaders. Clearly the ventilated tent was a result of Beth's and my own miscommunication, and the leaders were protecting us from the consequences of our mistake. On this glaciated mountain in the snow, such generosity was life itself.

That night, the winds blew sharp and cold. In the leaders' tent, Beth and I listened to snow hitting the outsides of the tent as we stayed warm in our own sleeping bags. As the night progressed and the snow continued to fall, our tent became even warmer. By morning, we awoke to bright clear blue skies, puffy white clouds, and at least six inches of snowfall.

Bud and Roger told us they had slept soundly.

On one of our last phone calls, Tom talked about suicide, a topic he had raised before. I tried to enumerate the reasons not to do it, foremost among them the pain it would cause his family and friends. Of course, we agreed, that's not a reason to live—just a reason not to die. We joked about the billboards we saw around Duluth that winter that proclaimed "#1 Cause of Suicide: Untreated Depression!" as if this were some kind of discovery. "Well, what else would it be?" Tom scoffed. "What would the #2 cause be?" I responded. Tom said he wanted to hang himself off that sign, after drawing an arrow from its insightful analysis to the place his body would be. The conversation took an upward turn from there, and after awhile I thought it was safe to hang up. You can't keep someone on belay indefinitely. At some point, they have to climb or fall on their own.

Months later, Tom chose to hang himself with a climbing rope rigged in a doorway inside his apartment. Dave, the best climber on the North Shore, was the one to find Tom the next day when he didn't show up for work. Dave said the knots were perfect, of course. The eerie thing about Tom's death was that Tom's feet were touching the floor. There was no overturned chair, no sign of struggle. Tom had simply put the rope around his neck and leaned back. Had he chosen to live in his last moments of consciousness, all he would have needed to do was to stand up.

What breaks my heart is that he used the climbing rope. This rope was Tom's connection to the climbing community and to me as his climbing partner. In climbing lore, there are stories of unbelievable heroism, where climbers are buried alive by snow or falling rock. When their broken bodies are found, one hand is still gripped tightly around the rope—the brake hand—proof that climbers belay the lead climber even in death. Tom's suicide made us feel as if one of us had committed the unforgivable sin in climbing: we had let go of the brake hand when Tom was climbing.

Why does anyone climb? Many of us do it as a way to get outdoors, in the same way that other people go fishing or hiking. We climb to participate in a community of climbers, usually a fun-loving group of jokesters who still remember what it means to play, to find joy in being useless and silly and unproductive, a group who temporarily thumb their noses at the Puritan Work Ethic. We go for the physical thrill of it, for the pleasure of using our bodies' own strength and cunning, the adrenaline rush of fear and desire on the rock, the incredible sensuality of life rubbing up against death, the interdependence of climber and belayer. We eroticize the clinking of stoppers and belay devices as we hike in to set up anchors, the dusty, supple feeling of a 10-mill. climbing rope as we stack it with our hands. Almost all of us see vertical rock and feel desire, a movement inside our bodies toward the rock that can't fully be explained.

"It's an 'up' thing," we say.

Many of us climb as a way of learning how to move with fear instead of becoming paralyzed by it. Risk, the tension between fear and desire, is at the crux of climbing: in order to fulfill your desire to move on the rock, you have to move through fear and let go of safety; you have to release your current holds in order to find new ones. Being "gripped" or paralyzed with fear can cause you to cling to the rock unskillfully, making even a neutral situation unsafe. There's a saying that in the mountains, speed is safety. You need to keep moving, keep flowing, to stay in balance.

With all the risks of possible injury and death, there is a fearsome intensity to climbing. Moving with fear and desire on rock and ice compels the climber's full attention, a single-minded focus on the present moment as if our lives depended on it.

After five years off the rocks, with little experience on snow and ice, I decided to climb Mount Baker. Ever since I'd moved to Bellingham, Mount Baker's snowy summit had dominated the landscape of my days. Its presence was palpable even through the density of rain clouds that obscured the summit nine months or more each year. To many Bellingham climbers, this volcanic mountain was a symbolic, spiritual home. It embodied unthinkable desire. I had to go there.

In late June, the confirmation materials for the Mount Baker summit climb arrived in my mailbox. I had been accepted. Along with a gear checklist, medical release form, and information sheet, the envelope contained a self-screening questionnaire designed to provide a reality check for the novice mountaineer. In bold letters, it asked, Are you more than 20 pounds overweight? Do you consider yourself to be in *Good* (not fair) physical condition? Are you committed to continuing a regular cardiovascular program of swimming, biking, aerobics, or running for one hour, four times per week, between now and the climb? Are you familiar with packing and carrying a 50-pound pack, hiking on trails, putting up a tent, lighting a backpacking stove, and completely caring for yourself outdoors, away from "civilization"? Are you willing to make the financial investment this climb requires? The screening questions dispelled any doubt about who was privileged to climb the mountain.

At the pretrip meeting three days before the climb, our expedition group met to review goals, route, and equipment. We went around the circle introducing ourselves, giving just our names and our motivations for being on the climb. There were the thirtysomething married couples from Lummi Island—Dede and Carl, Annie and David—who wanted to climb together on the same rope. There were the single people of indeterminate middle age: Mark, a tall, silent pilot, with a rock-solid build; Jamie, equally tall, a child psychologist, whose wiry short hair and wiry build exuded an energy even in stillness; John, a garrulous accountant with a truck tire of extra weight around his middle, who publicized his wealth and extensive travels; and me. As the two women climbing without mates in attendance, Jamie and I gravitated toward each other to discuss tents, stoves, and meals, while Mark paired up with John. Then the leader, Bud, reviewed the route and regulations.

We would take the southern approach this time, driving around Baker Lake to the Shreiber Meadow trailhead. From there, we'd hike in through the Sulphur Creek Drainage, and after numerous stream crossings, ascend the slopes and approach the Easton Glacier along an arête known as the "railroad grade." The trail was level and smooth, earning its name, but on either side the slopes dropped steeply away. Climbing six miles and 2,500 vertical feet, we'd ascend partway up the glacier to set up base camp at an elevation of 6,500 feet. We'd make dinner, pitch our tents, set out our ropes and ice axes for the climb. Then, we'd try to sleep. At midnight, we'd rope up and climb the remaining 4,000 feet to the summit, ascending the Easton Glacier up to the volcano's crater for the first 3,000 feet, and finishing with a fairly brutal vertical ascent up 900 feet known as the Roman Wall.

Anyone who couldn't make the climb, Bud said meaningfully, would be comfortably situated at a rest spot with a sleeping bag and Ensolite pad so that the rest of the group could summit. I wasn't the only one who cast a surreptitious glance at John to see how he handled news of his probable fate. But Bud looked at each one of us in turn, asking if we agreed. We did.

I wonder how many of us thought silently, I hope it's not me.

The day before the climb, I went to Bellingham's local mountaineering store, Base Camp, to pick up my rental gear. From the crevasse rescue course, I knew that the items I didn't own would again cost me seventy-five dollars to rent: plastic snow boots, 12-point crampons, an ice axe, Gore-tex snow pants, boot gaiters. In addition, the summit climb required extra gear to be purchased or rented—a third Nalgene one-quart water bottle; synthetic liner gloves, heavy snow gloves and mittens; a headlamp for our predawn summit ascent; several packets of electrolyte mix to add to my water bottles as an aid in fluid retention, keeping my body well hydrated and at less risk for altitude sickness—and these totaled another sixty-five dollars. Along with the $175 registration fee, the Mount Baker summit weekend alone would cost me $315. If the two preparatory classes were included—snow climbing (thirty dollars) and glacier travel/crevasse rescue (seventy-five dollars for registration, seventy-five dollars for gear rental)—it was clear that the project of summiting Mount Baker was costing me three weekends of free time, a certain reserve of psychological and emotional wealth, and $500. Collectively with seven other climbers, we were putting out a total of $4,000 for this chance at the summit.

Why mention money when the subject is wilderness? In her *Sinister Wisdom* essay, "Full Time Debt, Part Time Money," Caroljean Coventree writes that one of the barriers between classes is that we don't talk specifics about money. And it's no wonder: the figures reveal that the risk of climbing Mount Baker was cradled in a cushion of safety and privilege.

Maybe I wasn't so daring after all, if this was how much security I needed in order to take a risk. For at the same time that I had chosen to summit Mount Baker, my desires were pulling me toward another unthinkable risk: quitting my job.

After Tom's death and my own lead fall a few years later, I had just stopped taking risks. I stopped climbing. Without the environment of rocks and climbers as my compass, I had stopped living my life based on desire. Instead, I worked. I did research. And slowly, I began making choices based on safety alone.

No wonder that in the middle of my life's journey, I discovered that I had gone off route. Somehow, I'd gotten away from my own path in mountains and tracked onto the main route in the office because, well, because it was there. Because it seemed the inevitable path. Because there were plenty of ledges and handholds, good spots for placing protection, and even a few challenging moves along the way.

I was out of place.

At the age of forty, I found myself in my second tenured position as a university professor, with a comfortable income, lots of insurance and retirement and health benefits, a three-bedroom home, two-car garage, and a wonderful partner. All this was supposed to make me happy. Part of it did. For the rest, I was miserable. And Shawn knew it.

Where did we go wrong? Shawn and I had chosen this place as a step forward for both of us in our work. It offered the natural environment we had dreamed of and the chance to have a real home together. As soon as we moved, we threw ourselves wholeheartedly into the project of making this place home. We got involved in local politics, in ecodefense and in human rights issues. We explored the land, learned the social and ecological histories, spent time with our neighbors and coworkers. Bioregionalists agreed: these were the strategies for making ourselves at home. Why weren't they working?

As queer transplants, we were sending roots into shallow soil. Small-town Western culture was proving to be an impervious surface: rampant heterosexuality, born-again Christianity, and European American rugged individualism did not welcome our kind. In town, a grand canyon of class divided the long-term residents, mostly employees of the resource-extractive industries, from the influx of middle-class civic administrators, medical professionals, and university faculty. Progressives—a group that bridged college students and community holdouts from the 1960s—protested the oil refinery and the paper mill, while locals employed at both industries brought home high wages and a lowered tolerance for environmentalists.

While the natural environment filled us, the cultural environment was taking everything we had. It wasn't enough to drive ninety minutes south to Seattle or north to Vancouver just to walk down the street holding hands without it being seen as an act of civil disobedience. It wasn't enough to attend the annual Evergreen AIDS Arts Auction, or the occasional film at the town's only independent theater. It wasn't enough to call our friends and family long distance, or network with activists in the nearby cities. Both of us needed community right where we lived, a queer human community that even the friendship of the wild earth couldn't fill. After working all day, I wanted to go off duty, punch out—but neither of us could. The workplace followed us home.

Shawn's job was mobile; mine was not. Could I just quit?

As a same-sex couple in a state that offered us no human rights, no legal protections, and no partnership benefits from the workplace, I had to think about my economic well-being independently of Shawn. And somehow the job I held in the academy had successfully foreclosed the idea that I could do any other kind of work. It was this, or nothing. Colleagues in the academy reinforced this idea. There was nothing else out there for them. Leaving was not a possibility. Whether or not they were happy, whether or not they worked where they had wanted to live. They began counting down the years to retirement. They made compromises; they played it safe. They exchanged happiness and passion in the present for the promise of security in the future.

Listening to my colleagues explain why we couldn't leave university teaching, I realized that I was hearing something deeper than fear. The university gave us Letterhead. It gave us Business Cards with our Titles beneath our names. It gave us phone, fax, mailing and e-mailing privileges; it gave us travel budgets and conference fees. When it all boiled down to essentials, my colleagues told me, the university gave us our identities. Only in connection to the university were we Professors. On our own, most of us were just overeducated people writing obscure essays of dubious importance. My colleagues wouldn't leave the university because they feared that without it they would be no one.

No wonder I was gripped at midroute. The university had become the container not just for my desires, but for my identity.

And that identity depended on hierarchy and alienation. Being a professor meant being One Who Knows. And the implicit conclusion to that phrase, ". . . more than you do." The arrogance of this belief went against all my ethics of social justice. I didn't want an identity based on comparing myself, separating myself, elevating myself against others. I didn't want others to be less, so that I could be more.

And yet this container, this identity had been my invisible anchor and belay over the route where I had been climbing. To change routes, I would have to change anchors. I would have to find my identity somewhere else.

Hiking up the railroad grade to the Easton Glacier, I began to doubt my ability to make the summit. The altitude was already making my head spin, and I was panting with each step. I tried to focus on letting go, appreciating the beauty of thick-furred marmots, the tongue of glacial ice and crevasses curving steeply below, appreciating the tiny yellow, white, and pink flowers that dotted our trail's edge. These dainty plants lived here year-round, flowering and surviving. Surely I could take a lesson from their hardiness and manage two days of climbing at altitude.

Then the railroad grade ended, and we stepped out onto the glacier. The promise of a tent site, a place to drop pack and breathe freely, gave a little punch to my steps. Slowly, we passed several rocky outcroppings, saw other tents pitched here and there across the snow, and kept going. After passing two more outcroppings, I decided our leader Bud was not someone I would want to travel with in the future. I imagined him on a cross-country car trip, checking out each budget motel, asking for a room key to view a sample lodging, then returning to the front desk and handing the key back to the clerk, shaking his head no. This nasty narrative fueled my hiking until we topped the glacier's shoulder, and the snow swept up clean and smooth before us.

"This will do nicely," Bud turned around and smiled at us, dropping his pack. "We just cut off half an hour from tomorrow's ascent. You'll appreciate it in the morning."

After a dinner of pasta with pesto and sun-dried tomatoes, Jamie and I sat on the rocks drinking licorice tea and watched the changing skies. Stark blue alternated with thick dense clouds; light and shadow chased each other across the snow. By 8:30 p.m., we were ready to lie down, but the light stayed with us until after 10:00. Resting comfortably in my sleeping bag, dozing in and out of consciousness, I began talking to the mountain. I wanted it to know that we were here, hoping for the summit, and needing its permission to make the ascent. Over and over I repeated my petition to the mountain, deepening my intention, until I felt the connection had been made.

And then it was midnight.

Still burping pesto, I couldn't stomach the idea of eating oatmeal, and gratefully accepted Jamie's surprise treat of hot chocolate. It seemed unreal that we needed a full hour just to get into our pants and snow boots, start the stove, use the "facilities," fasten our climbing harnesses and carabiners.

By 1:00 a.m., ten climbers stood in a circle around ice axes planted stiffly in the snow, the climbing ropes coiled and draped over each axe. Beneath our boots, the soft snow of earlier evening had hardened into ice, yet the air seemed warm and still. Above our heads, a million stars outshone the waxing half moon. The area within our circle glowed with the illumination of ten climbers' headlamps.

"This is it," Bud said simply. "We've all checked harnesses, ropes, and carabiners. Any last thoughts before we head out?"

"I have one," I spoke unexpectedly, surprising even myself. "I'd like us to address the mountain, and I wonder if others feel the same way. If only a few people wanted to do it, we could step away from the group for a moment."

Headlamps nodded. Then Dede asked, "Do you have something you'd like to say?"

"I do." And as the climbers turned to face an unseen summit, I spoke the words I had been repeating that night in my mind.

"Mount Baker, Koma Kulshan, Great White Mountain.

For years we have lived at your base, watching you through winter storms and summer snows. Each one of us has seen your magnificent beauty, felt your energy, felt pulled to climb closer to your summit.

We are here, now, because you have called us.
Guard our journey; guide our steps.
Tell us what you have wanted us to know. We are listening.
And please, bring us safely home.
Thank you.

The group murmured and nodded. Roger took the lead, and we began the climb.

In her essay "Stupidity Deconstructed," Joanna Kadi explores the ways that the university system is intricately linked with our society's economic system. "People with power at the university," Kadi writes, "will do their part to reinforce and promote the capitalist explanation for class difference—smart rich people, stupid poor people—in return for continued benefits and privileges from the current structure."

When I was growing up, being smart meant being good and deserving of privilege. I never forgot the dollar I earned for every A in elementary school; I got nothing for any other grade. What I learned from this system of reward was that if you weren't the best, you weren't anything. Although Tom and I had different class upbringings, we both got this message loud and clear: only perfection counts. In my dollars-for-As, I got other messages too: intelligence equals money. If you're not smart, you won't get paid. And conversely, if you don't have money, you must be stupid. Happiness, pleasure, desire—these were nowhere in the equation. And somehow, who I was got mixed up with what I did, and what I achieved. My identity became anchored in my *A*s.

Looking at the institutionalization of oppression in this society, and thinking about class, I realized that my core identity, "I am intelligent," simultaneously required and denied the education I had received from private schools, the support I had received from parents, the nutritional food and fine clothing, the piano lessons and summer camps. This was race and class privilege, yet I had taken these academic achievements as something I had earned wholly on my own, something that was mine by rights.

It was not.

This "intelligent" identity was another form of unearned privilege. Why were Tom and I in such different locations in the classroom, even though we were the same age? Given the same opportunities as I had received, many other students might excel as I had; my abilities weren't so unique. And though the university values my particular type of intelligence, many other types of intelligence exist as well: the intelligence of designing and building a birdhouse, balancing a budget with no money, captivating listeners with stories, understanding a poem.

Surely there must be a different way to teach, a way of working as a professor without being attached to identity, a way that would allow me to pursue my deepest desires—and encourage others to pursue theirs. As Joanna Kadi asks, "Who does the academy serve? Can universities be transformed into places where everyone is welcomed and respected?"

I was ready to let go of this core belief, both for the pain it had caused me, and for the pain it was causing others. But, what would I put in its place?

If I wasn't intelligent, who was I?

Climbing the glacier one step at a time in snow and darkness, I was strangely calm. The few hours we'd spent at elevation had allowed my body to acclimatize, and my only real difficulty was footing. The three climbers roped above me barely left boot prints on the glacier's crusty surface. The slope wasn't yielding to their kick steps.

Around 3:00 a.m., after we'd passed 8,000 feet, I noticed my hands were stiffening, nearly freezing to my ice axe through my thin liner gloves. The wind had picked up, and the clouds had rolled in, blotting out the stars. All visibility was constricted within the glow of my headlamp. Not wanting to stop the climb, I waited for another mountaineer to call for a clothing change, then gratefully slipped on my Gore-tex jacket, pulled up the hood over my climbing helmet, and pulled on my hand mitts. Warmth is life.

As we continued the ascent, clouds thickened into a misty white fog that became snow. Our rope team slowed. The stronger climbers above me—our leader Roger; Mark, the pilot; and my tent mate Jamie—kept pulling me forward, but the climber behind me, John, kept pulling me back and calling for frequent rest stops. Whenever we stopped, the sweat from our exertion chilled against our bodies while the winds blew the snowflakes horizontally across the glacier. Looking up the mountain, I could barely see Roger in the lead, doing jumping jacks to stay warm. Trusting the clear night when we began, Roger had worn only polypro leggings and shorts, foregoing the snow pants because it was too warm out. Now he was French stepping sideways up the mountain, one leg crossing over the other, and slapping his thighs with each step. All my previous mountaineering training kicked in, and I remembered: protect the leader, and you protect the group.

"John!" I snapped. "Roger is getting chilled. We cannot stop this much and still keep warm."

"Okay," John gasped. "Climbing!"

"Climb on!" I replied, the universal call-and-response of climbing that lets the climber know his belayer is ready.

When we reached 9,000 feet, John called for another rest break and began vomiting. Looking downhill through blowing streams of snow, I could see him leaning over the rope, his headlamp illuminating his convulsions.

"John is nauseous!" I shouted up to Jamie. "Pass it on! We've got to find a sheltered rest stop."

Word came back through Jamie: 500 more feet. Then we could rest in the summit crater just below the Roman Wall. I could barely see five feet, much less imagine 500.

Up. By now, most of us were side stepping or trying to edge with our snow boots, wishing we'd already put on our crampons. The boots barely bit the slope, and sliding then regaining balance took more energy than getting a foothold to begin with. With John struggling and pulling on the rope behind me as if it were a towrope, my steps had slowed to a shuffle. Finally, Roger gained the ridgeline and disappeared into the summit crater.

The stench of sulphur from the caldera offered odorous welcome. Stepping and sinking unexpectedly into porous slopes of pumice and snow, our rope teams descended halfway into the crater, down to a shelf wedged against the mountain. Here, the crater was perceptibly warmer and somewhat sheltered from the winds.

"We've got some decisions to make," Bud said as climbers dropped packs, pulled out warmer clothing layers, and huddled together. "It's taken us longer than we planned to gain 3,000 feet. It's now 6:30 a.m., and we're at 9,500. The final ascent includes 900 vertical feet up the Roman Wall. The route is totally exposed. There will be no resting place. It should take us another three hours to go up and get back to where we stand now. By that time, the snow will have softened, the crevasses will begin to open, and we will still have to descend another 3,000 feet to base camp." Bud paused to let this information sink in. "What do people want to do?"

"Summit," said Carl.

"Summit," said Mark.

As we went around the group, only Dede and Annie expressed concern about the group's ability to make the climb. Bud supported this concern. The original plan of leaving anyone behind in the crater with a sleeping bag and pad was no longer feasible due to the weather conditions: while we were away climbing, the remaining climber could become hypothermic and be unable to descend the mountain when we returned. Nor was Bud comfortable with the idea of splitting up the rope teams and sending one back to base camp while the other summitted. The group had to stay together.

Weighing our individual desires for the summit against our well-being

as a group, we realized that a weak climber on an exposed ascent in blowing snow and whiteout conditions could put the whole group at risk. We
didn't have an emergency situation in the summit crater, but we had all the
pieces for making one.

Desire, and fear. Risk and safety. Individual and community.

By 7:00 a.m., we were on the climb down.

Driving back to Bellingham, our van stopped at Everybody's Store in
Acme, an old-time grocery store with a range of items so broad you could
get everything from food to fishing tackle. John bought cafe lattés for the
entire group. He didn't pretend that good coffee could compensate us for
losing the summit. John was simply sharing what he had.

I got more than a coffee out of the climb. In the summit crater, where
John's money couldn't buy us a thing, a group of individual mountaineers
became a community that recognized its interdependence.

Like the firm handshake of an old friend, this identity was the anchor
I had been seeking.

In itself, climbing doesn't make the world safe for democracy, end institutional heterosexism, or transform an oppressive economic structure. To do
any of these things, as climbers, we have to take what we've learned on rock
and ice and bring it back to our daily lives.

Mount Baker is still out there.

Silver Lake

Mist hovers on the lake, rising like steam from a cup of hot tea. Clouds of mist hang on the hillside, enveloping huge stands of hemlock and Douglas fir, western cedar and vine maple, alder and birch. Each morning I awake at 6:00 a.m. and take my coffee out to the cabin's deck, where Shawn, Sequoia, and I sit in silence with the mist. We watch as osprey soar and dive into the lake, fishing for breakfast. Bald eagles fish here, too, or sometimes steal breakfast from the osprey. This morning, a lone kayaker paddles silently across the lake. Later, he is joined by two other canoes of slow, silent fishermen who don't need the fish quite like the osprey and the eagle do. Instead they need the silence, the sensation of floating on water and mist, listening to the quiet roar of creeks and streams pouring off Black Mountain into Silver Lake. They need to watch the light of morning, the sun finally cresting Black Mountain and pushing down the shades of night with its stark blue-gold radiance. There's no way to explain such needs. Day after day, morning after morning, dawn after dawn, they bring their fishing poles to pacify the war gods of ceaseless production, and float on the lake, doing nothing at all.

Sitting out on the cabin's deck, or inside looking through big picture windows onto the lake, I've seen orioles and blue jays hopping on vine maple branches, a pair of great gray herons standing on the dock below, a kingfisher shooting across the railing with his rat-a-tat-tat jackhammer cry. I've learned to recognize hairy red-headed woodpeckers, tiny green calliope hummingbirds, raccoons, and garter snakes. Last night I heard the laughter of a loon, one of the pair who inhabits this teacup of a lake.

Near midday, Sequoia and I take our usual walk down the dead-end road, crossing the yards of silent cabins that sleep at the end of the lane, past signs that read "End of County Maintained Road" and "Private Property—No Trespassing." I climb a three-tiered split-log fence; Sequoia slips underneath. Then we cross two more gravel roads and begin bushwhacking through forest, leaping over mossy fallen logs, stepping among sword ferns and salal, climbing and slipping uphill to where the silver chain-link fence ends abruptly among fir and hemlock trees and, simply, walking around it. There. Same forest, but now we are in Silver Lake Park, where we can follow footpaths and horse trails for miles through the woods.

This summer, forty-five minutes from town and halfway up the Mount Baker Highway, Silver Lake has become my Walden Pond. Unlike Thoreau, I don't have another home within walking distance: Shawn and I sold it after the Mount Baker summit climb, put our belongings in storage, and moved to the mountains to consider our future. Before work resumes in the fall, we'll have to make some hard decisions about place and workplace, relationship and identity. As part of the process, I'm trying to get acquainted with greater Whatcom County, with the land, the mountains, and the people who live outside of Bellingham.

To stay here comfortably, sheltered from the days of occasional rain that occur even in July and August, we've rented the smallest available one-room cabin on the lake, yet it's hardly a minimum-impact shelter. Our summer home came complete with television, VCR, and a satellite dish for cable; running water, electricity, and a water heater; refrigerator and stove; indoor toilet, shower, and stacking washer-dryer unit for laundry. If I wanted, I could wash my dishes in the dishwasher, heat my food in the microwave, sit in a hot tub overlooking the lake, watch cable television shows, listen to the radio, audiotapes, or compact discs. Instead, I listen across the lake to the creeks cascading down from Black Mountain, the sounds of swallows and black-capped chickadees, the occasional thud of oars and paddles against gunwales. Because I do use the computer, the telephone, and the reading lamps even for one twilight hour, my presence here impacts the land. I draw electric power from the confinement of Baker Lake at Diablo Dam, from the strangulation of the Columbia

River at Bonneville. Worst of all, perhaps, is the fact that I can walk from this cabin's deck right down the stairs and out onto the dock, living in a proximity to water that would never be allowed in cabins built today. Coming here to learn about wild nature, and hoping my personal relationship revives its original wildness, I find myself concerned with my impact on the land, with the ecological impacts of local economy, and the effects of those who have lived here before me.

For guidance, I look first to the Nooksack, whose traditionally migratory, subsistence lifestyle was better suited to the land than mine will ever be. I inherit my way of living from the later waves of Chinese and European American immigrants who came to the Pacific Northwest and tried to make a living off the land. Very few of their descendants are still following the old ways of logging, mining, and fishing. These days, the harvest is meager, the impacts more severe. Across the lake, high on Black Mountain, I see the diagonal line of a logging road still pressed upon the forest, and the semicircular arc of skyline logging beneath it. In this one patch the mountain is scraped raw, skinned down to the bone like a child's knee, bleeding after some rough play. I want to kiss the slopes and make them better, or at least take the hurt away. I still struggle with the fact that, regardless of my love for wild nature—the earth's, my own, or my partner's—it's the economics of my culture that shapes each of these relationships.

The town closest to Silver Lake is Maple Falls, just under five miles away. Where Silver Lake Road crosses the Mount Baker Highway, Maple Falls is little more than an intersection, a meeting place for local businesses. On one corner, there's Der Storehausen, a multipurpose grocery, beverage warehouse, home repair, video rental, and camping supply store. In the same complex, there's the local realty, a tiny two-story hotel that also houses the Baptist meetings on Sunday mornings, and a hair salon called Mountain Do's. Competing with Der Storehausen on the opposite corner is Maple Fuels, a gas station that grew into a small grocery, espresso shop, and Laundromat. The town's only liquor store is tucked discreetly behind. Across the street is the town hall building and public library, open Wednesdays 10–7, and Saturdays 10–5. On the fourth corner, there's a school bus parked in an empty lot. Its painted side advertises the river rafting company that takes people down the North Fork of the Nooksack

River twice a day. This summer, only one person has died so far, a good year by anyone's standards. Depending on the annual snowfall and summer rains, the rafting season usually ends by mid-August, and the river guides are trying very hard not to lose any more of their clients.

Farther down the main highway, the town boasts its own post office, and the best all-around coffee shop, bar, and lounge on the mountain. Built some time in the 1940s, the Frosty Inn has a dark barroom with booths on one end, and an open, high-ceilinged fireplace room on the other, with wood-grained wall interiors from end to end. The food is average, but eating there allows you to overhear the morning's fish stories, local news, or descriptions of stream crossings, flowers, and wildlife sightings. The Frosty's exterior would look like any other cabin-business in a mountain town—except for the life-sized figure of Bigfoot, striding toward the front door.

The mounted head of a Bigfoot is also displayed as a trophy above the cash register at Der Storehausen. Every September for the past ten years, the town has held a Bigfoot-on-Baker festival, complete with mountain-bike race, parade, crafts fair, and golf tournament, culminating with a night of Sasquatch tales around the campfire. Although town boosters organized the festival as a way of supporting the local economy, part of the area's slow shift from resource-extractive industry to recreational tourism and a service-based economy, one wonders if there's more than a seedling of truth to this annual celebration of humankind's mythic ancestor.

Called Pekosia by the area's original inhabitants, the Nooksack, this water became known as Bachelor Lake and Fish Lake before the name Silver Lake was chosen. Before it became a Whatcom County park in 1969, before these 411 acres of land were enclosed as a private resort, the forest was homesteaded by a Norwegian American settler, Embret E. Gerdrum.

In 1890, the Gerdrum family arrived in Whatcom County from Norway after a brief stopover in Chicago, where their only daughter, Ethel, was born. The Gerdrums settled on Silver Lake, and Mr. Gerdrum built their homestead with four-by-twelve planks, handhewn from a single cedar tree. Nestled into the base of Red Mountain, the original house was two stories tall, with a living room, kitchen area, and bedroom on the first floor, and a stairway leading to an open attic space upstairs. When the first home burned to the ground in 1903, Gerdrum built another one just like it, right in front of the place where the first house had stood. From 1900 to 1919, more than thirty-three logging companies formed, reformed, or vanished around the mountain communities of Maple Falls, Silver Lake, and Glacier. Like many European American settlers, Gerdrum made his living here by cutting down the trees. Logging.

Today, the Gerdrum homestead is unequally divided by Silver Lake Road, with the county park getting the majority of the land on the lake side, and the Black Mountain Forestry Center on the other. Park and Forestry Center entrances open mouth to mouth. Campers turn one way, loggers the other. The former Gerdrum home has been converted into a forestry museum, with idle and ancient logging machinery encircling a 105-foot-high lead tower in the field beside the house. To persuade visitors about the continued importance of the timber industry for the local economy, the Forestry Center offers "high country tours" of its logging roads and clear-cuts on Black Mountain every Sunday, June through August. But when I visited the center, it appeared there had been no takers. I was the sole tourist.

The museum housed artifacts from ways of living on the land over a century ago: hand saws and rotary saws, tools and photographs, a wall of glass-and-key post boxes from Maple Falls's original post office, and upstairs, a long canoe hollowed out from a single tree, still fragrant with the sweet odor of cedar. By the cash register downstairs, some tintype photograph postcards showed the area as it had once looked: the block-long Fourth of July parade in Maple Falls, 1905; the tree-lined dirt road connecting Maple Falls to Silver Lake; the lily pond thick with floating logs in front of the Gerdrum and Caulkins Mill, before it was bought out by Silver Lake Manufacturing Company in 1906.

A century later and a few miles down the Mount Baker Highway, the logging community celebrates its continued presence on the mountain with an annual logging show. For one weekend in June since 1963, the Deming Logging Show brings together loggers from all across Washington to celebrate their craft, look over the newest tools of the trade, and take care of their own. This year at the Deming Logging Show, I hope to learn something about how these folks have been able to make a living on Mount Baker. The lesson begins before Shawn and I even enter the fairgrounds.

At the front gate, a massive slice of cedar trunk from the glory days of logging, perhaps ten feet tall, marks the formal entrance to the fair. Parked around the stadium, there are rows and rows of excavators, bulldozers, backhoes, and log loaders, followed by lines and lines of fully loaded logging trucks. Inside the Log Show Fairgrounds, crafts tents and wooden pavilions form a horseshoe surrounding the staging area, the pit, and bleachers. Here's a tent full of woodcarvings for sale, and behind it stretch the campground and the barbecue pavilion. Logging families from all around Washington have camped here for the weekend. Their trailers and RVs look pretty much like those at any other campground, except that in place of red-chili lanterns, or a sun-moon-stars string of lights hanging from their pop-up trailer porches, there are American flags. We say nothing, but I can tell from the stiffness in how Shawn is walking that we share the same feeling: we are out of place. Environmentalists trespassing among loggers. Queers infiltrating straights. Are there more of us here? We aren't quite sure how to carry ourselves, whether it's safe to stand and look at the machine saw slicing logs into boards and shaving off the bark, or whether our curiosity will betray us and we'll be thrown out. Without our consent, our white skin serves as a form of protective coloration; we see no people of color the entire afternoon.

At the barbecue, slabs of copper river salmon are advertised, laid across iron grill slats, and the wood fire smells warm and smoky. Around front at the buffet, we can see the menu: salmon, chicken, or beef; coleslaw, fries, potato salad; soda pop, coffee, milk. It's no organic picnic for a vegetarian. I nod to the women serving the salads and move on.

There's a blacksmith shop next to the displays of old yarders, lines, and chokers, and Thorie Finsrud's slice of cedar trunk. This twelve-foot-diameter piece of tree comes from a Deming red cedar cut in 1895 at 1,008 years of age. Just moved to the fairgrounds in April, the trunk section had been on display at the Deming Tavern since 1936. Outside the Washington Women in Timber building that houses both the Logging Museum and the Ladies Auxiliary Kitchen, we notice a grove of trees with low wooden signs posted at each base. There are men's names on these signs, with dates here from the past thirty-five or so years. At the American Legion stand, where women are selling souvenir T-shirts, ball caps, suspenders, sweatshirts, and mugs, I learn that Memorial Grove was established when the Deming Logging

Show acquired the fairgrounds property in 1967. Each time a logger is killed in the woods, a tree is planted to commemorate his life. The eloquence of this gesture moves me. I do not understand why it seems so right to plant a tree in memory of someone who spent his life cutting down trees.

Back in the arena, we take our seats in the bleachers to watch as a fully loaded logging truck pulls around the circle, stops, and the driver hops down from the cab. Booming over the PA system, the grandstand announcer explains the event while the driver gets into the seat of a shovel machine with automatic tongs. For this event called Best Load of Logs, the trucker has had to select logs so that they will bring the total load up to the required weight, but not exceed the legal limit. Logs must be loaded so that they fill the bunks of the trucks, but don't hang out the ends. As we watch, the driver uses the tongs to remove each log from the truck bed and place the log in the sawdust of the arena. We can see that the ends of the logs have been painted and branded. Logs are loaded according to size and kinds of trees, the announcer explains, so a single load may carry logs of several different owners. After the driver has unloaded his truck and received his applause, the reloading begins, and a second competition takes place.

"Now, we all know these logs used to fit on that truck," the announcer jokes, "and this contest is to see which driver can reload the truck for speed, balance, and safety. Loading logs is an art," the announcer assures us, "one of the creative arts and only a select few have the gifts to handle the job properly."

The next event, Trailer Backing, tests the driver's skill in backing up a fully loaded logging truck on a curved mountain road, simulated in the arena by a curved lane of orange cones and a goal stick at the end. As trucker after trucker tries his skill in this event, the difficulties become evident. Trying to balance speed against skill, few drivers can back up their trucks quickly enough without running over a few cones or demolishing the goal stick. The event is complicated by the fact that drivers can only use their outside mirrors—the rearview window is obscured by a load of logs.

At 1:00 p.m., the show officially opens with a formal welcome from the announcer, and a hand-over-heart rendition of "The Star-Spangled Banner." Then the announcer gives us the annual report: "Whatcom County has not suffered a logging fatality since we met here last year. That record has been kept for the last eight years."

The applause is deafening.

"Let's spend a minute in total silence," he continues, "to honor all those who have been injured on the job in the past year."

The entire arena falls silent. Heads bow. Even children sit quietly. And then the show begins.

Captivated by watching loggers display their skills before friends and family, Shawn and I watched event after event. Cable Splicing. Wrapper Throwing. Axe Throwing. And Pole Falling, a crowd favorite. In this event, four loggers stand at different poles around the arena. The object is to use an axe to cut front and back within a specified range on the pole, planning the log to fall so precisely that it splits the watermelon target. The crowd whooped and cheered as the poles fell. Only one logger made his target, and he exuberantly shared his split watermelon with his competitors.

In Speed Climbing, loggers dashed up sixty-foot poles to ring a bell at the top of each tree. For Hand Bucking and Double Bucking, loggers used a seven-foot bucking saw to slice an end off a log twenty-six inches in diameter. For Choker Setting, loggers had to run to a large log, jump or crawl over it, grab a choker, and speed back over the large log to set their choker around a smaller log, then finish up back at the large log. The weight and unwieldiness of the equipment could be seen in the way the men moved once they had picked up the chokers. "Get up! Get up!" the announcer encouraged one young logger who had fallen while leaping the large log and dropped his choker. "If you're going to fall, fall *towards* your work, son!"

As the announcer toured the arena with his cordless microphone, he reminded us of the reason for all these events. Each year, all funds raised at the Deming Logging Show go to support "busted up loggers," meaning any Whatcom County timber worker who is injured on the job and put out of work two weeks or longer. Workers who can't return to the woods get checks for the rest of their lives—even if they are able to find other employment. Evidently the logging companies don't offer adequate long-term disability benefits, dental, medical, or much of anything else. The loggers have learned to care for their own.

But where were the women? I'd seen them around, serving at the barbecue, cooking and cashiering and sewing at the Women in Timber building, hawking memorabilia at the Souvenir Shacks. Women's place in the logging community was confirmed in the show's program, which reminded us to give "a special 'thank you' to the Ladies Auxiliary" because "they do the jobs the rest of us don't like doing." The only events that featured women were the kids' tree climbing, open to boys and girls alike, and Ma and Pa Bucking (not Ma and Ma). For that competition, the program stated, "We wanted to have an event that the ladies could have a chance to earn a trophy. We would like to have more because without them we would have a pretty tough time. Besides that we like to get them in shape to cut some firewood. A logger usually has a long winter." Watching the men swing axes and chokers as "poles" fell around them, it was hard to know whether I wanted to get more women into logging, or get men out. Like my students who spend summers in Alaska killing or canning the salmon that symbolize the same wilderness they have come to explore, these loggers perform jobs that depend on destroying the very forests they love. Living in a cabin on Silver Lake, I would face the same dilemma if I tried to work here after my savings ran out.

As a Norwegian American, I found my history in the little towns on Mount Baker held no keys to the future. For cheap labor in clearing the trees over a century ago, men of my ethnic heritage had smuggled Chinese workers across the border from Canada, hiding them just north of Silver Lake at the old Comosun Ranch. As entertainment for the loggers, entrepreneurs in Maple Falls had operated two houses of prostitution, north and south of town. In *The Trail through the Woods,* Frances Todd tells stories of unmarked graves for women and infants, as up to twenty-five girls worked in these houses at one time. That would have been my line of work, had I lived here then. Now, from what I'd seen at the Deming Logging Show, I could enter the contemporary logging culture only if I went straight, learned to cook and sew, and married a real logger.

On the night Shawn and I decided to sell our house, we had huddled outside on the back deck talking, sheltered under the dining room's bay window. All around us, the incessant rain drizzled. Once again, I had raised the question: was this the right time to have a child?

Shawn exhaled a long stream of smoke, her left hand curled around her cigarette with an arched flair I had always loved, much as I hated her smoking. "This isn't where we want to settle," she began, giving voice and definition to a feeling we both had been resisting. "We're not going to raise a child in a place without a community of queer families. And once you have a child, it's harder to move." She paused to take another drag. "Besides, after I finish my master's degree, I need to make some money. When would we have time to have a child?"

It was like the conversation we'd had when we commuted between Duluth and Minneapolis, only then Shawn had joked, "What are you going to do with the kid, tie it on the roof rack while you commute?"

And she was right: our work lives, our activism, and our backpacking left no time for raising a child—whatever that entailed. As would-be parents, we had no clear idea what kind of resources parenting would require, but we suspected it was expensive in all ways: time, finances, emotional presence. Then, there was the question of how the child would be conceived.

While there was no doubt that I would be the birth mother, the source for the other 23 chromosomes had never been decided. I wanted the father to be a known donor, a presence in our child's life. Before Shawn and I had become a couple, I had asked my dear friends Jim and Gary if they would be my donors someday, so that when my child asked, "Who's my daddy?" and started to launch a soul-wrenching search for identity and origins, I could just say, "Oh, snap out of it—it's your Uncle Jim right down the block." But Jim and Gary had refused; it was too much responsibility for them, even when I assured them there would be no financial obligations, no coparenting arrangement needed or wanted.

We had even asked Shawn's older brother Mark and his wife, Missy. They had two beautiful children, and wouldn't feel a need to compete with us for parenting rights; their roles as aunt and uncle would be enough, and then our child would have a biological link to Shawn and her family too. Mark and Missy had several gay and bisexual friends; they were part of a pagan community, and one close friend of theirs already had a nontraditional parenting arrangement in place. One evening together we asked, hoping they would be able to handle our request. Mark seemed surprised but willing, while Missy joked about how likely it would be for us to get a sperm sample, since Mark had difficulty even peeing in a cup at the doctor's office. But the conversation ended there, and Shawn wasn't willing to ask them again.

This was the stalemate: Shawn wanted to get sperm from a bank, to look in a book and choose a donor profile that matched her features. Since she would be biologically unrelated to the child, it was important to her that there would be no competitor for the role of coparent. No matter what arrangement we made with a known donor, Shawn felt, the presence of a biological father in our child's life would marginalize Shawn's role. Lesbian couples with children were already vulnerable to legal challenges from homophobes and known donors alike. What if the unthinkable occurred and we separated after the child was born; what rights would Shawn have as coparent? Shawn wanted to ensure that she would never be torn from a child she had nurtured from conception to birth and beyond.

Looking through the books of potential donors, I discovered I couldn't change my own position. Origins of all kinds had already been too important in my own life. I had loved my own father dearly, and I felt that a father's nurturing presence was a birthright for my own child as well. No matter how loving we were as parents, I couldn't face the day when my own child would ask me, "Who's my daddy?" and I would have to look that child in the eyes and say, "It's N437."

To create a secure family for our child I wanted more parents, not fewer. Shawn wanted the same security through different means. While we deliberated, we delayed, and my sense of limitless opportunities diminished. Each year I lost another twelve or thirteen opportunities to have that child; each year brought us closer to the certainty that one day, there would be no more choices.

If we were to have any chance at all, we needed to move.

Nestled in a long north–south basin between Black Mountain on the east and Red Mountain to the west, Silver Lake is exactly the size of a lake you'd want for a friend. At a mile across and three miles long, it's too large to be called a pond, yet small enough that one can canoe its circumference in about an hour after dinner and become acquainted with its shorelines, its sandy beaches, and shallow recesses where the water lilies congregate. Shawn and I often set out just as the shadow of Red Mountain cooled our side of the shore, and paddled out twenty feet or so into the light of the setting sun.

With Sequoia as duffer, we would canoe north, inspecting the tiny lakefront dwellings that stood between our cabin and the main road. Built in the first half of the twentieth century, these summer cabins were set close

to the lake and now seemed more charming in their diminutive simplicity. Most had one main room with a fireplace or wood-burning stove to
serve as living room, dining room, kitchen, and guest room, with just one
bedroom off the main entry, and an outhouse still leaning close by. In the
1940s electricity was extended down Silver Lake Road; across the lake,
homes are just receiving electricity this year. The slower pace of technol-
ogy here has been good for the lake, good for the land. There's some open
shoreline after these older cabins, a public boat launch on the lake's very
northern tip, and a large beach and Boy Scout camp just east of the launch.
Jim and Julie, other longtime residents on our lane, tell us the land for
the Boy Scout camp was donated as a single parcel by former residents of
the lake who were involved in scouting. Julie says she has raised two boys
and volunteered as a den mother for so many years that when she hears
the boys shouting and singing across the lake, she gets nostalgic. We do
not. We often wonder what the Boy Scouts are learning over there in their
camp with the Indian-sounding names, since they surely have not learned
the first principle of lakefront wilderness ethics: sound carries.

After the Boy Scout camp, there's more open shoreline, room for
a stream to cascade down Black Mountain and have its own little delta
across the lake from our cabin. Much farther south, the more opulent
cabins invade the shore. Then we come to the lily pads of the lake's southern tip, and sometimes push our way through them, paddling under low-
hanging tree limbs to the place where Maple Creek begins its laughing
departure from Silver Lake. The creek travels four and a half miles through
the same valley as Silver Lake Road, finally bouncing and rippling down
a thirty-five-foot descent that gave the town of Maple Falls its name over
a century ago. Just below the town, the creek joins forces with the North
Fork of the Nooksack River, where it will run, ripple, and meander out to
Bellingham Bay.

Every time we drove through the intersection at Maple Falls, Shawn and I
would see the big yellow school bus and the sign for River Riders, the rafting company offering guided trips down the North Fork of the Nooksack
River. In addition to mountaineering, this ecotourism might be giving the
town its needed economic boost. I imagined a rafting trip guided by a nat-
uralist, whose narration would teach me more about the ways of water, the
history of glaciers and snowmelt, the interdependence of land and water

creatures whose survival depended on this river. Enticed by these imaginings, I called the rafting company to find out the details. Taking groups of rafters at a rate of fifty-five dollars per person, River Riders offered a two-and-a-half-hour rafting trip over twelve river miles of the Nooksack, and a lunch afterward. They put no more than six people in a raft, plus one guide. "We travel light on the Nooksack," the woman explained over the phone, "because it's a less forgiving river." Other rivers the group rafted in Washington included the Wenatchee, the Skykomish, the Methow, and the Tieton. I signed us up.

The next Saturday morning at ten minutes before 9:00 a.m., Shawn and I met the River Riders buses parked in a grassy open field just beyond the library. The morning was sunny and cool, perhaps sixty-five degrees. Already, cars for the 10:00 a.m. raft trip were pulling into the lot, and people were putting on wet suits. After signing the required release of liability, we lined up with the other rafters and picked up our wet suits, booties, life jacket, helmet, and paddle. Anxiety made its presence known as an energetic ball of tension at midchest. This could be fun.

Aboard the River Riders bus, we took our seats among teenagers and twenty-year-olds. Baffled, I searched the bus for other older people, and found very few, mostly men, and two women. What kind of raft trip had we signed up for? As if in answer, one of the river guides hopped up the bus stairs and popped in a cassette tape. Disco, at blasting levels. "Shake Your Bootie" and "Got to Be Real" rocked through the bus. Four other guides climbed on, one slipping into the driver's seat, and we were off. At the front of the bus, "Buddha," a chubby river guide with triply pierced ears and pierced tongue, discoed in front of the open bus door and shouted out the rules of the bus.

"Remain seated! Do not disturb the driver! Do not shout!"

On the driver's rearview mirror was a sticker that read "We Love a Safe Workplace." Our raucous crew was set for adventure.

Still squirming in my seat, I turned to face the two women guides sitting behind us.

"Oh, what lovely earrings you have on!" one guide immediately remarked.

"Haight-Ashbury, San Francisco," I replied, "a birthday gift two years ago."

"Of course," her companion snorted. "You wouldn't get that kind of thing around here."

"Really?" I asked, hoping for more information. "Do you two live in Bellingham? Or are you camping up on Mount Baker for the summer?"

"Heck no," the first woman scoffed. She was a lean, petite woman with a deep tan and long glossy dark hair tied in a ponytail. "See this tan? You'd never get that up here. I got it from the Wenatchee. We worked yesterday in Oregon and drove up last night."

"Got in at 2:00 a.m.," the guide beside her added.

Clearly, the guides were not local naturalists, nor was the raft trip going to be the one I had imagined. In such cases, it is better to set aside all prior expectations and accept whatever comes, on its own terms. I faced forward, and spent the rest of the bus ride practicing letting go.

Just past the bridge by the Douglas Fir campground, the bus pulled over. An array of eighteen rafts was lined up along the roadside shoulder, and three other buses pulled up behind us. Rafters and river guides gathered above the steps to the river to hear the safety lecture. There, a blond young man climbed up to stand on the stair railing and cheerfully shouted the precautions.

"Rule number one: stay in the raft. Rule number two: do not fall out of the raft. The water is cooold! How cold, guys? Two raisins and a Cheeto, guys. Cooold!"

If we did fall out, in spite of our instructions, we were to grab hold of the rope that encircled the raft. If we could not do that, we should extend the paddle, handle first, back toward the boat in the hope that someone would tow us in. If this did not work, the shouting guide told us, our Personal Whitewater Adventure would begin. In this case, we should float downriver feet first, keeping our hips raised, and avoid downed trees and boulders.

"Think of a pasta press," the guide advised us. "This is what a tree will do to you. *Avoid the trees.*"

After the safety presentation, we were assigned to our guides, who led us to the rafts. There, our guide, Will, a lean young man in his midtwenties, reviewed the rules for our rafting group.

"Rule number one: we are a team. Rule number two: I am the leader. When I tell you to do something, you do it. Immediately!"

Will led us in practicing the various strokes we would use: forward paddle, reverse, left forward, right forward, high left, and high right—meaning everyone would need to slide left or right in the raft, thereby raising the opposing edge off any rocks or trees we might be stuck on. Our group of six inexperienced rafters responded quickly, and we were ready to ride.

Carrying the raft down the steps to the river, we waited under the high-way bridge and watched the Nooksack rushing past.

"The hardest part of the river comes first," Will explained, "so it's crucial that your paddling is *perfect* from the start." Adrenaline surged through my arms and shoulders, biting into my chest. This would be an adventure.

The first twenty minutes on the river sped by in a blur; the guides hadn't exaggerated. After putting in to the water and quickly pulling into an eddy to wait for the other five rafts and the single kayaker in our "pod," we set off. Our raft practically flew through "the Canyon," a high-walled section of the river complete with boulders, drops, and lots of over-the-edge waves that doused us with *Cooold* water. At the first opportunity, Will pulled us over to the next eddy with two other rafts, and we turned to watch the other rafts come by.

"This water was a glacier about twelve hours ago," Will reminded us. "No wonder it's cold!"

Our next challenge was "the Nozzle," a section of the river where our course shot us between two huge boulders, with a third boulder embed-ded just off the middle. We came through this drenched and screaming. I began to see the river trip as a kind of outdoor Disneyland. What connec-tion were we making with the water, with the land?

"See that logging road up there?" Will pointed to a swath of clear-cuts and a logging road that ascended diagonally up the mountain. "There's actually a house back there, and some hicks. A couple of our guides were bicycling up that logging road, getting high and thinking they were all alone, when suddenly these hicks appeared with shotguns and said 'Yew git raht outta hyar, yew damned hippies!' Will's rendition was a cross between a Texas accent and a Southern drawl.

Evidently the antipathy between the river guides and some of the locals was mutual.

As we floated downriver and the water grew calmer, we had our first real chance to look at the trees, the rocks, and the birds. Alder. Sedimentary rock, sandstone and shale. A duck family, hen and chicks. A bald eagle up on the hillside, in my binoculars appearing larger than a toddler. Farther downriver, the water opened out, running in two wide streams around a sand bar in the middle. We took the lower stream and looked up to watch water cascading over the rocks and sand from the higher stream branch. Beyond, the mountains rose abruptly from the valley, a characteristic of land forms in western Washington.

At the confluence of the Glacier River with the Nooksack, brown water met milky green water and flowed side by side, white foamy waves resting above green depths. Farther downstream, three rivers braided together in a roaring rush of energy that made my heart wild. There was nothing to fear, no rapids, no downed trees. Just the joy of meeting, of pouring one into another, of joining, dancing, merging into a whole new river, spinning, churning, rolling, brown over milky green over brown again and again until a new river took color and flowed on.

Up in front, the four rafters were discussing what they would do next. The river trip hadn't ended, but in their minds, they had already moved on. After the high-voltage stimulus of the rapids, the river's amusement park appeal had vanished.

I had wanted this river trip to offer a way of experiencing the river from the river's perspective, a way of funding the local economy. But River-Riders-dot-com was no "environmental ed" group, and no local operation. All the youth we saw dancing, shouting at us, and guiding us down the river were from Seattle—and they didn't own the organization, either. There was probably some big adult money behind an operation that could afford to run rafts on five rivers in Washington as well as a few in Oregon and Idaho. My vision of the rafting biz in Maple Falls as a form of ecotourism, a shift toward a more sustainable economic base for the locals, faded. Sure, rafters who came to Maple Falls would patronize the local businesses, the stores and the lodges and the gas station, but was that enough to support the people who lived here? And why were adventure trips selling better than local environmental education?

Wildness encompassed more than outdoor adventure, more than local economic security. Wildness was in the essence of the mountain, and it still eluded me.

Stopping by the Maple Falls library one Wednesday when I saw the door propped open, I was stunned by the singular theme dominating an array of books exhibited in the library's corner on local issues. Bigfoot has a long history in Whatcom County, in both the legends of indigenous cultures and in contemporary news reports. From Grover Krantz's *Big Footprints: A Scientific Inquiry into the Reality of Sasquatch* and Kenneth Wylie's *Bigfoot* to Myra Shackley's *Still Living? Yeti, Sasquatch and the Neanderthal Enigma,* John Green's *Bigfoot: On the Track of the Sasquatch,* David George Gordon's *Field Guide to the Sasquatch,* and Robert Michael Pyle's *Where Bigfoot Walks,* this topic had received serious attention. Safely out of view from the library's front desk, I leafed through each one of the books and quickly found I needed to borrow the entire lot before anyone from the college entered by chance and caught me studying this creature of cryptozoology.

Back on deck at the cabin, with the books scattered across lawn chair and table, I learned that the Pacific Northwest—particularly the western Cascades—was a primary location for Bigfoot sightings. David George Gordon's *Field Guide to the Sasquatch* lists just a few of the recent encounters. In the fall of 1967, at the height of the sockeye salmon run, ten separate Sasquatch sightings were reported by local fishermen and residents of the Nooksack river delta near Marietta. The creature was seen entering, swimming in, or leaving the river, and in one report the Sasquatch was reeling in a fisherman's gillnet. In November 1975, a Lummi Nation police officer reported hearing a high-pitched screech after several sightings by reservation residents. Campers in Deming reported sighting a Bigfoot that same year, and in December 1980, the director of the Seattle-based Project Bigfoot reported finding more than 200 Bigfoot tracks in the woods just south of Slater Road. Most people who set out to find Bigfoot never do; the sightings are the result of chance encounters in less populated or wilderness areas near water or mountains.

Also known as Sasquatch (evidently a term derived from the various indigenous names for the creature—Soss qíatl, Sokqueatl, Sasqíatl, Saskehavas), the Bigfoot is identified by its large footprints (sixteen inches long by seven inches wide, on average), massive height and weight (seven to eight feet tall, weighing over 250 pounds), furry dark body, powerful odor, unearthly vocalizations, and nocturnal behavior. Though their drawings differ considerably, taxonomies of the primate family tree in Gordon, Shackley, and Krantz suggest the Sasquatch is of the genus *Gigantopithecus,* a creature part ape, part human. Gordon makes the most inclusive suggestion that Sasquatch could have evolved from any of three hominid stocks:

Homo erectus, Homo sapiens neanderthalensis, or *Australopithecus robustus.* Fossilized remains of four giant jawbones found in southern China and northern Vietnam suggest *Gigantopithecus* was ten feet tall, weighing over 900 pounds. How the creature could have made it to North America and taken up primary residence in the Pacific Northwest, is still up for grabs.

Although reports of apelike beings sighted in coastal areas and mountain ranges from northern California to British Columbia come from European Americans, there are stories of giants that seem half-human in legends across native North America. According to Peter Mathiesson's *In the Spirit of Crazy Horse,*

> most traditional communities in North America know of a messenger who appears in evil times as a warning from the Creator that man's disrespect for His sacred instructions has upset the harmony and balance of existence; some say that the messenger comes in the sign of a great destroying fire that will purify the world of the disruption and pollution of earth, air, water, and all living things. He has strong spirit powers and sometimes takes the form of a huge hairy man; in recent years this primordial being has appeared near Indian communities from the northern Plains states to far northern Alberta and throughout the Pacific Northwest. (xxiii)

In many Native American legends—Hopi, Ojibwe, Cree, Athabaskan, Lakota, Dené, Huppa, Salish, and many more—there are tales of a hairy giant, a great elder brother who brings a messenger from the Creator.

From an anthropological perspective, the message of Sasquatch could confirm our species' relationship to other apes, and hence our place in the animal family. As Gordon explains in *Field Guide to the Sasquatch,* though human and ape ancestors separated between five and ten million years ago, there are few early hominid remains, and "no one has been able to definitively trace the bloodlines of ancient hominids or fully determine the relationship between humans and modern-day apes." For evidence, what we have are footprints, myths, "eyewitness" accounts—and one home movie, shot near Bluff Creek, California, on October 20, 1967. Two young men from Washington, Roger Patterson and Robert Gimlin, had chosen this area to search for the Sasquatch based on the hundreds of footprints found there. When they came upon the Sasquatch, Patterson was ready with his 16-mm movie camera, and recorded about a minute of footage, shot at a distance of between eighty and 100 feet. Sasquatch researchers studying the film have used the creature's build and stride to dispute its authenticity, but to date no one has been able to fully discount the film. Meanwhile, images from the film are reprinted in almost every Bigfoot volume, and etched indelibly in the minds of North Americans. On the cover of Gordon's *Field Guide to the Sasquatch* is an etching from the Patterson film; on the back, a still photo of the same pose is reprinted. In both images, one feature is especially evident: breasts. Large, pendulous breasts. Our most popular, most credible image of the reputed "missing link" between human and animal is a female.

I wonder about Bigfoot's scream, which is widely reported in all the sightings, a scream so unearthly that those who hear it say they will never forget. Because all reports say the Bigfoot is shy, reclusive, becoming aggressive only when assaulted, I can only imagine her scream is the sound of our wild animal selves, fighting for survival. Does Bigfoot scream for her lost children, or does she scream to ward off sexual violence from these would-be photographers? Does she scream for the forest, for herself, or for both as the same? Is her voice raised in defense, or in grief? I imagine that scream coming out of me when I look at the clear-cuts across the lake, think about the dams on the Columbia, the oil pipelines in Alaska. It's not popular, that scream. But it's here.

Some evenings around suppertime, when the winds off the lake had calmed down and the air was still and warm, parasailers and hang gliders tried their luck by soaring from the high logging roads off of Black Mountain. Our neighbors in the next cabin, Walt and Darlene, were no strangers to the air. Five years ago, Darlene (already in her sixties) had decided to fly tandem with Bellingham's only certified hang gliding instructor, James Fieser, of Whatcom Wings.

"You've got to shake things up every once in awhile," Darlene told me smartly, looking up from her gardening where I had found her, as usual, that evening. "It's so still when you're up there," she explained. "And it's like your best dreams."

One time, the instructor had told her, an eagle had flown up to him and coasted for a while beside him, under the glider's wings. The image of human and eagle alike on the wing, high above Silver Lake, suggested a symmetry of species, a memory of lives forgotten but not gone. Wilderness in the forests and rivers was reflected above in a wilderness of air I had never considered.

Every year at the end of August, the Can-Am International Hang Gliding Competition takes place at Silver Lake. With Shawn frequently away at job interviews in Seattle, the cabin was lonely in the evenings. It was time to visit the hang gliders.

"It's better to be on the ground, wishing you were in the air, than it is to be in the air, wishing you were on the ground."

Six men in their fifties stood at the edge of a field, watching three hang gliders in the sky. The field at Silver Lake Park that served as landing zone was surrounded in a wide arc by alder, cedar, and maple trees, with two old barns at the far end. Nearby, the group camping site was filled with trucks and RVs and tents, with people and dogs roaming freely. And in a row beside us were the colorful hang gliders that had already landed, their wings lightly touching the ground.

But if this was the mantra of so many pilots, why did they fly?

"Did you ever have those dreams that you were flying?" Konrad asked. A tall man in his late fifties, Konrad still wore the long blond hair of his youth, now completely gray, and a bandana tied around his head. Of course I'd had those dreams, and spent countless nights flying over the tops of jacaranda trees that lined the street where I grew up. "Then you have to fly," he said simply. "Not everyone has those dreams."

"It's not natural," Gary conceded, stooping to take the battens out of his glider's wings like so many tent poles. "But once your feet leave the ground and you're airborne, you're either scared and never want to do it again, or you're hooked. When I first started, I came up three, four days in a row, every week. I just couldn't get enough."

Snickering, I pointed to the pirate's flag that hung from the nose of Gary's glider, and then the name Bad Dog emblazoned on his flight suit. "What's this all about? Haven't you grown up yet?"

"Oh, no," Joel piped in, peering around from his own landed glider's wings. "Now she's going to talk to us about adulthood." This bespectacled man with scruffy gray hair and beard rolled his eyes and shrugged. "What's the point in growing up? Now we can actually afford better toys."

"Tell her about your dreams," Konrad urged him, then added, "Wait 'til you hear this."

Joel stepped over to speak with us, a willing confidant. "Not only did I have flying dreams," he told us, "I actually had out-of-body experiences. Some nights I could feel myself lifting out of my body and soaring above the trees and highways. That was before we had TV," he explained. "So when I saw those helicopter shots of the highways, with the red taillights all going one direction, and the white headlights coming the other, I had this jolt of déjà vu." He paused, trying to gauge how I would react. "I'd already seen those red-and-white lights in my dreams."

I knew all about following my dreams. That very morning, I had driven down to the group campsite at Silver Lake field, dropped my weekly garbage in the large trash bins, and joined a group of ten or fifteen men huddled around one of the picnic tables. I walked with confidence, not wanting to draw attention to myself as a newcomer, and a woman at that. In twos and threes, the guys eyed me curiously while a man with a short ponytail read off the rules. "Does anybody want a copy of the rules who didn't get one?" he offered at the end, and I stuck out my hand for a sheet. Then the pilots began introducing themselves to me. One guy wasn't as polite as the others. "Who are you?" he asked pointedly.

"I'm a groupie," I admitted, glad to have it out in the open.

"Oh, yea!" The men laughed and punched each other. "We don't get many groupies," one man said. "You're welcome here."

"Do you want to go up to the launch pad?" another pilot offered. "We need a driver. Do you think you can drive that truck?" and he pointed to a large Jeep with three hang gliders tied on the roof, looking something like skis in a travel bag.

"Sure," I said. And I was in.

But now I wasn't so sure. With just one accident, one shift in wind direction at the wrong moment in flight, a hang glider pilot could be killed or injured for life. I didn't have to search for hidden information. There was Zdenka, watching the glider landings from her wheelchair at the edge of the field. Five years ago one of her wing wires had snapped just before landing, and she had crashed into the roof of one of the barns. Instead of killing her, the landing had permanently paralyzed her entire left side. Then there was James, who had crash-landed a tandem flight (not

Darlene's) and shattered his right femur. And Michael, whose tandem crash-landing had killed his rider, a woman in her early thirties who, like me, had shown up and offered to be a driver in exchange for a tandem flight. So why did these pilots keep flying? And why was I so compelled to do it myself?

At the familiar yellow metal gate that bars all of Washington's logging roads from general public access, one of the pilots hopped out and turned the combination so that the arm swung free. Amazed, I asked the driver, Michael, how hang gliders were granted access to these logging roads.

"We've got an agreement with Crown Pacific," Michael explained as we drove through the gate and waited for the pilot to close and lock the swinging arm behind us. "They want the land to have some recreational use. In turn, we agree not to sue them for any accidents or mishaps on our part. Works pretty well," he chuckled.

If the mountain hadn't been logged, the roads wouldn't have been built. The hang glider pilots wouldn't be able to haul their expensive gear four and a half miles uphill to launch over Silver Lake, while their wives, children, or girlfriends waited patiently back at the landing zone. Confronted with the social and economic contexts that made this environmental recreation possible, I fell silent.

On the long bumpy drive up Black Mountain to the launch area, five pilots in Michael's Jeep debated the safety of paragliding versus hang gliding, rigid wing versus flexible wing, and then complained about insurance companies who defined hang gliding as an uninsurable, "unnecessary risk." I thought about the loggers, whose daily work involved "unnecessary risk." And here I was, willingly riding to an unknown destination with a group of strange men whose names I barely knew. Here they were, preparing to step out into the wind with some artificial wings, hoping to fly. These were all old stories—pilots, loggers, inquisitive women—and the insurance companies would scoff at us all.

After nearly an hour of driving up dusty, potholed switchbacks, we reached the launch zone. The mountain was completely fogged in, so thick I could barely see beyond the parking area. From the lake below, the morning had seemed clear and breezy, with just a few clouds hovering atop Black Mountain. Here at launch zone, nearly five miles above the landing at Silver Lake Park, the mountain vanished twenty feet below the dirt berm that edged the logging road. I walked along the road where pilots were assembling their gliders and approached a man in a baseball cap holding a clipboard and cell phone. Mikey was a pilot who had decided to sit out this weekend's competition and serve instead as launch director, determining who and when to launch. Between phone calls with the landing zone director, Mikey assured me that everyone would fly. What we needed were launch windows, clear openings in the fog, when the clouds parted and the fields and lake would seem a hand's distance away.

All along the logging-road-turned-glider-launch, pilots were assembling their wings and walking around in their flight suits, the double-leg pouch flopping behind them like a dragon's tail. Around the launch zone, wildflowers had begun to reclaim the mountain. There were purple lupin, cow parsnips, green hellabore, and pearly everlasting in abundance. The remaining stands of fir trees still scented the cool mountain air. Above the crunch of gravel, as pilots shuffled and adjusted their gear on this high mountain road, the rushing sounds of a creek could be heard flowing nearby. In late August, it was still fifty-five degrees out, with thick damp fog in the North Cascades.

The pilots were a friendly group, quite willing to explain the equipment, the wind, and the desires that moved them to fly.

"I'm not a very social guy," Joel told me, looking away from me to check the lines out to his wings. "I don't know how to make small talk. This is a way to have a common language."

"You don't think of anything else up there," another pilot explained, while stepping into his flight suit. "You just push down your fear and go. You become one of the birds. A big bird."

"One time a golden eagle flew right with me," Steve volunteered, tagging on to the conversation as he suited up. "But then I spoke to him, and that broke the spell. He came for my glider every time after that, flying straight for me with his claws out, then tucked in and flew right under me. I learned my lesson," he concluded, nodding to a small crowd who had gathered to hear his story.

"What'd you say to that eagle, anyway?" I had to know.

Steve paused a moment, then shrugged. "'Hey, birdie.'"

We all laughed.

"But just imagine being accepted as 'one of us' by these birds," Gary urged us. "I've watched a red-tailed hawk flying fifty feet below me, circling on the same thermal. Sometimes the hawks don't like you, and they'll ride at the ends of your wings so you can't rise. Yup," he chuckled, "you're up there playing flight games with the big boys then."

The group broke apart, and I kept walking. Some of the pilots showed me their various tools for navigating the space once they were airborne. Compasses. Altimeters. Variometers. Expensive gear. Every pilot flew with a helmet and a parachute. They were ready.

Back with Mikey, I saw the first pilot ready to launch.

"How do they become airborne?" I asked Mikey, feeling like a stranded version of the flying nun.

"Come over here," he replied, stepping out to the launch and motioning me to follow. There, just a few feet away from the logging road's rim, the winds blew strongly up the mountainside. Mikey pointed out some pink ribbons flying from sticks posted twenty feet below us. I hadn't seen these before, but their motion told Mikey what he needed to know: the winds were at ten to fifteen miles per hour, sufficiently strong to keep a hang glider airborne.

"The wind is always there," Mikey almost whispered, "waiting for us. It's a spiritual thing." All they needed now was a launch window.

When the clouds finally opened, Mikey nodded to the first pilot, who took a few running steps off the launch pad and lifted easily into the air, shoving his feet back into the insectlike leg pouch and zipping it closed. Transformation.

One by one throughout the afternoon, silently as the wind, the launch windows opened, and pilots with hang gliders stepped through the clouds to become dragonflies, raptors, or just boys whose long-ago dreams of flying had finally come true.

One summer isn't long enough to get to know a place, though I surely tried. Every day Sequoia and I took walks in Silver Lake Park, on the horse trails up Red Mountain, and the logging roads up Black Mountain. After the busy weekends of campers and RVs, on Mondays we had the park campgrounds to ourselves again. We picked up empty Cheez Whiz containers, beer cans, ribs and chicken bones in the park, depositing these (Sequoia needing a little persuasion to surrender the bones) in the trash or recycling bins; after all, this park had become our backyard. On the afternoons when it was sunny, I sat on the cabin's deck and watched electric blue and black dragonflies mate and flutter, listened to the lake slapping the docks, the sound of wind in the trees. I tried to surrender my own story and let the place take me in, listening and watching, exploring and asking questions, using field guides and maps and history books.

In the final two weeks before my departure, a sense of urgency crept upon me when I realized I hadn't yet seen the namesake for Maple Falls, the thirty-five-foot waterfall mentioned in pioneer narratives. I had listened to the water cascading off of Black Mountain into Silver Lake; I had canoed to the lake's southern end, where the stream carried the water away. But now, perhaps since I, too, was leaving Silver Lake, I needed to know where the water went next. How could I retain the wild serenity of the lake as I went on to pour myself into other pursuits? The water could teach me, if only I could find it.

The falls weren't marked on any of the maps I held. On a hunch, I phoned Silver Lake Park and asked to speak to a ranger. Mike Barnes picked up the call. "That's a question we get a lot," Ranger Barnes answered easily. And he told me how to find the falls.

That evening instead of our usual walk, Sequoia and I piled into the dust-covered car and drove the four and a half miles down Silver Lake Road, sharing the valley between Black and Red mountains with the unseen Maple Creek, flowing from Silver Lake to the North Fork of the Nooksack River. At the height of logging operations, the town of Maple Falls had almost filled the Nooksack's North Fork Valley between Black Mountain and Slide Mountain, if the old photos in Todd's *The Trail through the Woods* told the truth. For nearly two decades at the turn of the century, the falls were at the center of the town, and several mills were built on their banks to utilize the water. But as the logging industry declined, and the economic base shifted from logging to tourism, the stores had taken over. There was no visible trace of the falls at the intersection of Silver Lake Road and the Mount Baker Highway.

I had almost missed the trail through the woods behind Der Storehausen and the Baptist hotel room-church. Once I'd found it, the trail seemed worn and familiar, the ground packed solid from the small feet of many children and animals. There was no sign, no tourist directive to the falls.

But the trail knew the way through vine maple and Douglas fir, down a steep embankment, and I followed, as the sound of rushing water grew louder and stronger. Climbing up a few mossy boulders and fallen logs, I was rewarded with a hidden gem. From pool to pool, Maple Falls dropped and cascaded down the thirty-five feet, veiled in a foliage so dense it was hard to imagine this was the same place that had been logged bare and used for mill sites a century ago. If I had any chance of finding the Sasquatch in Maple Falls it would be here, underneath the tourism and commerce of the little town, where the wild waters of the real maple falls now run free and unmarked. Looking down into pools seven and ten feet deep, so clear they hardly seemed tangible, I took off my shoes and climbed the rest of the way down to the creek, leaving only my footprints in the damp, sandy soil.

YEAR FOUR *Oil and Water*

Nature-based cultures tend to the psychic severance implicit in human
life by trying to mend it—by living in ecological participation with the
natural world and by creating, and re-creating, connectedness among
themselves and the world with ceremonies and healing practices.
Western civilization addresses the severance by covering it up, shoveling
it under, dramatizing it, acting it out, making it worse, and perpetrating
it on others.

—Chellis Glendinning, *My Name Is Chellis and
I'm in Recovery from Western Civilization*

a woman can't survive
by her own breath
      alone
she must know
the voices of mountains
she must recognize
the foreverness of blue sky
she must flow
with the elusive
bodies
of night winds
who will take her
into herself

—Joy Harjo, "Fire"

Explosion

I

In the beginning there was only water, and you were a part of it. Never mind what else you have heard. This was your first relationship, your connection to water. And the quality of this relationship, the character of your beliefs about water, shapes all relationships in your life. The way you do one thing is the way you do everything. You cannot separate one relationship from another, treat this water with reverence, that water with waste. Because water returns. Water knows there are no separations. You too should know this, for water has been teaching you, from the beginning.

Imagine a creek flowing through the length of your life, from your birth to your death. Yes, your death.

Water precedes you, water survives you.

Consider the silence of blue-ice glaciers, ancient in their solitude, melting. Each winter the snowfall thick and wet, fluffy, or crisp and dry. Each spring the snows melting, glaciers growing and melting. Water flows down pine needles and cedar bark, flows down rocks and fallen logs, flows through moss and soil and sand.

The lake gathers rainfall, gathers snowmelt and the plenitude of creeks. The lake overflows, spills, falls, exuberance of fullness, joy in motion, streaming downhill now, swelling the creek bed where it has made this journey so many times before.

You have never seen this creek, the hidden water that flows through your days and nights, from one season to the next. Without it you would not live. You rely on this unseen water to flow forever. It has flowed here before you were born, before you stepped into its flow, and you imagine it will outlast you, outlast whatever you might do to this water. You believe it is limitless, unending. You know its persistent force has carved rocks because you can see them, see the way water flows through stone, leaving its imprint in kettles, in the basins of water where rocks circulate, in the interlaced fingers of water and stone embracing at the falls.

Water becomes you. But Narcissus-like, you look at water and see only your self. You believe you are alone. You are afraid. You need to control this fear, this aloneness, this terrifying separation.

You see the power of water and you want power. Power will give you control. You build dams and concrete channels and ditches, believing that by doing this you will control the power of water, the fertility of water, the fear of your separation. But water is patient. There are laws that govern the way of water, the ways of energy and power, the ways of land. There are consequences. Water bears no grudge, extracts no retribution. Your own actions, skillful or unskillful, determine the outcome. Your own relationship to water will poison you or save you. You decide.

You believe blocking the flow of water gives you power.

You believe blocking the flow of feeling gives you power.

You believe harnessing the animals, fencing off the land gives you power. And for a while, these strategies work.

But there are consequences. That which is diverted, divided, suppressed, always returns with greater force, and when it returns, no one can control it. No one.

II

Imagine a family. Picture the elders first. How many do you see? Where are the children? The sisters and brothers, aunts and uncles, cousins and nephews and grandchildren? How many people are needed to form a family? Can you be a family of one?

Look at it another way: is there a limit to the relations of family? Is there a certain number of people allowed in a family until a limit is reached? Do you say, "Families may only have ten people"? "The eleventh person will not be included." Or do you point to the basis of inclusion, the things that bind you, one to another, and say, "Yes, this person too"?

How do you recognize a family?

Do family members have to pulse with the same blood, or will love create a family where the blood does not run alike? Do the people have to be the same age and gender, or can they be many? Do they have to have the same skin color, the same culture? Do they have to pair up boy-girl, boy-girl, or can they pair up wherever love joins them? Do they have to be the same species, these family members of yours, or will you treat other species as family too? Is the land part of your family, or are there limits to the flow of family relations?

When you say "family," are you talking about who will be included? Or for "family" to have real meaning, do you have to leave someone out?

III

Create a small town. There will be the usual schools, groceries, public works and sanitation, restaurants and hotels, city government and hospital, library and museum—just one of each. These are the service industries, the civil relations. Your town needs an economic base, and here it is: your town is founded around water. If the water were not here, your town would never have been built. Your town's first relationship is with water, and how you treat the water will determine how you treat everything.

Here's the catch: imagine that your town's relationship with water is based in denial. You pretend you don't need the water desperately. You pretend you can control it. You act as if you can do anything, take anything, discard anything, and the water will be there, as before.

You treat the land this way too. Your town's economic base is founded on destroying the very place where you live, destroying the place you have come to love, the place you call home. I know—it's absurd, but just play along. When we're done, you'll get to choose again.

Pretending the forest and the lake aren't connected, your town cuts the forest to build houses and roads, to build docks for motorboats and jet skis, and then drinks from the lake. Pretending the town and the land

are separable, your residents excavate coal mines beneath entire neigh-
borhoods, extracting the dark minerals and taking away the concrete and
wooden supports when the mines are exhausted, leaving only air to fill the
darkness, only water.

IV

Imagine another river flowing through your small town, your family, through the heart of your life. Like water, this river supplies power, the
energy to move. You use it like water, without thinking, without asking
much about where it comes from, and even less about where it goes after
you use it. (You think it goes away. You don't know where away is.) You
don't know how much there is of this force at any one moment. You don't
need to think about it, really, because it's always there.

This force is not like water. This force is deadly. It must be handled carefully, or it will explode. Those who drink it, die. Those who breathe too
much of it lose consciousness. Those who work with it use masks, gloves,
protective clothing.

To show the strength of your denial, you cross these two rivers at the
heart of your town. There. And then you say they won't explode.

V

In your town there are divisions among the people, people who
work and live together, people who rely on each other to survive. Your
relationships with other people mirror your relationship to water, your
ideas about family. Meaning is based on exclusion. Definition comes from
knowing what to leave out. Who you are depends upon who you are not.
Remember all this, and deny it.

VI

I could tell you stories about this separation, this denial, in your town.
You know about the women who worked on Twelfth Street between C and
D streets, close to the train station. You know about the "cribs," the places
where men in your town paid women for the pleasure of their bodies, until
protests from upstanding women closed down the district, dispersing the
fallen women. In 1910, those women were separate.

Right here on Cornwall Avenue, 780 men and women paraded their separation in 1926, wearing white robes, white pointed hats, white faces. Twenty years later, the Bellingham Hotel refused to accommodate Inez Malone's prior registration, explaining to her when she arrived that "we do not cater to the colored trade." Thirty-three Japanese Americans had just been evacuated to Tule Lake, among them two Bellingham High graduating seniors and six U.S. military veterans. The hotel didn't want to defy public sentiment.

Your denial is resilient. These stories are too old, you say. You pretend that if the stories were more recent, they'd mean something. Very well.

Do you remember a wooden cross set on fire in the driveway of a migrant farmworkers' camp near Lynden's raspberry fields? That was 1994. Do you remember the rock that was hurled against Jess Torcaso's head as she walked across the college campus, her attacker shouting "Dyke!"? That was 1998. Do you remember that Bellingham High graduating seniors have received complimentary newsletters from the National Socialist Vanguard for three years now? These newsletters explain the international Jewish banking conspiracy, provide the arguments that prove the Holocaust was really a hoax—information that must be necessary, helpful to graduating seniors who haven't learned enough about separation.

Ridiculous, you say. These are isolated incidents. Peripheral. They do not reflect the heart of this small town.

You're doing such a good job playing along with this denial. I'm almost convinced that you believe it. Now you're pretending that how we treat water and how we treat each other are separate.

And you still insist that power comes from separation.

What happens next?

VII

In 1908, the Young Men's Commercial Club of Bellingham bought a forty-acre plot around Whatcom Creek and founded Whatcom Falls Park. During the Depression years, President Roosevelt's Works Progress Administration built the park's fish hatchery and helped to construct a stone arch bridge over the falls. As the park continued to grow, it became a favorite place for fishing, swimming, hiking. The city put in horse trails, tennis courts, picnic tables, a playground.

In 1965, two parallel lines of 16-inch and 20-inch pipes were buried underground in Whatcom County. At Seattle-Tacoma International Airport, the pipes were combined into one 14-inch pipeline that continues south to Portland, Oregon. Starting at the oil refineries in Whatcom County, the Olympic pipeline runs through the city of Bellingham, beneath Whatcom Falls Park, thirty feet from Kulshan Middle School. Farther south into Whatcom County, the pipeline runs through Samish Park, crossing the lake at the wood-framed bridge near the swimming area. For the rights to place the pipeline across city property—rights that expired in 1994—Olympic Pipe Line paid the city of Bellingham a yearly fee of $500. For thirty years, the 400-mile underground pipeline transported more than four billion gallons of petroleum a year, and nearly all of the fuel produced at Whatcom County's two oil refineries, Arco's Cherry Point refinery and Tosco's refinery at Neptune Beach.

In 1968 the city's water-treatment plant was built near Whatcom Falls, and as the city expanded, power lines were laid nearby.

Betwen 1985 and 2000, Olympic Pipe Line Company has been responsible for at least twelve oil spills of greater than fifty gallons each in Washington State. These spills range from 1,000 to 168,000 gallons of jet fuel, gasoline, and diesel fuel. Early in 1999, Olympic Pipe Line applied to build a 230-mile fuel pipeline across the Cascade Mountains from Seattle to Pasco, crossing through three state parks. Thirty miles east of Seattle, in the town of North Bend, the pipeline would be buried beneath the Snoqualmie Valley Trail, three blocks from downtown and several hundred feet from an elementary school and a high school.

What happens next?

At 3:25 p.m. on June 10, 1999, the Olympic Pipe Line Company shut down its 229-mile pipeline from Ferndale to Portland when its Renton command center quit receiving information from the line. Employees tried to restart the line at 4:32 p.m. but found no pressure, indicating a break in the line. A few minutes later, an Olympic employee in Whatcom Falls Park reported smelling gasoline.

Gasoline remained in the pipeline during the forty-five minutes it was shut down. Gasoline was pumping through the line for about fifteen minutes after Olympic restarted the flow, and before operators realized something was wrong. During that time, 277,000 gallons of gasoline spilled into Hannah Creek, flowed into Whatcom Creek, creating a four-inch layer of gasoline on the water. From seven to eight feet underground, the gasoline emerged.

In late afternoon, three girls from Kulshan Middle School went swimming in Whatcom Creek. But when they noticed a strong gasoline smell, the girls decided to leave the water and go home. At 4:25 p.m., Bellingham's 911 line began receiving reports of a fuel smell and people having difficulty breathing near Whatcom Falls Park. By 4:45 p.m., Bellingham police and fire officials had responded and began blocking off the intersection of Iowa, Woburn, and Yew streets.

Don Alderson came home from work early on Thursday, preparing for a trip to California to see his daughter graduate from high school. Later in the afternoon, Alderson smelled gasoline fumes and checked his car to see if it was leaking. Then he noticed that the water in Whatcom Creek, the water flowing along the border of his half-acre property, the water was turning amber. Alderson wasn't thinking clearly by this time, so his golden retriever, Chester, did the thinking for him. When Chester fell down thrashing, foaming at the mouth, his eyes rolling back into his head, Alderson put the dog in the car and drove a block away. Firefighters were gathered there for some reason, and they gave Chester an oxygen mask. Minutes later, a fireball roared down Whatcom Creek, and Alderson's home went up in flames.

"We thought it was an earthquake," said one man who lives near Whatcom Creek. "All the glassware and bottles shook in our house."

"The smoke looked about three miles wide with multiple thermal columns," said a Bellingham firefighter. "I'd estimate it rose about 20,000 feet. My heart just stopped."

"I thought it was Mount Baker erupting, just like Mount St. Helens," said one bystander. "But the smoke was too close for a volcano."

The force of the explosion blew out seven windows at the city's water-treatment plant. Inside the plant, twenty one-ton tanks stored chlorine, about one hundred feet from the pipeline.

The blast knocked out power lines from Puget Sound Energy, cutting electricity from 5,800 residences and businesses.

The explosion ignited a firewall that burned the creek gorge and incinerated its inhabitants at temperatures between 2,000 and 3,000 degrees.

An eighteen-year-old who had picked up his diploma from Sehome High School earlier that day, Liam Wood was fly-fishing in Whatcom Creek when he was overcome by gasoline fumes. Liam drowned in the water before the fire ever reached him. Stephen Tsiorvas and Wade King, two ten-year-old boys playing with bottle rockets in Whatcom Falls Park, weren't as lucky. Their bodies caught fire in the explosion, and to stop the burning, they jumped into the creek. Blinded by the flames, they couldn't see, and couldn't imagine, that the creek itself was on fire. Rescuers soon found the boys, but could not undo the damage fire and gasoline had done to skin and internal organs. By 7:00 a.m. the next morning, both boys were dead.

About a mile and a half of creek was devastated by the fire. Three days after the explosion, Fish and Wildlife Department workers counted thousands of dead trout, salmon, crawfish, and frogs. The burned bodies of red-tailed hawks, robins, and a river otter were found. The worst-burned animals crumbled to dust in the workers' hands. There were no signs of insects, birds, fish, mosses, trees, no sign of life in or on the banks of the creek. Smoldering trees continued to burn and fall. Rocks had bowling ball–sized holes blasted into them. Mudslides brought soot-covered rocks and trees down into the creek. Permeating the area was the overwhelming smell of its scorched remains.

VIII

Are you still there? Do you see that how we treat the water resonates, influences, shapes how we treat each other?

Even your little town sees this now. Its people are asking, How do we heal a charred landscape, cool a boiling stream, resurrect the bodies of three boys, countless hawks and songbirds, 30,000 fish? It takes the force of an explosion, a burning cross, a plane flying into a building to break through the walls of denial, to expose the suffering that grows with separation. Only then do the people ask, How do we honor the work of the body, paint the white sheets with rainbows, open the doors to the hotel? What can we change to ensure this violence never happens again?

People volunteer to help in the healing. For the boys who lost their lives in the explosion, for the families who grieve, the people of your town leave flowers and notes, stuffed animals and balloons at the cordoned-off entrance to Whatcom Falls Park. For the creek, the people volunteer to help in cleaning out debris, stabilizing stream banks, replanting the burn zone. They establish a Wayside Memorial Park, and place a carved cedar sculpture there in memory of Liam Wood. They persist in demanding civic and individual restitution from the corporations, compel the companies to make amends to the boys' families. The townspeople lobby and succeed in passing national pipeline safety regulations.

On the one-year anniversary of the explosion, a Critical Mass bike ride provides healing by reconnecting toxicity, power, and transportation. Just after 10:00 a.m., a crowd of more than 150 bicyclists and hikers departs from Bloedel-Donovan Park at Lake Whatcom and follows the creek's four-mile journey through Whatcom Falls Park, through the industrial zone of Iowa and State streets, down to the bay. There, the people play violin and guitar, sing and speak to honor the water, the three boys, and the townspeople's resolution to draw on a different energy source for power, one that works with the energy of life, not against it. They tell each other that as a people and a nation, this reliance on oil will destroy us, destroy the water and the land. The people plan a bicycle revolution.

One year after the explosion, the Tribes Project performs a play at Ferndale High School about race and prejudice, friendship and difference. The play is written and performed entirely by teenagers and is warmly received. The following year, students at Ferndale High elect a homecoming queen and transgender drag king by popular acclaim, and no amount of protest from adults in the community will sway them to change their minds.

One year after the explosion, Keepers of the Water forms to plan artworks that illustrate flow, works that purify water at the same time that they educate viewers. Their Living Water Gardens project will clean and revitalize water damaged by urban runoff, industrial discharges and litter, using settling ponds, flow forms, and wetland paintings. Their goal is to create "a community in which everyone, from the moment they are born, will understand the deep connection between life and water."

The First Congregational Church of Bellingham takes a public stance as an "open and affirming" congregation that welcomes Christians of all genders and sexual orientations. Their inclusive stance joins with other public affirmations of diversity from the Unitarian Universalists, Beth Israel Synagogue, Faith Lutheran, Garden Street Methodist Church.

One year after the explosion, Tibetan lamas from the Drepung Loseling

Monastery in Karnataka, India, visit town to raise awareness about the loss of human rights in Tibet. Recognizing the need for healing, for the townspeople and the creek alike, the lamas spend a week constructing an intricate sand mandala of the Buddha of Boundless Life. As always, their art culminates in a ceremony that includes chanting over the mandala, then sweeping away its sands to show the impermanence of all things. Traditionally, mandala sands are poured into an inland body of water, where Tibetans believe the healing powers of the mandala can spread into the ocean and carry healing throughout the world. Whatcom Creek is well suited to this tradition. Carrying two twelve-foot-long horns to the water, and chanting in monophonic tones, the lamas bring the sands of the destroyed mandala to Whatcom Creek and spread healing into the water.

Everything changes.

Impermanence is water's kindest lesson.

IX

It's time for you to choose. What do you want to believe about separation, about family, about what kind of power, what kind of energy you will use to feel safe?

What kind of relationship will you have with water?

Body, Midlife

I have booked a passage on an oceangoing conch, and am looking out the porthole window at midseashell. My berth is very small, of course, and we are still docked on the sand, rocking a bit as the waves lap the seashore. Soothed by the undulations, I do not brace myself for the large wave that comes unseen and unannounced, curls over us and sends the conch spinning, tumbling, swirling into the salty depths. Immediately nauseous, I realize that I am not prepared to make this journey and really need to get off the conch when I hear the captain's voice over the loudspeakers.

We are at sea. No exit is possible until we reach the other shore.

Like it or not, the journey has begun.

Even now, I'm not sure how it happened. Through a series of seemingly rational decisions, each as sensible as the last, my partner and I had sold our house, put our belongings in storage, and rented a summer cabin while we investigated various career options in different cities. With no results at summer's end, we signed a lease on a tiny bungalow three blocks from Bellingham Bay, where through open bedroom windows we could hear the harbor seals barking at night. A month after I returned to work at the university, my partner accepted an excellent position with a new employer and moved to Seattle.

Seen from one angle, that year reflects incredible growth, a willingness to let go of the things that weren't working in what seemed, on the surface, to be a lifetime achievement of the American Dream. Seen from another perspective, that was the year I lost everything. Home. Family. Direction. Purpose.

If this story were personal, I would not write it.

Dante's journey from the Inferno through Purgatory and into Paradise begins with the realization that he is off the map. "Midway in our life's journey," Dante writes, "I went astray from the straight road and woke to find myself alone in a dark wood." At this point, Dante is not considering that he may have stumbled upon the path to Paradise—that one must lose the trail in order to find it. He is not thinking about crisis-as-opportunity. In climbers' lingo, Dante is "gripped." "I never saw so drear, so rank, so arduous a wilderness!" he laments. "Its very memory gives a shape to fear."

Though an arduous wilderness may sound like a good time to an experienced backpacker, the journey Dante describes is no medieval equivalent of car camping. (Notice that he calls it "*our* life's journey"—not just *his* life.) This is the bad news: there's no home, no hot shower, no sweetheart waiting after this hike. There's nowhere else but the trail. And Dante just lost it.

On such a journey, when the hiker goes off route and loses the map, all hiking companions, and the light, the expedition becomes a bit more daunting than a walk in the woods.

One day while blow-drying my hair, I noticed something unusual. When I leaned to one side, my face pulled down on the same side I was leaning. Startled, I tried the other side. My face shifted accordingly. Suddenly, where there had always been tight features, there was a little looseness—well, more than a little. There was enough extra skin to have it move around with gravity. Because my face was being pulled straight down every day, and I usually looked in the mirror while standing straight up, I hadn't noticed the sagging until I tilted my head to the side—and my face tilted too.

In the dressing room at the gym, I confided my observation to an older feminist colleague. "My face sags to the side I'm leaning on," I explained.

"That's good," she replied, unconcerned. She was in her late forties, and seemed to have worked out all her issues with aging. "At least it's moving with gravity. Imagine if your face were falling *up*."

The suggestion reminded me of my mother's face-lifts, the little skin tucks at her temples, behind her ears, and under her hairline, tucks that pulled her face *up*. I remember years ago when she first began sleeping on a slant board, her feet elevated in a line well above her head. I was very small, maybe only three years old, too young to understand. But I understood now: she must have made the same observation I had, while drying her hair on the sides.

For my fortieth birthday, I had wanted some sort of celebration, a gathering of all my dearest women friends, an evening spent outside in the snow, sitting around a bonfire and telling each other the wisdom of our lives. But my closest friends were scattered across North America like so many leaves in autumn, and the chaos of rupturing home and relationship left no room for celebration during my fortieth year. By the time my forty-first birthday began its approach, I was alone.

At midlife, it seems harder to meet people, harder to make new friends. Everyone's life is now running at full speed, with no time for additions. In a small town, most locals still have their high-school friends and extended families, and have no need for more people in their lives. At work, new colleagues were also frantically busy, trying to meet the demands of career and family. Scarcity wasn't the only problem: in truth, I had become more particular with age, more specific about the qualities I wanted in my friends. As a result, I spent most of my time alone.

Nonetheless, I wanted to celebrate a second fortieth birthday by hosting a pre-crone party, a ritual for building community and sharing wisdom. To this party I would invite women in their forties and fifties to talk about aging and midlife. Surely there were other women asking the same questions, taking the same journey, yet each of us feeling we traveled alone. This party would be a gift for all of us, a way of raising energy and renewing our strength, a ritual celebration of life's middle passage, of women's bodies, aging.

Instead of lamenting, with Dante, that I was lost and had no friends, I changed the question: if I had friends, locally, who would they be? Almost effortlessly, I wrote down the names of fifteen women. Women who lived in town. Women I had seen or spoken to briefly at the library, the book publication reading, the gym, the dharma hall. Women with whom I had exchanged phone numbers, each promising to follow up, but never finding the time.

I picked the date, planned the ritual, created invitations, and sent them out. Women responded enthusiastically. They were delighted with the idea of a pre-crone party. They wanted to discuss aging with other women as much as I did. The party would take place.

Dante. Jonah. Osiris. Odysseus. Why were all the quest narratives about men? In these stories, the women sit home and wait faithfully (Penelope). They try to rescue and keep the hero (Circe). They lead him to Paradise (Beatrice). Or they try to tempt him to his death (the Sirens).

What if the hero's story is only one narrative among many?

What if Odysseus were a woman?

I can see her now, standing before her ship's mast like some combination of Xena the Warrior Princess and Virginia Woolf's Orlando. Her rescue and reluctant affair with Circe. Her instructions to the crew on surviving the middle passage, resisting the Sirens and steering a course midway between Scylla and Charybdis. I imagine her lashed to the mast, her crew wearing headphones with the iPods turned up full volume to drown out the Sirens' song, a sound so tempting that all those who hear it have no choice but to follow it to their deaths. Only Odysseus wants to hear the women, and live. She has decided not to block the sounds and sights of sensual pleasure, because then she would miss the call of seagulls, the splash of waves, the smell of saltwater and glint of sunlight off the ship's silvered prow. She knows what will happen if she acts, steps forward and tries to hold on to the music; she knows the difference between pleasure and happiness; she used to sing on those rocks, herself. As the ship passes by, and the Sirens sing their seductive song, Odysseus well remembers the strains of desire, even hums along with the chorus. This time, she composes herself.

In *The Heroine's Journey*, Maureen Murdoch augments Joseph Campbell's monomyth. Evidently the author of *Hero with a Thousand Faces* had told Murdoch that women don't need to make the journey. "In the whole mythological tradition the woman is there," he told her. "All she has to do is to realize that she's the place that people are trying to get to." Not surprisingly, Murdoch found Campbell's explanation "deeply unsatisfying."

Her search for a better story led her to Inanna, and the heroine's journey. Unlike Campbell's half-circle journey through the underworld and its three stages of separation, initiation, and return, Murdoch draws a full circle that seemingly doubles the hero's quest (and no wonder—women have often had to do twice as much as men, for the same amount of recognition). The heroine's journey begins with the separation from the Mother, the rejection and repression of the feminine in order to win favor in a patriarchal culture. Like Persephone's separation from Demeter, the heroine severs connection with the feminine and identifies with the masculine, entering the male-dominated world of power and success, career and politics, business and government. Inanna becomes Queen. She works hard, and by midlife wins the boon of success. This is what everyone wants. This is what will make her happy.

Why does she feel so hollow?

Inanna's journey offered the archetype I was seeking. We chart our lives by story, navigate by narrative. Discovering I had lost my way, I turned cartographer, and with Inanna began plotting my location.

In this dream, I am driving Grandma's old yellow Plymouth Valiant, my first car, and I am crossing the desert. It is only 8:00 a.m., and for some reason I have decided to cross the desert in summer, in the hottest part of the day, rather than wait for evening and drive across the sands at night. Not long after I leave the last town, the temperature gauge rises dangerously close to overheating. I turn off the air conditioning, put on the heat at full blast, crank down the windows by hand, and hope for the best. Why am I crossing the desert in this old car, at the hottest time of day?

Compass in hand, I traced the arc of relationships by which I chart my journeys, drawing two circles: an outer circle of dear but distant friends, and a closer circle of near and nearly friends. Joining the two circles would create a spiral, the perfect shape for raising and sharing energy. How could the two circles meet?

Sending the party invitations to distant friends, I asked them to write an open letter about their midlife journeys, their questions, insights, struggles. The generosity of these longtime friends poured forth in their replies. As the letters arrived, I taped them around my living room, kitchen, hallway, until every space on my walls whispered the words of women's wisdom.

Finally, the women arrived. Some brought cards, flowers, potted plants. Each woman selected one of the name tags I had made—hand drawings

of yogis meditating, of skis and bicycles, books and backpacks and bas-
ketry—wrote her own name, and safety-pinned the note onto her shirt.
Women toured the house, reading the letters decorating the walls. In the
kitchen, women were offered wine, tea, fruits, cakes. At the kitchen table,
the heart of the ritual began. Each woman wrote down her questions about
aging, using the multicolored paper-doll cutouts I had made of Barbie and
Ken (years ago, we thought Barbie knew everything—or at least, she *had*
everything). Completed question dolls were folded and placed in the faux
leopard handbag, snapped closed with a gold metal clasp.

When everyone had arrived, we gathered in the living room and created
a circle, passed the purse, pulled the questions, and sought the answers.

Body image, weight and shape. Sexuality. Memory. Eyesight. Mortality.
Loss. Creativity. Commitment. Finding one's life work. Changing partners. Spirituality. Activism. The myth of reduced sex drive. The gradual
invisibility of older women. Choice and intention. Starting over, again and
again. Everything in our lives was up for review.

And then the dancers arrived.

Four women, clad in scarves and coins, veils and skirts, beads and ban-
gles danced into our circle and gave us their siren call. We hooted and
admired, gazed and clapped. Then it was our turn. Pulling from the basket
of veils and *zills,* we outfitted each other and danced a circle of shimmies
and shudders, undulations and belly rolls. Librarians showed off the hip
toss while chanting bibliographic data. Activists shoulder rolled. An herb-
alist stopped the circle by pulling up her shirt and showing off her belly
undulations amid shrieks and cheers. One environmental educator danced
off into the night, leaving her reading glasses behind.

The pre-crone ritual raised energy by creating community out of a scat-
tering of individual women. Sharing this energy with the outer circle of
friends, I detailed the evening's questions and conversations, writing on
homemade stationery bordered with Barbies, name tags, and photos.

I had summoned allies for the journey, spirit guides, mentors and sister
travelers. Whatever came next, I had renewed confidence in my own ability to survive the trials because I knew I did not struggle alone.

Inanna's descent to the underworld is occasioned by hearing her sister,
Ereshkigal, weeping. Deciding she must go to comfort her sister, Inanna

enters the Land of No Return. At each of the seven gates to the underworld, Inanna loses piece after piece of her queenly regalia. When she finally meets Ereshkigal, Inanna has been stripped bare. Ereshkigal—who represents the repressed feminine in a patriarchal culture—isn't exactly grateful to see Inanna. As Murdoch explains, Ereshkigal is the part of the feminine that has been raped, exiled underground. She is raw, primal, sexual energy; she is feminine power split off from consciousness. She is women's instincts and intuition ignored and derided. In meeting Ereshkigal, writes Murdoch, a woman confronts her own underworld, the rage and fury left unexpressed for decades while she tried to please the fathers above.

No wonder that Ereshkigal speaks the words of wrath, fixes the eye of death on Inanna, and hangs her corpse on a peg to rot.

Welcome home, dear sister.

On a stormy Sunday evening in early June, a group of women gather on the porch of the old Fairhaven public library. The building is closed, but Lishanna has rented the high-ceilinged meeting hall upstairs, bought the seedling herbs and pots, selected the readings. We each take a plant and climb the stairs. On the gleaming hardwood floor of the empty hall, a circle has been laid at the center, a cluster of candles, flowers, and stones set upon a scarlet, gold-flecked scarf, with multicolored pillows and cushions marking its circumference. We remove our shoes and enter the space.

Lishanna invites us to introduce ourselves, say what brought us here, and name a woman we admire. Then she tells us the story of Artemis, hunter and eternal virgin, who eases the pain of other animals in childbirth, and thus embodies the paradoxes of celibacy and sexuality, birth and death. A virgin, Lishanna explains, is a woman unto herself. Using the body paints she has brought for us, we draw moons on each other's bodies, arms, legs, and feet, taking the symbol of Artemis for ourselves. Lishanna passes out paper and pens, inviting us to tell our stories more fully, in writing. This time, she says, we must tell the story in the third person, "she." Lishanna believes that if we can step outside our experience, perhaps we can see ourselves with more compassion.

I have written this story before. In that story, I was twenty-five, married, in graduate school. There was no money. My husband's anger frightened me. He would support whatever decision I made, but offered no feelings of his own. I went alone to the clinic, paid for the abortion myself. Afterward, we didn't discuss it. My grief cooled, hardened, closed off. Two years later, I filed for divorce.

I write the story again, telling about the girl who wanted to hold that tiny embryo within her until it became a child, the girl who wanted to create a life filled with writing and activism and parenting, the girl who lived in circumstances that allowed for only one life to flourish, not two. She had to choose: Who would live? Who would die? And she made a promise to life, that she would give back a hundred times more for the life she would take. She would use her creative energies in defense of water and animals, mountains and trees, people living and working in desperate and degraded surroundings. She would take the fertile potentiality of one being and offer it as communion for many. She said, This is my body.

With this promise, she made the right choice. She never wavered on this point. She knew the history of illegal abortions in her own family, a matrilineage of women using hatpins and ergot, doing whatever was necessary to control their own fertility. Preserving her own life, she did not sin, and because she was unrepentant, there was nowhere to speak of her grief. Her sorrow became silence, became stones in the belly and hard knots in the chest.

That was the old story.

This time, sitting in a circle with other women, I wrote beyond the ending, told the rest of the story. The girl had become a woman. And she had fulfilled her promise to life. She had organized and acted, written and spoken and marched. With only the embryo of her imagination she had made the decision. Over the next sixteen years, she had fulfilled the promise, and brought forth life. Many lives, her own among them.

We told our stories. The other women, all in their midtwenties, were still very close to the experience: two months, eight months, or four and a half years did not offer enough time for healing. Yet each of us still stood at the threshold of grief, afraid to enter. This was the reason we had gathered.

Lishanna took us down. With closed eyes, we followed her guided visualization connecting our bodies to the stars with a force of light that flowed down into the crown of the head, down the neck and shoulders, through arms and hands, backs and bellies. Lishanna invited each woman to imagine her own womb, a place inside the body that belongs to her alone.

Imagining the mouth of that womb that opens out and down to origins, down to the earth itself. Imagining the sounds that would be uttered, emanated, voiced from that mouth to the listening earth.

Listening. Winds whoosh through luminous red rock canyons. We hear low moans. Sobbing. Silence. And then the screams. Winds screaming. Women's bodies screaming, voices screaming, raging, echoing off high walls and colored windows, off bare wooden floors, racing down hallways and out screened casements. Screaming. Again. And again. And yet again.

On waves of sound, the stones I had held onto in place of something else, the stones of grief and silence and loss were released, skipping across crest after foamy crest of sound, flying beyond the candlelight circle, out into the rainwashed night air.

Below the grief, a precious desire lay buried, curled up, knees to forehead, breathing. It was still waiting, two decades later. I still wanted a child.

"I want you to imagine a gold light," Lishanna resumed, "just below your navel. It is strong. Steady. Glowing."

Slowly, the gold light expanded, filling up from belly to chest and torso, pouring down arms and legs, following a cord of light out the top of my head and down from my spine to the earth. I saw my body illuminated, glowing, alive and life-giving.

"This gold light is the force of your fertility," Lishanna continued, "your creativity, flowing back to you and out into the world. Take a moment to feel the power of your own creativity, and envision what you will bring forth with this life force that is yours to use as you choose."

In the silence that followed, Lishanna handed out smaller sheets of paper, and we wrote down our intentions for manifesting creativity. When everyone was done, we gathered up our seedling plants and papers, went back downstairs and out to the porch. There, we set fire to our intentions in clay pots, and planted our seedling herbs on top of them. The circle was opened.

It was still twilight at 10:00 p.m. when I left the library and drove the road home above the waterfront. Suddenly, they appeared: two deer, a doe and fawn, trying to cross the highway. In a moment, I had pulled my car sideways across both lines of traffic, set the flashing hazard lights on high, checked my seatbelt, then waited to exhale until cars from both directions slowed to a stop, keeping their distance.

Warily, the doe sniffed the air, then bounded across the highway. Her fawn followed, the two of them disappearing into the blackberry bushes above the bay. In their place, only the gold glimmer of fertile twilight remained.

When Inanna fails to return to her throne some days after Ereshkigal's greeting, her dearest friend, Ninshibur, raises a cry as promised, beats the drum, and circles the houses of the gods. But few will meddle with the ways of the underworld. Finally, Ninshibur persuades Enki, god of waters and wisdom, to send two creatures made of dirt down to the underworld as messengers. There, they find Ereshkigal groaning in pain. As Enki has instructed, they don't fix anything for her; they can't change anything in her life. They simply grieve with her. They empathize. They offer compassion. They sing her lamentations with her.

And Ereshkigal is finally heard. Empathy turns her toward the pain, allows her to move into it, through it, out the other side. Ereshkigal heals. Inanna returns to life.

But to ascend from the underworld back to her kingdom, Inanna must find a substitute to take her place. Her solution—sending her husband, Dumuzi, and his sister, Geshtinanna, for half a year each—parallels the story of Persephone, who also heals the split between the two worlds by spending half the year in the underworld with Hades, and half in the daylight world with Demeter.

In the heroine's story, the daylight world and the underworld are linked, interdependent. The heroine's journey expresses the wisdom of the cycles of change, the insight that suffering and death have meaning that is a part of strength, courage, life.

In his book *A Year to Live,* Stephen Levine teaches readers how to live as if this year of life were the last. His discussions of forgiveness, letting go of the need to control, healing old wounds, and expressing gratitude are all part of the conscious life review that, if practiced with intention, allows one to live more fully. At midlife, we are offered the opportunity to practice conscious aging, to make peace with impermanence, to show up for the present moment because it's the only life we truly have.

For that part of us that identifies with an agile body and an unforgetful mind, writes Levine, aging is loss. In *The Middle Passage,* James Hollis agrees. "Seen from the perspective of the first adulthood," Hollis observes, "the second half of life is a slow horror show. We lose friends, mates, children, social status, and then our lives." Barbara Sher takes a different approach in her book, *It's Only Too Late If You Don't Start Now.* "How will you live," Sher challenges, "now that you know you will not live forever?"

When I realize that I am actually going to die, preparing for my own death becomes a major undertaking. At a workshop on Death and the Dharma, Vipassana meditation teacher Rodney Smith invites participants to write a life review—in five sentences. It's a sunny Sunday afternoon in early May, a rarity in Seattle, and at least forty people are sitting in this church basement on Capitol Hill, diligently summarizing their lives. Admittedly, no one here is under the age of thirty-five; the absentees probably believe, as I did, that they will be exempt, immortal. After the workshop participants have completed the assignment, or given up trying, Rodney asks us, Is this how you wanted your life to go? Is this how you want to be remembered? What is important in your life?

To give us some perspective on death, Rodney tells us stories from his years of experience as a hospice caregiver, aptly summarized in his book, *Lessons from the Dying.* He tells us, "Every time I am afraid of death, it's about feeling there's not enough time. When we die, all time comes together. Facing our death means letting go of our attachment to self-identity. The fear resides in the holding on to life, not in the experience of death itself."

To prove his point, Rodney asks us to imagine our death. It's the last five minutes of our lives. Who is there with us? Who is not? What have we left unfinished? And how do we feel, now that we know our life is no more?

It is early evening, some time after dinner, and the warm gold of waning sunlight illuminates the desert sands. This time, I will cross the desert at night, on foot, following a sandy road flanked by high dunes on one side and stretching down to a valley on the other. Pleasantly, my path is already shaded by the mountains, though the rest of the valley is still bright with evening.

Soon, I walk past the sculpture of a cobra coiled atop the sand dune to my right, its hood beautifully flared. I have passed this cobra before and admired the work of its sculptor: every scale shimmers or is etched with sand from the dunes. The cobra's trail to its resting spot is clearly visible, yet the sculptor's footprints are nowhere to be found. The snake does not move, and though it is a sculpture, I pass it cautiously, as before.

After hiking a short distance, I see a second cobra in the same position as the first, coiled on the sand dune, hood flared. The last time, I did not come this far across the desert. I don't know what to expect. I am startled when the cobra opens its eyes, sways, then undulates its hooded body down low and up again. This is no sculpture. And it sees me.

I turn to run back, and just as I realize that the first cobra is also alive, the sand becomes knee-deep and I cannot run. When I face forward, the sand becomes a road.

The cobras are the guardians. The path is clear.

At summer solstice in the Pacific Northwest, daylight stretches well past 10:00 p.m. In the last hours of light, I walk the dog once more around the neighborhood so that she will sleep undisturbed. Tonight the skies have cleared from the rains, and there's a gentle wind blowing away the clouds that hide the moon. Sequoia and I are walking back to the house when I hear the tallest cottonwood trees in our neighborhood. They are growing across the street from one another, and with the fluttering of their green and silver leaves, they are talking to each other in a language I hear but cannot quite decipher. I move closer, and Sequoia follows. The breeze picks up, and I lie down to listen in the grassy boulevard between the sidewalk and the street. It is dark out, and no one is near. At first, Sequoia is impatient, checking back with me and going toward the house, until she realizes I will not be moving. Then she lies down beside me, and together we listen as the cottonwoods whisper their stories into the night.

No one waits for us at home; we don't have to be anywhere. We are women unto ourselves, Sequoia and I, animal bodies at midlife, listening, and there is all the time in the world.

YEAR FIVE *Impermanence*

We have all been uprooted to different degrees, and for different reasons, but not everyone is aware of it. Here/there, homelessness, border culture, and deterritorialization are the dominant experience, not just fancy academic theories.

—Guillermo Gómez-Peña

If you realize all things change,
there is nothing you will try to hold onto.
If you aren't afraid of dying,
there is nothing you can't achieve.

—Stanza 74 from the
Tao Te Ching, by Lao Tzu

Food and Shelter

Weekends from April to September, organic farmers from Bellingham and Whatcom County gather in the large parking lot on Railroad Avenue to sell their produce directly to the public. Under blue-and-white-striped tents, vendors cover their tables with clean cloths and arrange their produce to please the eye. Bright green and red-leaf lettuce, gleaming white cauliflower, rosy tomatoes, and the delight of peppers—red, green, yellow—are placed alongside the dark-green broccoli and red cabbage. One tent offers the industry of bees, while another displays hazelnuts, and in the late summer months there are tables and tables of berries—strawberries, raspberries, blueberries, marionberries. Nearby, flower vendors bring the changing blooms of the season: yellow and purple irises, white bells of honeysuckle or blooms of baby's breath, purple and pink sweet peas, fragrant orchids and dazzling blue hydrangeas.

Interspersed among the farmers are individual craftspeople as well, with the products of their cottage industries gaily decorating each vendor's stall. There's earthenware and pottery, earrings and beadwork, children's clothing and sweaters, dresses and slacks. At the end of one row, the Greyhound Rescue League displays the dogs that volunteers have brought to safety and are now trying to place. Another row features goats in a large goat pen, with goat treats available for a mere twenty-five cents on a table nearby. The cheerful goat herder chats with parents and children beneath a sign that reads "Cashmere Goats." A few tents away, two people look on enviously as their friend receives a five-minute massage, her face buried in the pillow and protective tissue of the headrest, her body limp with repose. And all along the market's back row there are food stalls and picnic tables, where the impatient and the hungry can sample spanakopita and Greek salads, tortillas with rice and beans, cinnamon-and-walnut breakfast rolls, cranberry-orange scones, coffee, and fruit juices. At one end, a harpist and a guitarist have assembled their chairs and music stands so that they enjoy the shade of nearby trees, while closer to the picnic tables, a soloist sings softly, alternating between his guitar and his banjo for accompaniment.

Food brings a community together. Families share breakfast; students and coworkers meet for lunch; friends gather over dinner. Sharing food and feeding one another affirm our good will. Food is a part of our rituals of celebration and of mourning, trystings and weddings, funerals and farewells. Feeding each other, we affirm our desire for life itself.

Food is also the way that we partake of the earth: at every meal, we consume water, air, soil, and seed, transforming the elements of earth into our very selves. I am part of the broccoli that this organic farmer raised in the county, part of the sunshine and water and dirt that fed these green flowerets. Eating is an act of transubstantiation, a sacred communion with the earth on which we feed and which, one day, our bodies will feed as well. But in the Pacific Northwest, a region of agricultural abundance, there are still people who go hungry.

At the exit from Bellis Fair Shopping Mall to Meridian Avenue, and the off-ramp from Interstate 5 southbound at Lakeway, people stand with hand-lettered cardboard signs that read "Homeless Vet—Please help—God Bless" or "Homeless and Hungry—Will Work for Food." One day I decide to watch, to sit at a discreet distance where I can see without being seen. The people with signs also see without being seen. They see cars and drivers who stop and stare straight ahead. They see cars that drive quickly, drivers who, in order to turn the corner, are forced to look where the people with signs are standing, looking at them. Sometimes, not often, a car window comes down, a hand with money sticks out. Sometimes there is a conversation. I watch this as long as I can stand it, which is not as long as the people standing.

After one afternoon of observation, I make a list of all the food banks, hot meals, and shelters in and around Bellingham, duplicate it, stash copies in my glove compartment. I keep single bills in there as well, for others to spend as they see fit—beer, food, cigarettes, they can decide what they need. I don't believe the list or the dollars will solve much of anything. It's the act of seeing, of clear visibility, that might confer some dignity on sign holder and driver alike. For it's the invisibility of the sign holder that shatters my own humanity. I can't claim to be anyone I would respect if my best response to suffering is to look away.

On weekday mornings at 6:20, I drive to the dharma hall for the 6:30 a.m. sitting. The morning sangha consists of a Zen priest, a yogi from the Shambhala meditation group, and two Vipassana practitioners—some days more, some days less. Driving down Holly Street through Old Town, I pass the Lighthouse Mission, where there's always a crowd of men standing outside, even when it's raining. Two blocks farther down, there's the Labor Ready office, its fluorescent lights illuminating the numbers of people already waiting in the building, or milling around outside, drinking from Styrofoam cups, waiting to be sent out on jobs.

The Lighthouse Mission, Labor Ready, the dharma hall—we are the only people out and about at 6:00 a.m. in Bellingham. It makes me wonder what else we have in common.

It's a Saturday afternoon in February, sunny, with crisp, bright-blue skies, and downtown Seattle is crowded with shoppers. Although living and working in separate cities, Shawn and I are still spending time together, still partners apart. This weekend we are looking at laptop computers, comparing models, prices. We stop at Starbuck's to buy two lattes ($5.50). The laptop is a necessity, Shawn advises, for I am struggling with my old Powerbook 520 and software copyrighted in 1987. The new laptops have faster speeds, newer software, and the ability to play movies and music and even edit videos. But a new computer will cost me $2,500 during the six months when I am writing and have no income; perhaps I can make do without it. Now a resident of Seattle, Shawn is baffled by my unwillingness to enter the twenty-first century. Her employer is buying her a pocket computer—more advanced than a Palm Pilot, she assures me. All of Seattle is online, on call, on caffeine.

We go to the Bon Marché, the Northwest's version of Dayton's, and I consider buying new shoes. I have been wearing the same ankle boots for five years. At the independent shoe repair store in downtown Bellingham, the two old cobblers know me well. Each year when I pick up my reheeled boots, we lament that the soles cannot be fixed (these days, shoes are glued together, not sewn); we delight in the shine of newly blackened leather uppers. I don't want new shoes.

Our shopping ended, Shawn and I take the escalator up to the second-floor women's room that I like so much for its antique elegance. Shoppers enter through the large ladies lounge, pass through the oval washbasin area with its brightly lit sink-to-ceiling mirrors, and on to the more discreetly lit toilet section with large stalls and shelves enclosing each individually decorated toilet and washbasin. Anticipating the unfolding of this triple enclosure, I am not prepared for the tableau that awaits us in the women's room.

Women are sleeping on chairs and couches in the ladies lounge. Elderly women. Women with wigs and hats, women with old coats and mismatched bags, women with newspapers and bundles of clothing and food. The Grandmothers.

Mechanically, I pass through the lounge, through the mirrored washbasin area, use the toilet, and wash my hands. I am struggling to assimilate what I have just seen. We must do something, I decide. We must take all the money that would have been spent on the laptop computer, money that would have been spent on the shoes, the clothing I no longer want or need, the overpriced coffees we just drank. We must divide it all up and give it to these women. Then we must go directly to city hall and demand that social services provide food and shelter, job skills training if it is wanted, a living stipend for all women over sixty-five, telephones, and whatever else these women need. I go out into the lounge and count the women, numbering how we shall divide up the sums.

Eleven. Eleven homeless women are sleeping in the ladies lounge at the Bon Marché in downtown Seattle. In February.

Shawn wants to go. She thinks my idea is well meaning but ineffectual. There are too many women. The problem is too big. It's like throwing your body into the Grand Canyon to plug a leak. Whatever you give, your whole life, still won't be enough. The problem never ends.

Two years later, Shawn joins the United Nations and works to coordinate humanitarian relief efforts in Iraq, Liberia, and later, Sri Lanka. And I remember her words from that day in Seattle: whatever you give, your whole life, still won't be enough. The suffering is endless.

How, then, shall we respond?

If you are hungry and homeless in Bellingham, you need to be prompt and eat fast if you want hot meals. At the Lighthouse, breakfast, lunch, and dinner are served seven days a week—for thirty minutes each meal. If you have transportation, you have more choices. At the Unitarian Church's Maple Alley Inn, hot lunches are served Wednesdays and Thursdays for two hours, and again at the State Street soup kitchen on Tuesdays and Fridays. It's mostly men who use these services, since it's mostly men who are homeless and on the streets.

For those who have access to cooking facilities, the Bellingham Food Bank and the Salvation Army give out food three or four times a week, once per family. There are other food banks in Whatcom County, a few run by Christian churches, and one on the Lummi reservation.

For homeless women there are more social services, most started in the 1970s, thanks to the women's movement against domestic violence. Lydia Place, WomenCare, Agape House, the YWCA, and Dorothy Place are shelters where women and children can find transitional housing, job placement services, financial counseling, wardrobe assistance, community, food. Some houses serve only single women; some serve women with children, and some focus their services on battered women. Some offer emergency housing, while others provide longer-term transitional housing. And the shelters are always full. In a town of 66,000, with a countywide population of less than 150,000, Bellingham's incidence of domestic violence means there are more women and children seeking safe shelter each night than there are places to accommodate them.

I talk with workers at the Opportunity Council, at the food bank, at Jobs with Justice, at Maple Alley Inn, and the picture of homelessness emerges. One in three homeless persons is a veteran. The others may be impoverished elderly, refugees or new immigrants, people with disabilities, or those recently deinstitutionalized from hospitals or prisons. They may be children or teens fleeing emotional, physical, or sexual abuse. Some are rejected by parents for their sexual orientation; some flee to escape violence or families abusing drugs and alcohol. Unable to obtain work due to their age, their lack of an address, or their inexperience, runaways resort to drug dealing, shoplifting, prostitution, and are often at risk of contracting HIV/AIDS.

The problems change for adults. Three-quarters of homeless men are over age thirty-five, and many are illiterate. Men become homeless through loss of employment, leading to loss of housing, and perhaps loss of family connections, all aggravated if there is substance abuse, physical or mental illness. Women usually have children, and will stay longer in desperate situations to hold on to whatever tissue of safety protects them from the greater vulnerability of the streets.

More than half of all families in poverty are headed by women. Over 90 percent of families in shelters are headed by women. They are, on average, about twenty-seven years old. Three-fourths are women of color. They move four times a year. Their support networks are limited. Most have less than a high school education. More than two-thirds are depressed.

Migrant workers are also part of the homeless population. There are significant language and cultural barriers between these workers and the food-service programs. There are fears about government agencies and the INS. Farmworkers face even greater barriers during the off season—no work, no housing, no income. Lack of personal transportation, and lack of adequate public transportation, place another major barrier to accessing support services for those living and working in the county.

The information is mind numbing. How can the Veterans' Administration be failing the people who have risked their lives for their country? How can children fail to care for elderly parents, or parents fail to protect children? Where is the continued support for ex-prisoners and deinstitutionalized patients once they leave confinement? Why are the social services of Whatcom County and Washington State failing to help these immigrants and refugees? Why isn't this country's minimum wage a living wage for working families?

Disbelief covers fear. If homelessness and hunger can happen to others, it might happen to us. Surely homelessness is a personal problem, a character defect. If we look only at the individuals, we can ignore the social structures that place people on the streets. We can pretend that there is no coincidence, no inheritance, no social connections that have delivered us the homes and jobs we now possess. We insist that we got what we deserved, paid our dues, received only our just reward. We are willing to provide Social Security for retired or injured workers because these beneficiaries have earned their rewards; taxes for other social programs are merely hand-outs. We distinguish between deserving and undeserving poor, donate ten or twenty-five dollars to the United Way, give a can of tuna to the food drive, and look away.

At the food bank volunteers' orientation, Crystal explains the guidelines for distributing food to the community. If people can show proof of a Bellingham address—their mail, their utility bill, their rent receipt—their household can receive food once a week. Just inside the food bank's front door, two volunteers are shown how to check people in, using computers and spreadsheets, providing people with a slip showing the number of persons in their household. Instead of *recipients* Crystal uses the word *clients,* and I like her immediately. The word *client* connotes choice, describes those who have judiciously contracted for a service, suggests a professional relationship with the volunteers. I notice that Vera, Elinor, and some of the longer-term volunteers have plastic name badges like those worn by grocery clerks. Everything we do, Crystal emphasizes, needs to show a respect for the clients and the foods disbursed.

Then she puts a box of food on the table, and the new volunteers perk up. The food bank receives donations from grocery stores, from customer donation baskets at the stores, from individuals, and from food drives, Crystal explains. Not all of these donations are edible. Shocked, I think back to the postal workers' food drive earlier that year, cringing as I watch myself go to the pantry and select foods that have sat there for months, foods that I had bought but really didn't like, foods I wouldn't eat. Those were the cans and boxes I set out for the postal workers' food drive. The less-than-desirable foods. The rejects.

And here they are. Crystal pulls out crumpled boxes of breakfast cereals and pastas, expired and even bulging cans of vegetables, sacks of rice and flour with bugs. Using the food as props, Crystal explains how we work with these donations if they aren't already sorted out in the stock room. Canned goods can last three to five years past the expiration date, but we must discard the cans with rust, dents, or bulged tops. Crumpled boxes of food are acceptable as long as the food inside is contained in a sealed liner.

Dairy products can be given out seven days after the expiration date, and products like yogurt, orange juice, cottage cheese, and sour cream can go even longer as long as there's no visible mold. Meats must be discarded if there is freezer burn. The only products whose expiration dates must be honored are those to be consumed by the most vulnerable, infants and the elderly. Baby foods, baby formula, and Ensure all must be thrown out on the date of expiration.

Then there's a test. Crystal hands around sample food items, and we are to decide whether or not these foods can be given out. Would you eat food from this can? Cereal from this box? Drink from this container? I am given a can of creamed corn, rusting at the top, with an expiration date of two years past, and the world cracks open. This food should not be given out. In fact, this food should not have been donated.

Right, Crystal nods.

On cool summer evenings when Sequoia and I walk through the neighborhood, I see fruit trees overflowing in every other yard. Blackberry bushes fling their tangled branches over fences, over empty lots, over rotting wooden garages, over parked and abandoned cars. The small white flowers have already fallen, and I keep close watch on these bushes, collecting jelly jars and pectin and waiting for the blackberries' late-summer ripening. Furtively, I check the fruits for ripeness. At some houses, the apples have fallen to the ground and lie scattered beneath the apple trees. I pick up a sample and mark the trees' address, pocketing the fruit for later scrutiny. This early in the season, the fruits have been bitter. The berries are still hard, and don't come readily off the stem. I fantasize about finding the sweetest apple and returning to the home where the owner says, "Take them all, I don't use them."

How much food goes to waste in Whatcom County? How much overripe fruit falls unnoticed from the trees and bushes, how much useable food is left over for the birds, the insects, and the animals to have their share? How much fruit goes back to the soil? For several years now, a gleanings project organized by Fairhaven students, Fruitful Gatherings, has collected unused fruits from trees and from farmers, unsaleable produce from grocery stores and the farmer's market, and given it to shelters and food banks. It makes me wonder why we grow lawns instead of food,

why we cultivate and fertilize and encourage the growth of purely orna-
mental crops, while people in our own community go hungry. I imagine
being part of a community where edible and decorative food is grown in
every yard, a community where ordinary walks could become meals, a
community where everyone could be fed.

Bellingham's food bank is tucked away on a side street in an industrial area
just east of downtown. Earlier that spring I had driven down one of these
streets by chance and seen people lined up outside the warehouse building at midday on a Friday afternoon. From the appearance of it, I got two
impressions. I thought it was a soup kitchen. And I knew I would work
there.

There's not much to the food bank, really. The front room is the distribution area, with bread shelves lining the entire left wall, and a long
L-shaped line of silver metal food service tables edged into the back and
far-right walls. Along the back wall are the produce shelves; dairy is in the
far-right corner, with grains and canned goods stacked along the right wall.
Each station has a little hand-penned card stuck into a plastic sleeve and
taped onto the metal table. The cards change weekly, depending on the
foods received. The cards tell the volunteers how many cans or servings
of each item to give out per household. Commodity foods provided by
the federal government are available once monthly to families who have
a proven address and who receive other forms of aid. Noncommodities
are foods donated by the community through food drives, grocery stores,
farmers, religious or civic organizations, and they are available to anybody
who walks in off the street. Though the food bank requests it, you really
don't have to have proof of address, a letter from an agency, or any other
type of certification to receive noncommodity food, but the allowances are
smaller.

The volunteer who trains me for my first night, Vera, is a petite woman
in her sixties or seventies. Vera volunteers at the food bank every day, packing and sorting the food as it comes in, or working distribution if they are
short on volunteers. When Eric, the assistant manager, passes by, he jokes
with me about Vera's zeal.

"We're going to send Vera to California to help them solve their energy
crisis," he says.

Vera waves him away and shows me how to set up the canned goods so that they are already portioned out per household. Tonight, commodity food recipients may have six cans of pears, two cans of green beans, and one can each of peaches and corn from our station. Vera arranges the six cans of pears in pyramid stacks of three, two, one as if she's setting up a store window display. She gives quite the air of a working professional with her navy polyester slacks and vest, her blue-and-white striped blouse, her plastic name tag "Vera," and her red lipstick smile set in deeply lined cheeks. Like the produce volunteers, Vera wears latex food-worker gloves, although we are only handling cans. By the end of my shift, I understand the need for gloves. My hands are grimy from handling greasy, dusty, dirty cans. But Vera's gloves aren't just about protecting her hands. Volunteering in a situation potentially ripe with shame and judgment, Vera's entire attitude is about dignity and respect. She wants the people who come here to feel that their food was handled in a sanitary way, whether it's a can or an ear of corn.

The row of produce is a bit harder to dignify. Although the apples at the end look fresh, the bananas are covered with black spots, the tomatoes display darker areas of damage, and the ears of corn are blemished as well. Each box of produce has a number posted on it, indicating how many of each item is allowed per household. I can only glance at the bags of lettuce, the quarts of milk and stacks of cheese, the bags of rice and jars of peanut butter before returning to my station beside the volunteer preparing her portions of beef stew and canned potatoes. It's time to open the doors on my first night of service.

The food bank is geared to supplement households who already receive other forms of aid but whose supplies have run out before the end of the month, or the end of the paycheck. Recipients range from working poor to homeless and unemployed. Households range in size from one person to fifteen, but the quantities of food allowed seldom vary. Even with my limited mathematical capabilities, I am angered by this apparent lack of logic. I ask Crystal about it, then Vera, and get the same answer from both. The food bank is only a supplement. Food is available from other sources throughout the community.

"With three meals a day available at the Lighthouse, the hot lunches at Maple Alley Inn, picnics from Food Not Bombs, and all the other services in town," Crystal assures me, "no one in Bellingham has to go hungry for even a day."

To prove her point, Crystal shows me the boxes stashed on the lower shelf of my metal food-service table. Full of boxed food and cans with pull-off tops, these boxes are labeled "No-Cook." These are to be given as noncommodity foods to people who have no place to cook food, and no can openers. It takes me a moment to imagine how this could be possible: no can opener. No pots or pans. No stove, gas or electric. No refrigerator. No home. I finally look at Crystal, adding it up. This food is for people who have nowhere to eat it.

"And I'm still trying to figure out," Crystal continues, so accustomed to the situations faced here that she needs no time to process the information, "what to feed my vegan and vegetarian homeless clients." She looks at me with new interest. "You're vegetarian," she lights up. "Maybe you can work on this, give us some ideas."

She puts the food box away and hurries back to the computer, where volunteers are greeting the evening's first recipients. I picture my rows and rows of vegetarian cookbooks at home. Some of my unexamined assumptions about food have just been put out for compost.

The food-bank recipients are nothing like what I expected, and it is serving them that shows me I even had expectations. The individuals who come are women and men, some in their early twenties, others in their thirties, forties, fifties. Sisters come in together, as do whole families: a mother with two girls under the age of seven; a heteronuclear family, the father with a long red braid and black cape, the mother with soft blond hair and no makeup, the little boy with dimples and a shy smile. Some single fathers come through, as do women with notes identifying their households as having four, seven, or nine persons. A number of dedicated bicyclists come through with bike helmets and panniers to hold their canned goods. One sight-impaired woman comes through the line, assisted by another woman in designer clothes and large rings on her hands. One person comes through holding a cane. There are several families from the Ukraine, Vera tells me, and I warm up to their wide faces and broad smiles, their accents and limited English.

Vera knows many of the clients, and they greet her by name. She smiles and talks to the babies, helps out the women struggling to get one reused plastic sack inside another for added reinforcement. Defying the old yarn that "beggars can't be choosers," Vera treats people as if they had choices. "You can have up to six cans of pears," she tells people from small households of one or two persons, "but you don't have to take all six, unless you want them."

"What do I do with these?" one young mother asks, bewildered by Vera's pyramid of pears.

Vera responds with an easy recipe for pear salad, which she explains as the woman bites her lip, nods, then smiles and takes four cans of pears.

Vera is right: the people do have choices. Some nod to Vera's suggestion and take only two or three of the six pear cans offered. Some refuse the green beans. The vegetarians and vegans make themselves known at the canned beef stew station, or by asking to exchange noncommodity canned salmon, mussels, or clams for vegetables instead. The labels on the cans we distribute are generics or grocery-store labels, or companies no one has heard of. Despite all Vera's attempts at dignifying the situation, this food is picked over and left over, close to or past expiration, ignored in someone's cupboard until it's finally donated.

But the people who come to the food bank have worked through all this information. Only a few people ask, "How do I do this?" and as the most experienced volunteer at the front of the line, Vera explains: take a bag or a box, show your slip with the number of people in the household, and choose some, none, or all of what is offered.

"Are you volunteers?" one woman asks me as she bags her green beans, peaches, and corn. I nod. "How can I help?" she asks frankly. "You are helping me. I can help too." I point out Crystal, and the woman steps over to meet her.

"We've brought you a gift!" A tall gray-haired man enters, accompanied by a smaller woman. Both are beaming. She reaches in a wrinkled plastic bag and pulls out two small, 35-mm film canisters. "Honey from our bees!" the man exclaims joyously. The woman says nothing but keeps smiling. She walks down the line, and I can see her patterned socks, paisley skirt, striped sweater, and patterned blouse are all just getting acquainted, like guests at a party. She is handing out small film canisters of honey to every volunteer on the line, smiling and nodding, as her companion packs his canned pears and calls out explanations to the volunteers ahead of us.

The people who come to the food bank aren't merely recipients. When they step into the line, a circle of community takes shape. I see the growers walking the cornfields, the farmworkers planting and harvesting, backs bending, hands picking, wiping away sweat and dirt. I see the trucks and drivers, the cannery and cannery workers, the grocery-store clerks and shoppers, the community donors, the volunteers, the clients, the children.

My father grew up in foster care during the Depression, when families were struggling to survive any way they could. After serving in World War I, my grandfather became a methadone addict, and my grandmother's flight from her husband was interrupted by the birth of her second child, my father, in an elevator of the St. Regis Hotel. On my father's birth certificate, he is listed as "Baby," with his given name written in later. After his mother divorced his father and remarried a healthier man, mother and stepfather soon produced a daughter of their own, and were unable to care for the two children from the mother's first marriage. I never met my father's older sister, Billyette, who was sent to the grandparents in Chicago. As the only son, my father was raised in various foster families and kept nearby, in Minneapolis, so he could see his mother. At least, this is the story he told, without emotion. My father seemed more annoyed by the severe winters in Minneapolis, by the snow that soaked through the new layers of cardboard in his shoes. He praised the Burts, the foster family who finally took him in and raised him to adulthood. My father wasn't one to detail the past, and I accepted his stories without question.

For many families in America and around the world, the Depression never ended. In Whatcom County, children still go to school without food, return home without knowing where home will be tomorrow. It's like a time warp here, with me renting a four-room house and bathroom all for myself, while entire families are crowded into one-room motels, living out of cars, in campgrounds, in shelters. It's 2001, year of the space odyssey, the yuppie and the caffeinated REI dot-com-ers, and it's still the Depression, in the same town. When I see six-year-olds on the food lines at the soup kitchens and the food bank, I see my father as a child in an oversized wool jacket, the snow seeping into his shoes like rain in the Pacific Northwest.

In the basement of the Unitarian Church on I Street, behind the Cat Clinic, Maple Alley Inn serves hot lunches on Wednesdays and Thursdays from 11:30 to 1:30. Behind the church and across the one-lane street, there's a small dirt-and-gravel parking lot with trees shading many of the spaces. At the intersection, a sandwich board sign sits out on the church lawn, announcing "Maple Alley Inn Open."

As soon as I arrive, the soup kitchen's coordinator for eleven years, Lillian, warns me that this experience will be nothing like the food bank.

"Many of the people who come here suffer from mental illnesses," she says frankly, "and we will serve people who are visibly intoxicated, so long as they don't disturb other guests." As part of my volunteer orientation, Lillian shows me into the storage room adjacent to the dining area, where she drops her voice. "We are very cautious about infectious diseases here in food handling," she continues. "Be sure to wash your hands before serving the food. Then hold the plate and pass it along to the other servers, asking how much people want of each item. Once you give the plate to the guest, you never touch it again. If they come back for seconds, they hold the plate, and you serve them. Then you must be sure the servingware never touches their plate, once they have eaten from it."

Obediently, I choose an apple-red apron and follow Lillian back to the kitchen, tying the apron strings behind me. There are four or five energetic women in their fifties or sixties bustling around in the kitchen, pulling pans out of the oven, reaching for serving spoons, gathering wooden blocks to set along the counter where the hot serving trays will be placed. Sally, Pat, Rose, Sarah—the women smile and nod as we are introduced, but keep moving. I anticipate joining an active team of recently freed homemakers who know how to put together a hot, crowd-pleasing meal.

"It's kind of slow today," Lillian observes, pointing to the few people already seated on metal folding chairs at dining tables spread with red-and-white-checkered plastic tablecloths, a fresh flower bouquet, water pitcher, napkins, and salt-and-pepper shakers placed neatly in the middle. With seven long rectangular tables set lengthwise and across the dining area, the place seems overprepared. There are only six people waiting, older men sitting and drinking coffee out of paper cups. One man is reading a paperback novel; another has the newspaper spread out before him. Except for the unwashed appearance of the guests, the dining room looks more like a bed-and-breakfast place than a soup kitchen. "Last week we served 92 people," Lillian says. "This week we'll be lucky to serve 50."

As she shows me the cupboards and closets of the large kitchen, Lillian explains the workings of the organization. Maple Alley gets its vegetables from Joe's Gardens, a community garden just south of the university, and gets gleanings from the co-op. The soup kitchen donates to the food bank, which in turn donates to Lydia Place, the shelter for homeless women and their children.

Lillian holds up the clipboard and sign-in sheet resting at the front of the serving counter. "Everyone has to sign in," Lillian explains, "but they don't have to put their real names. Any name will do. We just need it for the numbers." On the flip side of the sheet, the form asks for tallies of guests by gender, race, age, and whether they are regulars or new guests. "We use the data to get grants," Lillian says with a shrug.

Today's meal requires four servers at the counter, and two more at the dessert and beverage table out in the dining room. Lillian brings me over to Sally, an attractive woman in her late fifties, her blond hair neatly curled to her shoulders. With her glossy coral lipstick, large gold hoop earrings, and a white-and-tan slack suit, Sally could be dressed for shopping at the Bon. Instead, Sally is serving the baked potatoes, with barbecued pork ladled over them.

"Always ask the guest first," Lillian cautions. "We have some vegetarians, and they can have everything else but the pork."

Next in line is the shredded cheddar cheese, sour cream, and homemade salsa. "Do you think you can do that?" Lillian asks me very seriously. "It's not easy. You have to hold the plate and still put the servings on the pork-and-potato."

I assured her I was up to the task.

"Then pass the plate to Pat," Lillian continues, and here a cheerful woman waves to me across the kitchen, "and she'll serve carrots and corn." Lillian drops her voice. "A lot of the people who come here have dental problems," she continues. "They can't chew. So we cook the carrots until they're soft, and take the corn off the cob and cook it too, so they can eat it."

After Pat, another woman offers fruit salad, green salad, and bread.

"Now on the bread," Lillian explains, pulling me to the back of the kitchen, "we never serve bread with hard crusts, because of the chewing problem, and we always butter it first." She pauses. "Some of our guests have a problem with limits. When I first came here, I just put the butter out. One person took a quarter pound of butter for one piece of bread! It's just never enough," she says. "Let's go to the furnace room."

Down the hallway where I had first entered the building, I follow Lillian into a room branching off to the left. "I keep this room locked," Lillian continues her narrative tour of the operations. "This is where I keep frozen food—meats, vegetables, and so forth. You know, when we are running out of time to spend a grant, we have to get rid of it all at once, so I buy food and freeze it. But one day, I found people walking out of here with whole sides of beef," Lillian says, the amazement still resonant in her voice. "They had already eaten, and they were taking the frozen food. So now I lock it," she concludes.

And then it was time to serve. For two hours, people came to eat—lots of people at first, in a continuous stream that lasted for half an hour. After that, they came in waves. Clusters of men evidently on a break from work. A few women in their forties or fifties. One young family, a father, mother, and son. Another couple, two women in their sixties.

The guests seemed to know the procedure here. No one attempted to take their own plate until it was offered to them at the end of the line. No one came up for seconds until Lillian announced that seconds would be offered, and when the diners did return, they held out their own plates, evidently instructed in these procedures long before I came.

I tried to focus on serving the cheese, sour cream, and salsa without scrutinizing the guests, but there were a few who insisted on being noticed. There was Matthew, with his campaign buttons and political sloganeering. When Sally asked him who she should vote for, he asked where she lived, knew her ward and district numbers, her candidates, and their differences in viewpoints.

After Matthew, there was a gray-haired man with a bushy beard, a dirty blue overcoat, and hunched shoulders. When I offered him salsa, his "Yes, please" was delivered with such a mellifluous voice that I was startled. Smiling into his pale-blue eyes, I saw that he was the man with the paperback novel, an aging hippie who never left this college town.

The homeless are not who I expected.

A large man returns for seconds, holding out his plate eagerly as each server places a portion that is smaller than the first offering. "Do you want cheese, sour cream, and salsa, or all three?" I ask politely. "Oh, yes," he replies. "I'll take whatever you've got. I'm hungry," he says emphatically.

Many people thank the servers as they leave the dining room. One man tells us he has spent the morning working with school officials so that his daughter can get into the Head Start program. He is obviously proud of his efforts, proud of his daughter. He wants us to know that the food he consumes here goes to a worthy effort. He seems to need to justify his meal.

Does he deserve to eat?

Do we?

For many years, my efforts for social and environmental justice had taken the form of direct action protests, blockades, banners, marches and rallies, speechmaking and journalism, community education and grassroots film-making, eventually culminating in efforts to link local electoral politics with community activism. I wanted a wholesale transformation for this corrupt political-economic system, not a "patch" job it so it could keep on going. Handing out food to the hungry did not seem very transformative—that is, not until I started doing it.

In Buddhist and Catholic circles alike, there's the story about a group of people who approach a river to drink and notice bodies floating down-stream, drowning. The people on shore quickly organize and begin pulling the bodies out of the stream, laying them on the grass, working to resuscitate those they can. But the bodies keep coming. A few members of the rescue team decide to form a search party and hike upstream to see what is going on. They hope to find whatever is throwing people into the river and put an end to it. Meanwhile, the bodies keep coming downstream, and the other half of the rescue team stays behind, pulling people out of the water.

Social change is two-handed work. With one hand raised upright, fist or palm facing out, activism intervenes. With another hand outstretched, service connects.

Searching for details of my father's childhood, I once visited the Minneapolis School District's central office and requested his school records from the 1930s. They were still stored on microfilm, and after some time away in an archive, the clerk returned to me with three grayish-yellow microfilm copies of elementary school reports, grades, and evaluations from junior and senior high. For kindergarten, my father attended Emerson school; for first and second grades, Lowell Elementary. In fourth grade, he attended Loring, then back to Lowell; in sixth grade, it's Hamilton, but by seventh, it's Phillips. Ninth grade is Jefferson, tenth is Central, eleventh is North and by this time I am practically shouting encouragements and attaboys from the future and, by golly, it's a wonder that he actually graduates Central High School in June 1940.

The addresses change with the schools—James Avenue, Fifteenth Avenue, Franklin, Nicollet, Second Avenue South—and his grades change as well. He begins elementary school with all As and Bs, and attendance rates of eighty-six, eighty-eight, and eighty-nine days per school year. By eighth and ninth grades, all the address changes have affected his education. He's getting Cs in English and literature, Ds in math, social studies, typing. His attendance has dropped to sixty days. Then something happens in eleventh grade. A "nervous disorder" is recorded on his Family Record. He is moved from Central, starts the year at North High School and drops physics, gets Ds in bookkeeping and in his favorite subject, English. Midyear, he switches back to Central and finishes with an A in English, Bs in public speaking and social studies, and merit marks for glee club. By twelfth grade he is taking advanced writing and theater production on top of all his regular classes. What happened? It's the address. It stays the same. He's living with the Burts, at 4247 Upton Avenue North.

When the children come to the food bank with their parents, I think about their addresses. Low income and temporarily homeless families can move two, three, four times in a year. Often the schools change with the move, and the children lose friends, favorite teachers, peer groups, routines. They lose their place in the textbooks too. Tests report these students as "learning disabled," "developmentally impaired," "hyperactive," "underachievers." But when tests measure learning, they don't measure the learning of new names for new classmates at midyear, learning new rules and new routines, learning how to pick up in the middle of a new textbook and keep the same grades. The tests don't measure breakfast.

Clearly, service work needed to be done; people needed to eat. But each week at the soup kitchen and the food bank, we were feeding many of the same people. Our service wasn't changing the circumstances of people's lives. And I began thinking about the ways that education had failed to reach students on the margins of society, those who most needed literacy and marketable skills. I began thinking about ways to serve that utilized more of my skills, and nurtured survival skills in others. I began wanting to go upstream.

One Wednesday night in September, Whatcom Literacy Council holds an open house at Bellingham's Technical College. About fifty adults are here, ranging in age from twenty to eighty. These people are interested in volunteering two nights a week for a year, working one-on-one, teaching English, reading and writing, to someone they have never met.

And the need is shockingly great. One in five adults in the United States is functionally illiterate, which translates into 30,000 adults in Whatcom County alone. In the year 2000, Whatcom Literacy Council volunteers tutored 382 students—seventy-eight in basic literacy, and 304 in English as a foreign language. In Whatcom County alone, the Literacy Council serves students from thirty-one countries, but the highest numbers come from the former Soviet Union, Mexico, and Vietnam. The literacy-poverty link becomes clear: without immediate employment or literacy skills, even hardworking Ukrainians need food supplements. Literacy is the key to work opportunities. The volunteers tell us more: three out of every four food-stamp recipients have literacy problems, and children of illiterate parents often have literacy problems as well. In prison, the rates are even higher: 70 percent of adults and 85 percent of youth in prison are functionally illiterate. According to those working to end hunger at America's Second Harvest, only 36 percent of food recipients hold a high-school diploma or have passed the GED; another 40 percent of food recipients didn't finish high school. Why?

In his book about "those who fail," *Lives on the Boundary,* Mike Rose describes how it is the American educational system—not the students—is failing to teach those students whose life experiences place them outside the white, middle-class norm. There are complex ties between literacy and culture, Rose argues, and these ties are often invisible to those who teach, largely because the teachers themselves come from the middle classes. The teachers learn to rank students based on their abilities to absorb a specific curriculum; they seldom learn how to investigate "failed" papers for the wealth of clues revealing "knowledge that the assignment didn't tap, ineffective rules and strategies that have a logic of their own." Along with educators such as John Dewey, Paolo Freire, Ira Schor, and Ilya Prigonine, Rose believes that education must serve marginalized communities if our nation's historic belief in democracy is to become a reality. But the educational system does not work in an economic and political vacuum. In the end, Rose struggles "between a celebration of individual potential and a despair over the crushing power of the environment," recognizing that education is "being asked to do what our politics and our economics have failed to do: diminish differences in achievement, narrow our gaps, bring us together."

At Bumbershoot, Seattle's annual music and arts festival held at the Space Needle grounds on Labor Day weekend, I meet Anitra Freeman in the Publishers' Display Building. Anitra is a staff writer for *Real Change,* the newspaper by, for, and about homeless people in Puget Sound. I am reading her posters when Anitra starts a conversation with me about writing. She tells me about her program, StreetWrites, that teaches poetry and creative writing to the homeless, and urges me to check out her Web page. The idea of homeless people writing poetry, organizing online classes, and publishing newspapers—homeless people taking back the power of the word, naming their own experiences, and writing from their own perspective—electrifies me. This is what Bellingham needs, I tell her, describing my work at the food bank and the soup kitchen. Anitra responds with the same enthusiasm, showing me the past five annual publications of writing and art from the Homeless Women's Forum.

Something clicks.

There is a different way to teach, with a different institutional structure—one that serves working-class students, first-generation and rural students. I buy a copy of Anitra's journal and start planning.

In Buddhist cosmology there are several hell realms—burning or freezing hells, biting or piercing, tortures of all kinds, both physical and psychological. In the Hungry Ghost realm, miserable beings with huge, swollen, empty bellies and long, pencil-thin necks suffer without relief. With their tiny throats, Hungry Ghosts are continually yearning, famished: they sit at a banquet table filled with delicacies, unable to feed themselves because they are trying to eat the food with very long spoons.

Through his work with the homeless in Yonkers, Bernie Glassman recognized the suffering of Hungry Ghosts as something we have all experienced right here, in the present moment. "I saw that even though there is enough food in our society to feed everyone, many, many people hunger for food," Glassman writes. "I saw that even though some people have more than enough food, they hunger for power. I saw that some of us thirst for appreciation or fame. Others are starved for love." Responding to this great hunger, Glassman created the Zen Peacemaker Order and took a bodhisattva vow, dedicating his life "to offering the supreme meal to all of us hungry ghosts in the ten directions."

In his book, *Instructions to the Cook,* Glassman describes an ancient Zen scroll depicting heaven and hell. In both realms, the Hungry Ghosts sit at the same banquet table, but in heaven they use the same long spoons to feed each other.

"Ending homelessness does not mean fixing broken people," Anitra explains on her Web pages. "It means fixing a broken system."

She lists the situations I have learned to become familiar with—domestic violence, alcoholism, drug addiction, mental illness, poor work habits, lack of social skills, lack of education—but these are not the root cause. "There are people with each of these problems who are still housed," Anitra writes. "No one becomes homeless just because they have problems. They become homeless because they don't have the economic resources to deal with their problems."

Anitra's explanation is breathtakingly clear. Combine low-wage work with escalating housing costs, throw in a few personal problems, and exhaust the social support network of family and friends. This is the shake-and-bake recipe for homelessness.

Anybody can do it. Take a middle-class person with a decent job and some overextended credit-card debt. Say he forgets to pay his auto insurance and buys a cell phone or a snowboard instead. His descent into homelessness can begin with one car accident, a lawsuit or personal injury that puts him out of work, out of a job, out of a relationship, out of a home.

This is one reason housed people look away from the homeless. It's not because we are so far apart. The metal serving table at the food bank, the kitchen counter at Maple Alley Inn, the distance from our car to the curb—these aren't far enough. We have to accent the divisions. That's not me. That couldn't happen to me. He must have done something wrong, made some error of judgment, had some lapse of character. She must be stupid. They must not have tried hard enough.

Instead of assuming the homeless are incompetent, Anitra suggests, why not assume that something is blocking them from actualizing their own inherent competence. Most people know what they need in order to thrive, and may just need some help in removing the obstacles that stand in their way. And while it's important to ensure that people have the basics of survival—"because dead people aren't going to get ahead in life," Anitra wryly observes—providing these basics alone is merely "servicing poverty, not ending it." Targeting the most common obstacles means providing services in four critical areas: domestic violence intervention; universal health care, including mental-health treatment and treatment for addictions; training for real jobs, for work that pays a living wage; and education. Education for empowerment.

This is just the start. There's a continual need for achieving the more revolutionary goals as well: a fair economy, nationally and globally. An ecological and economic democracy. And most important, an end to individualism, to the belief that any one of us can truly flourish in the presence of hunger and homelessness.

"This is the Buddhist teaching nobody wants to hear," Ajahn Geoff said jovially, sitting on the low teachers' platform at the dharma hall. "Buddhism is so trendy these days, until people hear the teachings on suffering and interdependence. Interdependence is all really good until you understand it also means 'inter-eating,'" Ajahn Geoff continued, adjusting his ochre monk's robes and looking carefully at each person in the room. "We are literally—economically, psychologically, energetically, spiritually, materially—feeding off of one another. Eating each other. And there's a lot of suffering in that," the monk acknowledged, "and a lot of compassion too."

"Look at those pears!" Ruth was holding up a yellow-green Asian pear from the box at the end of the produce line. "Gleanings from someone's yard, I'm sure," she added.

Gleanings. All around Bellingham, fruit was falling, falling on gravel and grasses, falling from bushes and branches, ripe and rotting fruit. Apples and pears, plums and berries. Gleanings were the excess fruits, the ripened fruits, the picked-over fruits. Fruits nobody needed, nobody wanted. Gleanings could feed us all.

At the food bank and the soup kitchen, we are nobody, everybody. We are slow learners, savoring excess fruits. We are bodies that hunger, work, create. We are cooking and serving and feeding each other.

The Dance

On the northwestern shores of Lake Whatcom at Bloedel-Donovan Park, where the lumber mill once consumed the trees, a longstanding celebration of earth-based spirituality takes place each winter solstice. People gather for a ritual dance that celebrates the end of shortened days, the beginning of hope and light. The winter solstice dance brings together nearly 200 people, solely by word of mouth. Each year I see people I have known in other contexts—in classrooms or faculty meetings, in city-council audiences and dharma-hall sittings and activist gatherings—come to this light-filled gymnasium, take off their shoes, and join hands in a circle around the celebrants, Leslie and Kenyth, who lead the ritual.

Initiated in the late 1970s by the choreographer Deborah Hay, the "Grand Dance" of the winter solstice has spread throughout earth-based communities across the nation. Every community improvises with the music and the movements, but the ritual's three-part structure remains the same: we begin with the Seven Surrenders, enter into a dream of solar return, and cycle into a healing dance of regeneration.

Hours before the ritual is scheduled to begin, Leslie arrives at the community center and cleanses the air with incense, calls in the four directions, and performs the entire ritual with the other dance leaders so that they become the embodiment of the dance. When the full community gathers, joins hands, and the ritual formally begins, Leslie again invokes the four directions as a way of focusing the community's energy and intentions. A sacred clown moves within the circle, sprinkling the air and the people with scented water drops. Then Kenyth and Leslie instruct us in the movements of the Seven Surrenders, as volunteers wearing gold sashes step forward to demonstrate each of the movements and to serve as guides throughout the dance.

To enter fully into the process of regeneration, we must first let go of everything that stands in our way.

The ritual begins as those in the great circle step forward, joining the hands of their neighbors behind them, and moving to the first surrender of outward focus. They walk, stop, and bow deeply. As each person does this, over and over, others step into the circle to join them, and the circle becomes smaller, denser, until those within the circle step under the clasped hands of those remaining, and at last there are only four, then three, two, and now everyone in this large gymnasium is stepping, stopping, and bowing deeply. We are embodying the surrender of outward focus, letting go of the need to achieve, to accomplish, to perform, to produce.

The dance leaders initiate the next movement, and slowly people notice and catch on as they are ready. With the second surrender, we walk, cast off an imaginary cloak from our shoulders, remove the mask from our faces and cast it aside, dispelling old self-images with a clap and an exclamation, "Ha!" We turn, walk, and repeat this surrender of self-image as more and more people join in this movement of release. With the third surrender, we bend over to find the veil that has separated us from the rest of the world, lift the veil over our heads and release it at the top. Turning in place, we repeat the movement, surrendering our idea of a separate self.

We walk again, facing north or south, and through the vigorous shaking of one arm extended at our sides, wordlessly we tell our personal story until we are exhausted of doing so. (This takes some time.) Then we cross arms, placing hands on opposite shoulders to offer compassion to ourselves for this story, and face hands palms outward, to share that compassion with others. Then we tell the story again. Release it again. Again. With these movements, we enact the fourth surrender, letting go of our personal story.

In the fifth surrender, we let go of rigidity, of fixed beliefs and ideas, and the conviction that we are right. Through movements that shake the body, fling the arms, and flop the legs, all fixity is jiggled loose.

In the sixth surrender, we surrender pain to light. In this movement, we discover a ribbon of light emanating from a place in the body that needs healing, and follow this light on a journey around the room until it spins us in place and is released.

For the seventh surrender, we let go of our attachment to the idea of human stature, of our separateness from the animals and from the rest of nature. We drop to the floor and hang out on all fours. When every participant has surrendered these various forms of separation, like Salome's Dance of the Seven Veils or Inanna's ritual descent through the seven gates, our interdependence is fully revealed. The ritual community is created through dance.

On my desk is a sculpture of the Shiva Nataraj, or Shiva dancing. It depicts the Hindu god of destruction, four-armed Shiva, dancing in a circle of flames. Shiva's dance is the movement of creation, preservation, and destruction in the universe. This dance did not happen just once, at some mythic beginning that will someday come to an end. The dance is happening now, continuously. The speed of Shiva's dance is seen in his radiant hair, which flies out from his head in all directions. His four arms are in continual movement, captured only for a moment in the Shiva Nataraj, a sculpture created during the ninth or tenth century during the Chola Dynasty of South India. In his upper right hand Shiva holds the two-sided drum, symbolizing the pulse of creation. In his upper left hand he holds the fire of destruction and purification. Shiva's lower left hand points outward, signifying that "there is a way out," for Shiva's dance of creation is surrounded in a circle of flames signifying samsara, the cycle of continuous rebirth, old age, sickness, and death. Shiva's lower right hand is held upright, palm facing out, in the gesture of preservation that means "fear not." Preventing us from recognizing the dance that connects all of life, delusion is symbolized by a dwarf on whose back Shiva is dancing. Seeing through the delusion of separation is the "way out" and the reason we have no need to fear.

Other aspects of Shiva's dance seem to have older associations. Shiva wears serpents, signifying his control over the powers of nature. The third eye in his forehead and a crescent moon in the crown of his matted hair both represent illumination, insight. The skull he wears as a crown symbolizes that Shiva conquers death. The arms, the hair, the circle of flames, the lifted foot all symbolize the rapid movement of Shiva's dance. But it is Shiva's startling femininity that made me look for the woman behind him.

And this is how I discovered Kali, the four-armed goddess of creation, preservation, and destruction. Most commonly in the drawings Kali is not behind but on top of Shiva. In her right hands she makes the sign of "fear not" and offers blessings, symbolizing her creative powers. In her left hands, she holds a bloodied sword and severed head, symbolizing the destruction of ignorance and the dawn of knowledge. She wears a necklace of skulls and a girdle made of dead men's hands. Her tongue protrudes from her mouth; her eyes are red, her face and breasts smeared with blood. Kali signifies the birth-and-death Mother Goddess of ceaseless creation. Her necklace of heads signifies knowledge and wisdom; her girdle of hands signifies the severing of karma. With her lolling red tongue she consumes all things, enjoying all the world's flavors.

Kali's wild dance with Shiva is one that threatens to destroy the world, and we are invited to take part in that dance. What part will it be?

Still attempting to evade Kali's dance, Shawn and I went camping one August weekend on the northern banks of the Columbia River near Goldendale, wandering at twilight through tall stones standing in two concentric circles around a massive tablelike altar. When we returned to Seattle late Sunday evening, there was a phone message from Shawn's father. On Friday night, while we watched the sunset from Sam Hill's Stonehenge replica and tried to stave off the forces of dissolution between us, our sister-in-law, Missy, had suffered a severe asthmatic attack. She had stopped breathing before the ambulance could arrive. Lying in the intensive care unit at the hospital, Missy straddled the river between life and death. She was thirty-nine.

Shawn and I learn the news about Missy through terse phone conversations, piece it together from Shawn's parents, from her brother Mark's numbed narrative. Then we all tell it again, recounting the story as if there must be some mistake. The details become so vivid, so ordinary, it's as if we were all there as witnesses, watching, unable to intervene.

On that Friday, Missy went to work at the airlines. She went to church, to cantor for a funeral. She mailed Shawn's birthday gift, then met some coworkers for a drink. She went home to make dinner for Mark and the children, Sonya and Dave. It was a normal day.

That evening, Mark and Missy were at home watching television with their friend Karen; the kids were reading in their rooms. Missy got up to use the bathroom and returned, saying she was having trouble breathing.

Mark suggested using their son's inhaler, but Missy had already tried it. Her breathing was becoming more and more constricted. Mark and Missy knew that asthma ran along Missy's side of the family. Both mother and son suffered from it. They knew not to wait. Mark moved quickly, asking Karen to stay with the kids while he drove Missy to the hospital.

We are all there in the living room, urging him, Go. Go now.

But in the driveway, in the car, Missy's gasping got worse. Mark realized he wouldn't be able to help her breathe if he were driving. He yelled for Karen to call 911, pulled Missy out of the car to wait for the ambulance outside, in the warm summer air. He told her, help is on the way.

And she just couldn't breathe. Between gasps, Missy spoke. She told Mark, gasping, how grateful, for the life, he had given her, how much, she loved them, all.

And then she stopped breathing.

Help is on the way. Mark gave her mouth-to-mouth resuscitation until the ambulance arrived. The paramedics continued life support in the ambulance to the hospital, while a neighbor drove Mark, and Karen stayed with the kids. But the paramedics couldn't get the air into Missy's lungs. The bronchial tubes had collapsed. The medicine that would open her lungs had to be inhaled. The medicine that could be injected wasn't in the ambulance.

By the time they got to the hospital, Missy's brain had been without oxygen for over ten minutes. Her body was clinically dead.

They revived her. They put her on oxygen.

Missy did not wake up.

Shawn's parents pick us up at the Minneapolis airport, and although it is late at night, we go directly to the hospital. Missy has taken a turn for the worse, they tell us. On Saturday, the first EEG test for brain activity was "as bad as it could be," the doctor had said, and the follow-up test forty-eight hours later had shown no change. Now, Missy's body was in revolt. Her temperature had risen five degrees; her blood pressure had increased; her vital signs were dropping.

At the waiting room outside of the intensive care unit, Shawn embraces her older brother, Mark, and her younger brother, Todd. Mark looks exhausted. He tells us that we can go in to see Missy even at this hour.

The linoleum floors, the long hallway and swinging doors safeguarding the intensive care unit, the nurses' station with its cheerless balloons and flowers—it all seems surreal. This can't be happening. We have shared holidays and birthdays and vacations together, but we have no experience with death. There. The word has appeared. The personification of death has stepped into our family, and she is a vibrant woman of thirty-nine, a wife of sixteen years, mother of two. She sings in the church, decorates cakes, dances in a flower garland at her own midlife toga party. This is not death. This is not what anyone expected.

But here she is. We enter the room where Missy lies and for a moment I cannot even see her. Everything is white cloth and metallic silver, plastic tubes and tape, pulsing meters and blipping lights. Around the bed, there are photos of Mark and Missy taken last month on their trip to San Francisco, Mark and Missy on the Golden Gate Bridge, Mark and Missy on holiday with friends, photos of the kids at play, and taped at the base of Missy's hospital bed is an enlarged, life-sized photo of her feet and a swimming pool beyond, taken during their Greece vacation. A portable boom box plays Missy's favorite instrumental music. The signs of love and longing are everywhere visible, but Missy has not opened her eyes since Friday night.

Propped up in this hospital bed, her tongue thick and distended around the plastic tube, her hair stringy and greased back, Missy does not look like herself. Only her nails are perfectly polished, fingers and toes. Every other sign of her immaculate self-presentation has been stripped away. She would not like to be seen this way. Shawn and I take her hands, speak her name, tell her we are here, but expect no response. With Mark's permission, I unclasp the pearl drop earrings from my ears and put them on Missy. It is a futile gesture but it cheers both Mark and me just a little. Missy loves beauty.

When we return to the waiting room, Mark tells us he has decided to take Missy off life support the following day. She has always insisted that she wouldn't want to linger in this way. If she wakes up, he tells us, the brain damage from ten minutes without oxygen is such that "she wouldn't be Missy anymore." I was baffled. How could Mark hold in mind the paradox that "Missy was no longer Missy" and simultaneously acknowledge that "it was time to let her go"? Was Missy's selfhood equivalent to her brain function? Was it Missy's memories that had been erased? Her speech patterns? Her likes and dislikes, habits of mind, opinions and beliefs? Was her mind more essential to her selfhood than her body, which continued to live and function, though poorly, in this hospital bed? What if Missy woke up from the coma the next day and no longer decorated cakes, no longer wanted to dance and drink at the Renaissance Festival? Would she still be Missy if she woke up without her voice, couldn't sing as a cantor for the weekly mass? What if she woke up a Lutheran instead of a Catholic?

Would she still be Missy if she never woke up? How can we know that the real Missy is gone, so that letting go of her body is not a capital offense, a mortal sin?

Mark knew. The priest knew.

The next day, the Feast Day of Mary's Assumption, fifteen family members and close friends gathered around Missy's hospital bed. The nurses had washed Missy's hair, rearranged her sheets, and fluffed up the pillows so she looked fresh and clean. The room was crowded full of life support when the nurse removed Missy's breathing tubes and the intravenous needles. Then the priest read some verses. Mark said a blessing on Missy's life. And the woman—the daughter, the wife and sister, the mother, the body that lay in the bed—breathed her last rattling breaths. The nurse turned off the diminishing blips on the monitor, and silence overwhelmed the room. Silence. And then the loss, her children's anguish, and the noiseless tears of fathers, mothers, husband, sisters, brothers, friends, and priest.

She was gone.

Mark opened a bottle of Missy's favorite wine, a red wine just bought on their trip through the vineyards of Northern California, and poured little plastic pill-cups full until everyone in the hospital room, even the children, had a thimble of wine. We drank to Missy's life. It was like the end of a play, when all the actors have performed their parts. We were free to move around.

Eleven days after Missy's asthma attack, a full funeral mass is held at the Church of the Assumption. Songs are sung, Bible verses read. The priest delivers his own eulogy for Missy, pointing out the many ways that Missy brought people together, how she gave joy to her coworkers, to the parishioners at Assumption, to her children's school, to her family and friends. He asks us to look around the church, and it is true: the cathedral is overflowing with people who have loved Missy. At 10:00 a.m. on a workday following Missy's wake the night before, there are still more than 300 people who believe it is more important to be here honoring Missy's life than it is to be at work, or anywhere else. Even the archbishop of Minnesota has come to preside over Missy's funeral mass, and to say a few words of comfort to her children and husband.

The church's graveyard is just behind the cathedral, and stretches over a rolling hill, ending with a hedge of lilacs. The pallbearers rest the casket a moment as they pull on sunglasses, then follow the priest into the cemetery, on the little gravel road that winds across the hill, turns, and loops its way back to the parking lot. There are gravestones here from 1860, and numerous markers with Shawn's family name, the first great-great-grandparents to come over to America, infants who died in the first year of life, aunts and uncles and cousins, mothers and fathers, husbands and wives. This is what home is supposed to look like: it's where your dead are buried, and where, some day, you will be buried along with them.

The casket is placed on a trestle above the grave, and the priest offers words of comfort and life and hope. Everywhere around the mourners there are dragonflies, swooping and buzzing their delight on this late-summer day. The sky is a brilliant blue, too beautiful a day for death. When the priest finishes his prayer, Mark passes out the small white envelope boxes that read "Missy's spirit flies freely through the garden of matchless beauty." As Mark speaks of letting Missy go on, releasing her spirit, we carefully open the little boxes and the air is filled with butterflies, butterflies meeting dragonflies, butterflies soaring, butterflies resting a moment on Missy's casket, breathing with wings opening and closing, then soaring again.

In the church gymnasium, long tables have been set up with pink place mats, thermoses of decaffeinated coffee, and two long serving lines of tables heaped with food. There are sandwiches of ham and turkey slices laid between pieces of white buttered bread, the mayonnaise and mustard set out in separate bowls for the adventurous palates. There are bowls of potato salad, pasta salad, coleslaw, and dill pickles. On the dessert tables there are bars, a Midwestern specialty involving any combination of sweet items baked together into a single gooey mass and then sliced into squares or rectangles. Apple crisp bars and Rice Krispies bars, peanut butter and chocolate bars, Special K bars, lemon meringue bars, German chocolate bars and chocolate chip bars.

Going through the line together, Shawn and I skip the sandwiches and choose salads, pickles, and lemonade before sitting down. There are elderly ladies and a few good men scurrying around everywhere in the gymnasium, making sure that the coffee thermoses are full, that the salads and sandwiches and bars are being replenished, that there is enough of this meal to feed everyone.

Take this, all of you, and eat:
This is my body which will be given up for you.

With the bingo boards on the walls beside the basketball hoops, the performing stage at one end, and the poster boards of photos from Missy's life at the other, we share in the communion meal that Missy has given us. Finally, I understand. This is the food that matters most. Family. Community. An enduring relationship to place.

Kali's three forms, creation, preservation, and destruction, are manifested in many ways: in the phases of the moon, in the three stages of life, and in her three colors, white for Virgin, red for Mother, black for Crone. When Kali the Destroyer wore red, it symbolized the blood of life that she gave and took back. The dance of Kali teaches that pain, sorrow, and death are not to be overcome by denying them. They are woven into the texture of creation, so that realizing the fullness of life requires accepting the cycle of death.

When I chose Missy's red beaded dress for her burial outfit, I did not know that its blood-red color invokes Kali in her aspect as the Mother. Kali's mothering is accomplished not by protecting her children from the way things are, but by revealing their full mortality. Kali's dance releases her children, allowing them to act fully and freely, accepting the inevitability of death in the cycle of life. Kali's gift is the freedom of being fully present for life, a freedom that is possible only after full confrontation and acceptance of death.

I want to shake Kali and tell her these children, Sonya and Dave, are too young for such freedom. But I am out of step, and the speed of Kali's dance allows no intervention.

Because my eyes are always closed for this part of the solstice ritual, I can only imagine the sweetness of this image as more than 200 people in this gymnasium—adults, elders, and children alike—curl up on the floor, lying on their sides or bellies. Inviting us to assume the most comfortable posture we take when we fall asleep, Kenyth leads us in a guided visualization. We become smaller and smaller, dreaming into the darkness, into the longest night of the year. We pay attention to our breathing, to our complete dependence on the sun, and to our longing for the sun's return. It is dark, and we are near despair.

At the sound of a flute, we rise and begin searching for the sun, but without success. Then the group decides to imitate the sun as a way of inviting its return. We spiral to the center of the room, hum and jiggle, pressing together, arms upraised. At the sound of a gong, we spring into the wild energy of the seed-pod dance, jumping and leaping until each person lands down on the floor, rooting our own new growth from the seed of our intentions. By slowly rising to our feet, standing like trees growing to maturity, we grow ourselves into the present moment, where we harvest the seeds of our own clear intentions for the coming year. Around the room, people stand, picking invisible fruits from their own outstretched arms. When we have collected armfuls of what we deeply desire, we plant these seeds one at a time. Some dancers stay in one place, digging and dropping seeds where they are. Others plant a few seeds, and then move on to another spot in the gym, where they dig again. From intention to action to further intention, we are feeding and seeding ourselves, creating a forest of intentional actions and growth.

When the music changes, the dancers move joyously into a large circle around the room, skipping and swirling, anticipating the growth of the new seeds. People meet and clasp hands, spin and separate. We move on together; we move on alone. As the music fades, we reform the great circle and close the ritual. And we reassure each other: the sun does notice, and will return.

For two months I carried in my wallet the little card from the funeral, with the oval photo of Missy standing in the ferns at her midlife toga party, a flower-and-grape wreath atop her curling golden hair. For years after the dissolution of our relationship, I carried in my heart the image of my life partner, carried in my wallet the scribbled note promising eternal love.

Missy's death brought a final, unexpected clarity to my questions about home. The childhood trips to the High Sierras, the influences of mountains and water in shaping my sense of identity—these places shaped an identity

I had thought of as a stone sculpture, immutable. It was not. Identity was indeed shaped by place, and place was as powerfully social and economic as it was ecological. In five years, my partner's and my new relationship with place had changed our relationship with each other, revealing cracks in our connection that weren't perceptible at home. We had treated our relationship like a potted plant, independent of climate and context, able to be moved at will from the living room to the outdoor patio, and from one ecoregion to another. Instead, our relationship was part of an ecosystem, rooted in connection to other living beings and places, nourished by a flow of energetic interdependence that was invisible to us until we left it behind. Now, living in connection with new environments and new communities, we developed different desires. My partner wanted to travel the world. I still wanted home, and a child.

To enter fully into the process of regeneration in the solstice dance—to complete the descent to Ereshkigal and heal the split between the two worlds—we must let go of everything that stands in our way. Everything.

Only one thing remained. Career. Job security. The fruits and recognition of my life's work. Without these, how would I live? How could I let go, without something else to hold onto?

In Vipassana communities, there is a story about the monkey-hunters in Thailand, and how they trap their prey. The hunters use empty coconut shells, drilling a hole to let out the coconut milk and to hide a sweet within the gourd. The monkeys find the gourds and put their hands inside to grab the sweets. And then the hunters come. The monkeys are frantic. They cannot get the sweets out of the gourd: the hunters have made the opening just large enough for a sweet, or a hand, but not a hand holding a sweet. Because they cannot run or climb with their hands in gourds, the monkeys are easy prey.

If they would let go of the sweets, the monkeys could free their hands and escape the hunters. But the monkeys don't let go.

It was this story, and my empathy for monkeys, that finally brought me home.

Epilogue

The Headwaters

Along the banks of the Mississippi River, just below Minnehaha Falls, the off-leash dog park romps along sand flats that range from oak savanna to maple-basswood forest. Pink, blue, gray, and white stones mark a pebbled path between the packed wet sand at the river's edge and the dry, sinking sands that slope upward into shade. A tangle of footpaths winds through the prairie grasses and sedges, crossing streams, climbing sandstone cliffs, vanishing abruptly amid churning foot- and paw-prints, reemerging farther ahead in damp, packed dirt.

On this late-August afternoon, the air is thick with warm humidity, and pungent with the wet smell of the Mississippi River, this lifeblood current of a continent. On the beach below the cottonwoods, Sequoia sniffs five or six stones stacked atop one another, a tower of significance. "This is the place," they say. I nod to the stones and walk on. Around the thick trunk of another fallen cottonwood, still growing in sand and in water, the beach arcs upward, and there are more stones. Many more. Innumerable cairns stand sentinel on the beach. Some are made of five large rocks, equal in size and weight. Some stones are set in graduated stacks, large and chunky pink ones at the bottom, flat gray and smaller white ones at the top. Some are built with fist-sized pebbles. It's a wonder they don't topple over.

At the next inward-turning curve of the beach there are more. These cairns are lined up shoulder to shoulder, a council of cairns discussing the presence of place. "Here," they murmur. "Yes, here," calmly. "You have arrived," they proclaim. "This is the place."

Where the people throw sticks and tennis balls into the river so the dogs can play, there is talk of the cairns. Evidently these standing stones took shape at the same time as my return to Minnesota. No one saw them the week before.

The days become shorter, the air cools, the cottonwood and maple and birch leaves turn gold and red. No one disturbs the standing stones.

It is a Wednesday morning in early December. A group of five yogis and the Qi Gong instructor, Paul, stand in a hexagon on the bare wooden floor of the dharma hall. Winter-morning light blazes into the room, while outside, stark blue skies illuminate bright-white snow, glinting down in sprays and showers off tree branches and rooftops with the coaxing of wind. Each morning I am ecstatic to be living in Minneapolis again, home for bright-sunshine mornings, for meditation with my original dharma community. Home.

At Paul's instruction we gather the energy of the earth and pull it up into our body's three energy centers, the *dan tian*. We begin by pulling energy into the lower abdomen, and pushing it down through our legs. We gather energy from the air above us and pull it down into our foreheads, through our bodies. We reach before us and scoop energy into the heart center. When my hands bring energy into my chest, I can feel the brokenness there. Grief has left my heart a shattered vase, the aftermath of so much letting go. The energy flows through my chest, spills out and over and among the heart fragments, out my spine at the shoulder blades. With each motion I try again, and each time the result is the same. My heart will not hold water.

Four days later, on the sunny morning of winter solstice, I am walking with Sequoia near the confluence of the Mississippi and Minnesota rivers where we used to walk when she was a puppy. There is fresh snow on the ground, a thin layer of bright white just covering the brittle, brown fallen leaves. Sequoia is romping along the creek, dashing at other dogs, coaxing a bright-green tennis ball from a stranger. We round the peninsula and begin our return walk up the shore of the Mississippi where the cairns have begun to reappear, no matter how many times they are knocked down after the snow has fallen.

Climbing into the tangled roots of a cottonwood tree, I lie down to watch the river. Then, seeding my intentions, I imagine the fragmented vase of my heart submerged in the river, at the center, where the water is still flowing between the frozen edges at the shores. This time I feel my heart fragments immersed in water. I am still unable to hold the energy, unable to serve as a container, but here such holding is unnecessary. The water holds me instead, flowing around and through me. Immersed in this river, I no longer need to be a container, no longer need to hold on to my separate little vase full of energy. The energy surrounds me. My heart has broken open and is bathing in the Mississippi. I let go of the expectation that the pieces will be joined, that the unbroken vase is the best shape for my heart.

When we set out to find our fortune, wrestle our demons, or otherwise undertake the journey that can wait no longer, we expect to be changed. Change is why we go. Naively, we expect at the same time that the places we left behind will stand still, a freeze-framed photo that will await animation until our return.

On my return to Minnesota, that photograph became a shadowy background, enriching every present moment with a storied past. Here in this urban and natural environment, I greet my history with the land, the culture, the people. At Lake Como, I see faint shadows of myself walking year-round with the lover who left to go to the Peace Corps. There, I am ice skating in winter with my best friend and her two daughters, here, bicycling in summer with book bags hot against my back. Here is the run-down fourplex where I completed my last years of graduate school, its leaning and paint-peeling front porch the place where I wrote my final papers, night after night. There is the high-ceilinged duplex where I lived during the waning years of my first marriage; six blocks away is the ornate Victorian apartment where I was robbed of all my earrings. Beside this Uptown lake one steamy July night, my future partner and I walked, chatted, flirted. Five years later, at another lake, we swam with our new puppy, Sequoia. Here is the house in north Minneapolis where my father found a stable foster home, and flourished during his last years of high school. The apartment building where his mother, my grandmother, lived during his childhood is now the interstate. In all these places, the land retains stories that affirm my presence here.

As a European American, I feel grateful to find family roots that go back one generation, roots that must seem shallow to the indigenous inhabitants of this place, who can see their history reflected here for millennia.

Against all these images, a new present is taking place. Minnesota has changed culturally, politically, environmentally. No longer a homogenous mix of Finns, Swedes, Norwegians, Irish, and Germans dominating the visible culture, with the native Ojibwe backgrounded on reservations or in urban ghettos, and the African Americans gaining only token visibility, Minnesotans have diversified. The dominant culture's favorable qualities of Scandinavian hospitality, Lutheran social service, and socialist labor organizing have made the Twin Cities a welcoming choice for other immigrants and refugees as well.

First, the Hmong migration, which had begun in the 1970s after the Vietnam War, has stabilized. All along University Avenue in an area formerly called Frogtown, Asian groceries, restaurants, and shops proclaim this community's commitment to place. A second influx of immigrants began in the 1980s, prompted by civil unrest and failing economies in Mexico and Central America, and attracted by a combination of strong solidarity movements in the Twin Cities as well as agricultural work in Minnesota's farmlands. Then family brought family, farmworkers learned English and other trade skills, and another community settled down in the Cities. Along Lake Street in south Minneapolis, a new generation of Mexican and South American restaurants, groceries, clothing stores, and nightclubs has taken root. Finally, the most recent group was propelled here by famine and civil war in East Africa: Somalis began arriving in 1991, joined by Kenyans and Ethiopians throughout the 1990s. By the new century, they had formed the Somali Community Association, the Somali Women's Association, a soccer league, and a series of African marketplaces featuring the clothing, jewelry, foods, fabrics, cookware, and artwork of home, as well as the temples needed for the five-times-daily prayers of Islam. On the streets, in buses and in grocery stores, the women's traditional clothing of *jalaabiibs, hajibs,* and *khamaars* make this group the most visible of the three. The Twin Cities' new diversity offers the possibility of cultural exchange and education reminiscent of my childhood in Los Angeles.

Our political landscape has changed as well. No longer as reliably progressive as in the past, Minnesota has been influenced by the nation's conservative shift, and fiscal mismanagement at the state level has created a budget deficit where we once had a surplus. These conditions of false scarcity mean that education, health care, social services, and environmental programs must now compete for reduced funding. I worry about the coincidence of new immigration and the budget cuts to health and human services, the shift in funding for parks and recreation from unlimited public access to annual user fees and pay-for-parking lots at city lakes and rivers. The "new Minnesotans" will not be marginalized and segregated like the indigenous Minnesotans: their communities are already too well organized.

Minnesota's ecology has also changed, with more change imminent as global warming affects our precipitation. Whereas Minnesotans could always count on a big snowstorm by Thanksgiving, the winters since 1997 have seen less snowfall than ever before, with the snows coming late after Christmas, and the ski trails uncovered until late January. Reduced precipitation coupled with higher temperatures is predicted to affect the trees in Minnesota's Boundary Waters Canoe Area Wilderness, the cold-water fish populations such as lake trout and brook trout, the ducks and other water birds around the state. Some worry that mild winters and fewer subzero temperatures will also affect the human population, failing to build the hardy character and strong community ties that have characterized Minnesotans and inspired such films as *Fargo* and *A Prairie Home Companion.* To protect all these local residents, we lobby for increased funding to renewable energy sources and mass transit, for hybrid vehicles and carpool lanes.

There is nowhere else to go.

There are many facets to place, I have learned, and the ecological environment is but one component. As a bisexual woman in a same-sex partnership, I did not have the same experience of wild nature in the Pacific Northwest as *Outside* magazine and *Backpacker* claimed I would, rating the town where I lived as among the top ten in the UNITED STATES for those who love nature. Returning to Minnesota, I found a balance of culture and nature, history and economics that finally allowed me to feel at home. Once again I work at a university, but this institutional workplace values teaching as its primary mission, and focuses on serving rural, first-generation, and

working-class students. Here, teaching becomes a practice of empowerment and social justice, shaping my role as a mentor and guide. With place
and workplace finally in balance, my heart opened to love again.

This time I didn't ask water, though I walked by the Mississippi every
day. But once it was clear that I was truly single, I thought again about
the child. I knew I would have to act decisively. And I chose someone
with a heart of kindness, a man who moved earthworms off the sidewalk
after the rain and walked the nearsighted dog for an elderly neighbor. I
chose a teacher, an environmentalist, a feminist ally. With eyes wide open,
we began our child unconventionally, without a marriage contract or any
expectations other than shared parenting. A year and a half later, I pushed
our daughter from my body into water—the maternity ward's water-
birthing room used purified water, water from the Mississippi.

Four years after my return to Minnesota, I am traveling north for summer
solstice to the headwaters of the Mississippi, Lake Itasca. *Where does our
water come from?* I still feel drawn to make this pilgrimage to origins, to be
a true resident of this place. From experience, I know the river will have
something to teach me.

What I learn at Lake Itasca is that the river's history is shaped with arti-
fice and contradictions. The "headwaters" is simply a narrowed part of the
lake contrived to educate tourists, and built by the Civilian Conservation
Corps (CCC) in 1933–39. Photos of the unreconstructed headwaters taken
in 1903 show this area as a quarter-mile stretch of marshy bog, a process
rather than a point of interest, littered with logs from the clear-cutting
around Lake Itasca that continued until Mary Gibbs, the first woman to
supervise a U.S. state park, faced loggers at gunpoint to preserve the forests. Years later, another park superintendent decided that this quarter-
mile bog was an unfitting beginning for our nation's greatest river, and
his vision guided the CCC's tidy reconstruction with "natural-looking"
boulders that allow the visitor to walk across the Mississippi. It's our culture's first intervention in the river's course, but definitely not our last: the
river's original length of 2,552 miles has been shortened to 2,318 through
the straitening of its channel, the constriction of floodplains, the imposi-
tion of locks and dams.

The 1834 "discovery" of the headwaters is also a fabled history, as Henry

Rowe Schoolcraft's fruitless search ended when he finally asked for directions of the native Ojibwe. Ozawindib pulled out a map and showed him the headwaters, then had to guide Schoolcraft here himself. Throughout the nineteenth century, Lake Itasca's status as the source of the Mississippi was challenged by European American men who designated two different tributary lakes (each named after themselves) as its origins, then two other lakes feeding those lakes. This debate was resolved near the end of the century by a surveyor who observed that the entire basin functioned as the headwaters, but not until the river left Lake Itasca at its outflow did all the waters come together. On the Mississippi, the European American search for origins leads to a whole community of water, not an individual spring, creek, or lake. It's the same lesson, greeting me over and over like a good friend.

At the edge of Lake Itasca, the little girl I wanted for so long now sits in the sand, happily grabbing handfuls of sticks and dirt and showing them to her father. I want Lake Itasca to be *her* June Lake; I want to bring her to the headwaters each year so she won't have to search for it later. Already she has seen marsh marigolds and lady's slippers, watched ruby-throated hummingbirds and white-tailed deer, looked up at red and white pine trees over 100 feet tall. She has heard loons ululating in the quiet evenings, their calls carried on the whoosh of fluttering maples and birch. Now sitting on the lakeshore, she examines a pinecone from Minnesota's state tree, the red pine, a species adapted to withstand fire like the great sequoias of California. I wish for her the same resilience, the same healthy adaptation to environments.

There are the teachings of Buddhism, and there are the teachings of water.

According to water, home is not a static place or destination, not a noun but a verb, a process of creating relationships to place, to creatures, and to people. Being at home means accepting impermanence, entering fully into the cycles of life, stepping into the flow of relationships, a movement of energy, a dance of creation, preservation, dissolution, and re-creation.

In every present moment, home is where you are.

ACKNOWLEDGMENTS

Every writer looks to history for predecessors to authorize, inspire, or refute. We are not always so fortunate as to meet the writers who will become our muses. I was blessed: while searching for a way to articulate my emerging ecofeminism, in the summer of 1988 I attended a poetry reading given by Margaret Randall, Beth Brandt, and Meridel Le Sueur at the University of Minnesota. I still remember the humidity in that small auditorium in Coffman Union, the fans positioned in the doorways blowing the warm, damp air around fifty panting attendees. All three speakers were dynamic, powerful women, but at this reading, it was Meridel who presented a poem that moved me deeply. She was then eighty-eight years old, and still read vigorously. After the presentations, I went up to her and knelt by her wheelchair, took her hand and said, "In this poem, you have given words to what I have been trying to say for months." I tried to explain my ideas about feminism, ecology, and social justice while Meridel smiled and nodded. Then she astonished me by kissing me and replied, "They are your words now. Use the words."

"We think back through our mothers if we are women," wrote Virginia Woolf in *A Room of One's Own,* emphasizing the value of having role models for women writers. Like many daughters who don't recognize and thus can't appreciate their mother's struggles, successes, and wisdom until later in life, I didn't recognize the importance of Meridel Le Sueur when I met her for the first and only time, nor did I realize how her life and life's work made my own work possible.

Meridel Le Sueur was born on February 23, 1900, and she lived to be ninety-six years old. Her life and her activism epitomize many women's struggles for justice and for freedom in the twentieth century. At sixteen, Le Sueur marched in a parade on Fifth Avenue all dressed in white, participating in one of the demonstrations for women's suffrage. In New York, she lived in an anarchist commune with Emma Goldman, and continued her "communal sensibility" later with another group of women and their children in an abandoned warehouse in St. Paul, Minnesota. Her well-known essay, "I Was Marching," documents her participation in the

Minneapolis truckers' strike in 1934. Beginning in 1932 with her essay "Women on the Breadlines," Le Sueur chronicled the struggles of unemployed and homeless women at the economic bottom of society during the Depression. Le Sueur's notes to her unborn child, written throughout 1927 and published in 1935 as the story "Annunciation," mark her first published attempt to connect the body of woman with the body of earth, a connection that she felt linked her to all of life through the sacredness of fertility.

A writer committed to radical political thought and action, and a member of the Communist Party since 1924, Le Sueur and her work fell out of favor in the nationalist 1940s and McCarthyist 1950s. But Le Sueur persisted. In the 1950s, she began to travel extensively by bus, talking with people and recording their stories. The essays from this time emphasize the restless, persistent movement of the people she met, and articulate her vision of America as a people in motion. The idea of physical movement creating ideological movement was key to her, articulated as early as her 1934 essay "I Was Marching," and continuing on through her own actions and bus travel during the sixties to participate in protests and reform movements from Berkeley to Washington, D.C.

In 1983, Le Sueur traveled again, from California to Atlanta to Tulsa to Wounded Knee. In Atlanta, Le Sueur prayed at the Etowah Indian Mounds of the Creeks, and wrote poetry deploring "the great culture built on slavery" and "the darkness of capitalism." She bussed from Atlanta to Tulsa, where she spent six weeks in the homes of sister activists, writing furiously. From there, she flew to Wounded Knee for the tenth anniversary of the people's courageous struggle against occupying forces at Pine Ridge. As a gift for her food and shelter, Le Sueur left her journal notes from this circular trip in the hands of Tulsa activists Anne Dethrow and Mary McAnally, who published them in a limited edition chapbook of 300 copies in 1987, titled *Word Is Movement*. It was from this chapbook that Le Sueur read her poetry and prose at the University of Minnesota in 1988. The poem titled "Asking for the Stories of Our Mother's Rebirth" was written on the bus trip from Atlanta to Tulsa, and it was these words that Meridel Le Sueur gave me with a kiss:

> *It's just the earth*
> *just the plain pulsating rich turning earth*
> *winter green wheat and the earth for seven hours*
> *   without tree or river*
> *line circled against the sky which leaned over the flesh*
> *earth hums the three notes of a wolf howl*
> *the pure earth   just the naked flat swinging cradle*
> *of the naked earth.*

Miles and miles of pure earth.
I kept crying, pressing my face against the dirty wet
window.
It's the earth rolled in the dark
rolled east
alive stirring   immense with moisture and heat.
Flesh hum of global solidarity
hum   hum   earth great earth our earth
curving in space   breast   belly loins
just the skin of the earth
mother naked   the great curved earth
belly   skin   the great valley
just the plain earth   no cathedrals   no little shacks
flesh hum   erotic earth   mother skin
no mountains   decorations crops   just the skin
taut over the belly of the earth   just watched in marvel
pressing against the window and weeping
it's the earth   just the great earth
just pulsing over the global organs and magnum and depth
in the rainy night the moisture on the skin of the earth
and the teeming   humming   seething in the soil
millions of years old crone
billions of bodies mingling   beast   human
grasses   birds   insects

all pressed shining in the jeweled flesh
and it grows   flesh bone   grass beast
time and again   this black moist teeming solid sea
fresh ever teeming nitrogen earth

Recent feminist criticism has all but dismissed Le Sueur's writing. I want to reclaim her work, her activism, and her writing. As in the poem above, Le Sueur articulates one woman's passionate connection with the earth, her sense of humility and awe, her tenderness and fierce solidarity with all life. Her sense of identity is rooted in her relationships with oppressed people, working people, women, animals, and the land. Although her formal education ended with the ninth grade, Le Sueur spent a lifetime learning and reflecting. She was a Communist, a feminist, an environmentalist, a labor activist, a writer, a mother. Until her death, in 1996, Le Sueur never stopped organizing, speaking, and writing about the common woman, about the land and the people, about sexuality and the erotics of the earth, about social, economic justice and ecological health. She is a magnificent literary foremother whose activism and writing make possible my own.

A project of this duration could not have been completed without the assistance of many, many mentors. At Western Washington University, Janet Collins in the Map Library showed me historical maps of Bellingham, Lake Padden, and Whatcom County. Elizabeth Joffrion at the Center for Pacific Northwest Studies brought out archival boxes and guided my search for historical facts, anecdotes, and inconsistencies. Jeff Jewel, at the Whatcom Museum, showed me the old mining and logging maps for Lake Whatcom, humorously tolerated my random visits, and delighted in my searches. The water essays that later became "Women/ Water" benefited tremendously from the wisdom of Gordy Tweit at the Fairhaven Pharmacy, Joy Monjure's productions of *Water Whys,* conversations with Wendy Scherrer, of Nooksack Salmon Enhancement Association, and Anna Deeny's generosity in sharing her local knowledge about Padden Creek.

Others provided more literary or financial support. I am grateful to Vega Subramaniam, Debra Salazar, and Midori Takagi, who read and commented on an earlier draft of "Looking for Home." Sharman Apt Russell read substantial portions of the manuscript, Lorraine Anderson read and commented on the entire manuscript's first full draft, and Barrie Borich provided wise counsel on creative nonfiction writing during the manuscript's final edit. The first drafts of the essays "Family of Land" and "Wilderness" were written during one blissful, rainy springtime month at Hedgebrook, a women writers' retreat on Whidbey Island, and I am so grateful for the peace and solitude provided there. Fairhaven College granted me two unpaid quarter-leaves of absence, which allowed me the freedom of unbroken writing time. During one such leave, Paul Piper arranged a library reading for me at Western Washington University, giving a wonderful affirmation to my writing. Fellow yogis at the Bellingham dharma hall provided continuous community, support, and friendship to me throughout my periods of writing and not-writing. When I returned to Minnesota, the friendship of the Common Ground Meditation Center sangha, Patrice Koelsch, Carole Broad, and our teacher, Mark Nunberg, along with dear friends like Beth Bartlett, Jan Conley, Lisa Marie Bader, Jim Berg, Jo Haberman, Nancy O'Brien, Renee Pardello, Linnea Stenson, and Marianne Turnbull warmed and revived my spirit. A women writers' retreat on the north shore of Lake Superior, Norcroft, granted me a residency where I made final revisions to the manuscript and hiked the north shore at every writing break. There, the land and the lake gave so much to me, a generosity I feel deeply.

This book would not have been completed without the steadfast support and unremitting faith of my immediate family during the years of writing and rewriting. I am deeply grateful to Shawn Boeser, Charles Gherardi, Barry Greenwald, and especially to my mother, Beverly Gaard, who supported me through many dark nights of the soul. To Sequoia, a thousand tennis balls of joy. And to Flora, blessings. For me, your life will be the best story of all.

BIBLIOGRAPHY

Alighieri, Dante. *The Divine Comedy: Inferno; Purgatorio; Paradiso.* Trans. Allen Mandelbaum. New York: Alfred A. Knopf/Everyman's Library, 1995.

Austin, Mary. *Stories from the Country of "Lost Borders."* Ed. Marjorie Pryse. New Brunswick, N.J.: Rutgers University Press, 1987.

Barlow, Maude, and Tony Clarke. *Blue Gold: The Fight to Stop the Corporate Theft of the World's Water.* New York: The New Press, 2002.

Bean, Betty. *Horseshoe Canyon: A Brief History of the June Lake Loop.* June Lake, Calif.: June Lake Loop Women's Club, 1977.

Campbell, Joseph. *The Hero with a Thousand Faces.* Princeton, N.J.: Princeton University Press, 1972.

Cardea, Caryatis. "All the Pieces I Never Wrote About Class." *Sinister Wisdom* 45: Lesbians and Class. (Winter 1991/1992): 105–17.

Carson, Rachel. *The Sense of Wonder.* New York: Harper & Row, 1965.

Chödrön, Pema. *When Things Fall Apart: Heart Advice for Difficult Times.* Boston: Shambhala, 1997.

Coventree, Caroljean. "Full Time Debt, Part Time Money." *Sinister Wisdom* 45: Lesbians and Class. (Winter 1991/1992): 98–103.

Csikszentmihalyi, Mihaly. *Flow: The Psychology of Optimal Experience.* New York: Harper & Row, 1990.

Glassman, Bernard, and Rick Fields. *Instructions to the Cook: A Zen Master's Lessons in Living a Life That Matters.* New York: Crown Publishers/Bell Tower, 1996.

Glendinning, Chellis. *My Name Is Chellis and I'm in Recovery from Western Civilization.* Boston: Shambhala, 1994.

Gordon, David George. *Field Guide to the Sasquatch.* Seattle: Sasquatch Books, 1992.

Green, John. *Bigfoot: On the Track of the Sasquatch.* New York: Ballantine Books, 1975.

Green, Rayna, ed. *That's What She Said: Contemporary Poetry and Fiction by Native American Women.* Bloomington: Indiana University Press, 1984.

Hollis, James. *The Middle Passage: From Misery to Meaning in Midlife.* Toronto: Inner City Books, 1993.

Homer. *The Odyssey.* Trans. Richmond Lattimore. New York: Harper Perennial, 1999.

Kadi, Joanna. *Thinking Class: Sketches from a Cultural Worker.* Boston: South End Press, 1996.

Krantz, Grover. *Big Footprints: A Scientific Inquiry into the Reality of Sasquatch.* Boulder, Colo.: Johnson Books, 1992.

LaDuke, Winona. *All Our Relations: Native Struggles for Land and Life.* Cambridge, Mass.: South End Press, 1999.

Le Sueur, Meridel. *Word Is Movement: Journal Notes from Atlanta to Tulsa to Wounded Knee.* Comp. Anne Dethrow and Mary McAnally. Tulsa, Okla.: Cardinal Press, 1987.

Levine, Stephen. *A Year to Live: How to Live This Year as If It Were Your Last.* New York: Crown/Bell Tower, 1997.

Maathai, Wangari. *The Green Belt Movement: Sharing the Approach and the Experience.* New York: Lantern Books, 2004.

Mathiesson, Peter. *In the Spirit of Crazy Horse.* New York: Viking Books, 1983.

Mellor, Mary. "Ecofeminist Political Economy: Integrating Feminist Economics and Ecological Economics." *Feminist Economics* 11, no. 3 (November 2005): 120–26.

Murdoch, Maureen. *The Heroine's Journey: Woman's Quest for Wholeness.* Boston: Shambhala, 1990.

Oliver, Mary. *American Primitive.* Boston: Little, Brown & Co., 1983.

Pyle, Robert Michael. *Where Bigfoot Walks: Crossing the Dark Divide.* New York: Houghton Mifflin, 1995.

Rose, Mike. *Lives on the Boundary: A Moving Account of the Struggles and Achievements of America's Educationally Underprepared.* New York: Penguin Books, 1989.

Salzberg, Sharon. *Lovingkindness: The Revolutionary Art of Happiness.* Boston: Shambhala, 1995.

Shackley, Myra. *Still Living? Yeti, Sasquatch and the Neanderthal Enigma.* New York: W. W. Norton & Co., 1986.

Sher, Barbara. *It's Only Too Late If You Don't Start Now.* New York: Random House, 1999.

Shor, Ira. *When Students Have Power: Negotiating Authority in a Critical Pedagogy.* Chicago: University of Chicago Press, 1996.

Silverstein, Shel. *The Giving Tree*. New York: HarperCollins, 1964.

Smith, Rodney. *Lessons from the Dying*. Somerville, Mass.: Wisdom Publications, 1998.

Stauffer, Julie. *The Water Crisis: Finding the Right Solutions*. Montreal: Black Rose Books, 1999.

Storer, Tracy I., and Robert L. Usinger. *Sierra Nevada Natural History*. Berkeley: University of California Press, 1963.

Todd, Frances Bruce. *The Trail through the Woods: History of Western Whatcom County, Washington*. Baltimore: Gateway Press, 1982.

Upham, Warren. *Minnesota Place Names: A Geographical Encyclopedia*. Third edition. St. Paul: Minnesota Historical Society Press, 2001.

Wahl, Terence R. *Birds of Whatcom County*. Lynden, Wash.: Print Stop, 1995.

Whitney, Stephen R. *A Field Guide to the Cascades and Olympics*. Seattle: The Mountaineers, 1983.

Wilcox, Ken. *Hiking Whatcom County*. Third edition. Bellingham, Wash.: Northwest Wild Books, 1996.

Woolf, Virginia. *Orlando*. New York: Harcourt Brace Jovanovich, 1956.

Wylie, Kenneth. *Bigfoot*. New York: Viking Books, 1980.

CREDITS

YEAR ONE: HISTORY AND IDENTITY
Quotation by Rachel Carson. From *The Sense of Wonder*, copyright © 1956 by Rachel L. Carson, reprinted by permission of Frances Collin, Trustee.

YEAR TWO: PLACE AND WORKPLACE
Quotation by Meridel Le Sueur. From "Asking for the Stories of Our Mother's Rebirth," *Word Is Movement: Journal Notes from Atlanta to Tulsa to Wounded Knee* (Tulsa, Okla.: Cardinal Press, 1987), 33.

YEAR THREE: HOME/ECONOMICS
Quotation by Wangari Maathai. From *The Green Belt Movement: Sharing the Approach and the Experience*, rev. ed. (New York: Lantern Books, 2003), 112.
Quotation by Winona LaDuke. From *All Our Relations: Native Struggles for Land and Life* (Cambridge, Mass.: South End Press, 1999), 130.
Quotation by Mary Mellor. From "Ecofeminist Political Economy: Integrating Feminist Economics and Ecological Economics," *Feminist Economics* 11 (November 2005), 122.

YEAR FOUR: OIL AND WATER
Quotation by Chellis Glendinning. From *"My Name Is Chellis and I'm in Recovery from Western Civilization"* (Boston: Shambhala Publications, 1994), 135.
Quotation by Joy Harjo. From "Fire," by permission of the author.

YEAR FIVE: IMPERMANENCE
Quotation by Guillermo Gómez-Peña. From *The New World Border: Prophecies, Poems, & Loqueras for the End of the Century* (San Francisco: City Lights Books, 1996), 6.
Stanza 74 from the *Tao Te Ching*, by Lao Tzu. From a new English version, with foreword and notes, by Stephen Mitchell. Translation copyright © 1988 by Stephen Mitchell. Reprinted by permission of HarperCollins Publishers.

ABOUT THE AUTHOR

Greta Gaard is author of *Ecological Politics: Ecofeminists and the Greens,* editor of *Ecofeminism: Women, Animals, Nature,* and coeditor of *Ecofeminist Literary Criticism.* Beginning her activism with the animal rights movement, she developed organizing skills through diverse environmental actions, through the U.S. Green movement, and later through the movements against globalization. Most recently she has served on the board of directors for the Environmental Association for Great Lakes Education (EAGLE), working on issues of water privatization and local democracy. Formerly an Associate Professor of Humanities at Fairhaven College/Western Washington University, and an Associate Professor of Composition and Women's Studies at the University of Minnesota–Duluth, she now teaches writing, environmental literature, and environmental studies to rural and working-class students at the University of Wisconsin in River Falls.